Ancient Egypt

Ancient Egypt

A. Rosalie David

Phaidon · Oxford

Frontispiece: a drawing of the Great Sphinx at Gizeh from the *Description de l'Égypte* commissioned by Napoleon in 1798.

AN EQUINOX BOOK
Phaidon Press Limited, Littlegate House, St Ebbe's Street, Oxford OX1 1SQ

Second edition 1988

Originally published in 1975 by Elsevier-Phaidon as *The Egyptian Kingdoms* © 1975, 1988 Equinox (Oxford) Ltd

ISBN 0 7148 2472 0

A CIP catalogue record for this book is available from the British Library

Printed in Yugoslavia

CONTENTS

PREFACE

Traveling by air between Cairo and Luxor, the modern visitor to Egypt gains a striking impression of the landscape which helped to mold the character of the ancient Egyptians thousands of years ago. The Nile, winding on its sinuous course to the Delta, is still as in earlier times the life-blood of the country. Cultivated strips of fertile land, still tended with primitive tools and irrigated much as in ancient times, hug the banks of the river. The small fields, intensely green, contrast vividly with the desert close on either side, which often rises steeply to rugged cliffs.

From Cairo the visitor will have traveled to Gizeh, Saqqara and Memphis where the pharaonic civilization first flourished during the Old Kingdom. In Upper Egypt, making the modern town of Luxor his base, he may devote several days to the east and west banks of the river which once made up the ancient capital of Thebes. He will wander around in the vast complex known as the Temple of Karnak and the smaller and more compact Temple of Luxor, and on the west bank will be shown the mortuary temples, the tombs of the kings, queens and nobles and the remains of the village of the royal necropolis workers. The temples, hosts only to the birds, the tourists and the archaeologists, are now deserted; columns and masonry lie scattered about, and the ritual incantations of the priests have long been silenced. And in the barren valleys the tombs lie empty, looted long ago by robbers. Only King Tutankhamun still rests in his original tomb. But it is impossible not to be moved by the great temples, or to marvel at the freshness of the tomb paintings, with scenes of kings and gods adorning the walls, as if the artists had just slipped away back to their village over the mountain.

The fortunate visitor may go further afield – perhaps to Abydos to see what are possibly the finest reliefs in Egypt in the Temple of Sethos I; or he may visit the well-preserved and shapely temples of the Ptolemaic era – Edfu, Denderah, Kom Ombo, Esneh and Philae. Some will follow the river as far as Aswan and beyond, to the temples of Abu Simbel, recently rescued from the rising waters of the Nile. A few may perhaps reach Tell el-Amarna where the heretic pharaoh, Akhenaten, built his city and worshiped his single deity.

The ancient custom of burying possessions with the deceased for the afterlife, along with Egypt's dry climate, has ensured that Egypt's material past has been preserved to a greater extent than that of most ancient civilizations.

And a greater understanding of this civilization has been gained by the patient and arduous labors of several generations of Egyptologists, while spectacular discoveries have inspired people of every kind to learn more about these orderly and creative Egyptians. Finally, the decipherment of their writing has allowed us, at least to some degree, to enter into their minds.

Moreover we shall find that many aspects of the civilization of ancient Egypt are not strange to us. We can understand their attitude to the home, to the family and education. We can admire their elegant jewelry and clothing, and sympathize with their search for medical knowledge and for rejuvenating cosmetics. Their buildings still stand to demonstrate the skill of their workmen, architects and craftsmen. Yet despite our wealth of knowledge about the Egyptians, it must always be remembered that it is based largely on the preservation of possessions they provided for funerary purposes, and there is a temptation therefore to regard the Egyptians as a race "obsessed with death." In reality, it seems, their main preoccupation was not death but eternal life. The religious beliefs and the associated art forms of the Egyptians are perhaps the most difficult aspect of their civilization for the modern world to understand.

The history of Egypt spans many centuries, from its obscure beginnings through the first great upsurge of brilliance during the Old Kingdom, the periods of decay and renewal, the zenith of international power, prestige and wealth during the New Kingdom to the gradual, sad decline during the later years. When her internal resources were exhausted, Egypt became easy prey for successive waves of invaders. Some, like the "Sea Peoples," were unsuccessful, but others – the Ethiopians, Assyrians, Persians, Greeks and Romans – were able to subjugate Egypt for long periods of time. Yet not until the late Ptolemaic era, when a Hellenistic dynasty exploited the country, did these successive conquerors make any determined attempt to interfere with the deep-seated traditions and way of life they found in Egypt. Indeed, the invaders tended to become "Egyptianized," adopting many of the customs and ways of the country they had conquered.

The following chapters attempt to give the reader some idea of the men and women – great and humble – who created this tenacious and long-lived civilization, and of the Egyptologists who have rescued them from oblivion.

CHRONOLOGICAL TABLE

Period	Date	Dynasty and names of important rulers
PREDYNASTIC PERIOD	c.5000–3100 BC	
ARCHAIC PERIOD	c.3100–2890 BC	I Menes (Narmer)
	c.2890–2686 BC	II
OLD KINGDOM	c.2686–2613 BC	III Djoser; Huni
	c.2613–2494 BC	IV Sneferu; Cheops; Chephren; Mycerinus
	c.2494–2345 BC	V Sahure; Neuserre; Unas
	c.2345–2181 BC	VI Pepy I; Pepy II
FIRST INTERMEDIATE PERIOD	c.2181–2173 BC	VII ⎫
	c.2173–2160 BC	VIII ⎬ (Memphite)
	c.2160–2130 BC	IX ⎫
	c.2130–2040 BC	X ⎬ (Heracleopolitan) Achthoes
	c.2133–1991 BC	XI (Theban) Mentuhotep Nebhepetre I
MIDDLE KINGDOM	1991–1786 BC	XII Amenemmes I, II, III; Sesostris I, II, III
SECOND INTERMEDIATE PERIOD	1786–1633 BC	XIII
	1786–c.1603 BC	XIV (Xois)
	1674–1567 BC	XV (Hyksos) ⎫
	c.1684–1567 BC	XVI (Hyksos) ⎬ Khyan; Apophis; Jacob-el
	c.1650–1567 BC	XVII (Theban) Seqenenre; Kamose
NEW KINGDOM	1567–1320 BC	XVIII Amosis I; Amenophis I, II, III; Tuthmosis I, II, III, IV; Hatshepsut; Akhenaten (Amenophis IV); Tutankhamun; Horemheb
	1320–1200 BC	XIX Sethos I; Ramesses II; Merenptah
	1200–1085 BC	XX Ramesses III
LATE PERIOD	1085–945 BC	XXI Psusennes I; Herihor (high-priest)
	945–730 BC	XXII (Bubastis) Shoshenk I; Osorkon I
	817?–730 BC	XXIII (Tanis) Pedubast
	720–715 BC	XXIV (Sais) Bochchoris
	751–668 BC	XXV (Ethiopian) Pi'ankhy; Shabaka; Taharqa
	664–525 BC	XXVI (Sais) Psammetichus I, II; Necho II; Apries (Hophra); Amasis
FIRST PERSIAN PERIOD	525–404 BC	XXVII (Persian) Cambyses; Darius I; Xerxes; Artaxerxes
LATE PERIOD	404–399 BC	XXVIII (Sais) Amyrteos
	399–380 BC	XXIX (Mendes)
	380–343 BC	XXX (Sebennytos) Nectanebo I and II
SECOND PERSIAN PERIOD	343–332 BC	XXXI (Persian) Artaxerxes III; Arses; Darius III
CONQUEST BY ALEXANDER THE GREAT	332 BC	
PTOLEMAIC PERIOD	332–30 BC	(Ptolemies) Ptolemy I; Soter I; Ptolemy VII; Euergetes II; Cleopatra

CONQUEST BY ROMANS – OCTAVIUS RULES EGYPT 30 BC

INTRODUCTION

During the past 12 years, major changes have taken place in Egyptology. There are three areas where the advances are particularly evident: first, in the degree of international cooperation in various rescue projects; secondly, in the introduction of new techniques in archaeology, paleopathology and language studies, and in the willingness to adopt a multidisciplinary approach; and thirdly, in an awareness of the conservation problems which now affect the monuments and artifacts, and the need to find solutions for these.

The High Dam and its consequences. To some extent, this situation has been brought about by decisions taken in the political and social context of modern Egypt, namely, the building of the High Dam (el-Saad el-Aali) at Aswan. The decision to build this dam was taken in 1955 and it was completed in 1971. With its capacity to store surplus water in a great artificial lake (Lake Nasser) over a period of years, it was intended to enable the authorities to balance the effects of high and low annual river floods and to provide several million additional acres of cultivable land in Egypt and the Sudan, thus supplying more food for the burgeoning population.

At the end of the 19th century, a smaller barrage had been constructed at Aswan, creating an artificial lake behind the dam, and even this smaller project had caused some problems for the ancient monuments in the area. The collection of beautiful temples and associated buildings on the island of Philae was especially vulnerable. Until this time, they had always remained above the water level, but now, although they rose above the waters during the few months each year when the river level dropped during the Nile flood, for the remaining months they were partially submerged. The constantly changing conditions and the movement of the water threatened ultimately to destroy the wall scenes and inscriptions in the temples and undermine the buildings. In addition, the site was inaccessible to visitors for considerable periods.

With the construction of the new dam, conditions would worsen; Philae, lying between the old and new dams, would be completely lost, submerged in an artificial lake, and many other monuments would also be destroyed because of the new ultimate height of the water in Lake Nasser. Because the monuments in this area are of such importance, an international rescue operation was launched by UNESCO, and from 1959 various plans to save the monuments (the most famous were the temples at Abu Simbel and the Philae buildings) were

considered. The team included experts from various countries, and finance was raised in many ways. In all, 44 countries participated in the rescue operation. Egypt offered temples from the doomed area to several countries, where they were reerected in safety; the Temple of Dendur, for instance, is now housed in Central Park, New York, in a specially built extension to the Metropolitan Museum. To assist with fund-raising, major travelling exhibitions were organized, such as the notable "Treasures of Tutankhamun," held at the British Museum, which brought in considerable revenue to save the monuments.

At Abu Simbel, the temples of Ramesses II and his queen, Nefertari, had originally been carved out of the living rock. These awe-inspiring monuments had been built about 1250 BC, to impress the local population with the might and majesty of their Egyptian ruler. The modern rescue scheme involved moving the temples and reerecting them at a higher level at the same site, so that they would stand safely above the new water level which Lake Nasser was expected to reach. The temples were cut into the sandstone cliff, and the first stage in the project was to cut them into manageable blocks to facilitate transfer to the new site. To provide the temples with a similar setting in their new location and also to give them sufficient physical support, an artificial mountain was constructed behind them; an immense concrete dome was incorporated in the scheme, and to design this and the supporting scaffolding, the engineers used a computer. Today, this engineering feat is an eloquent reminder to the visitor of the effective marriage between modern technology and ancient buildings. Work on the smaller temple of Nefertari was completed in 1966, and on Ramesses II's own temple in the following year.

The island of Philae, situated some 175 miles to the north, at the First Cataract, posed different problems. In ancient times, it was a center of pilgrimage and worship for the family triad of gods, Osiris, Isis and Horus. Some monuments from earlier periods have survived, but essentially it is preserved as it would have appeared in the Ptolemaic period (c.250 BC). In this instance, the UNESCO experts decided to save the buildings by dismantling them and then removing the blocks to be reerected on another island, Agilkia, which lay about 500 yards to the northwest of Philae. Agilkia, at a higher level, would preserve the monuments above the new water line.

To this end, the buildings were dismantled, and each stone was marked and numbered to facilitate its replacement in exactly the right location at the new site. At Abu Simbel, this process had posed a major difficulty, because the blocks had to be cut out of the living rock from which the temples were originally carved; at Philae, the situation was easier in that the temples had simply to be dismantled, but there were other problems here to be tackled. It was necessary to build a coffer dam around the island and to pump out the water from inside this dam, so that the site could be drained to allow the work to progress. Simultaneously, the ground on Agilkia was blasted and prepared to provide a level site for the re-erection of the buildings. The project was completed in 1977, and today these temples provide visitors with a magnificent spectacle, either in daytime or as the setting of a son et lumière performance at night. Every year many tourists visit the Philae temples and also the remote site of Abu Simbel, which is one of the highlights of an Egyptian tour.

Although these two sites are the most famous successes of the rescue project, many other monuments, villages and cemeteries were also threatened by the water and some were excavated, recorded or rescued by UNESCO. In some cases, material could be removed for later study elsewhere; the extensive cemetery at Gebel Adda, opposite Abu Simbel, which contained burials of the Meroitic, Christian and Muslim periods, was excavated by the Smithsonian Institution and this revealed many skeletal remains which were taken to the USA for further study. Today, the visitor to this area can also wander around the open-air museum of monuments which were rescued by German archaeologists and reerected on a promontory near Philae; the buildings here include the impressive late temple of Kalabsha and the 19th-Dynasty temple originally situated at Beit el-Wali.

By the late 1970s, successful rescue of these treasures had ensured that multidisciplinary techniques, new scientific methods and international cooperation were key factors in the development of Egyptology. This approach is now evident in field archaeology, and also in research programs undertaken on material excavated many years ago and since held in museum collections.

The boats of Gizeh. At Gizeh, some 5000 years ago, King Cheops (Khufu) selected this impressive plateau which now overlooks modern Cairo as his site for a magnificent funerary monument, known today as the Great Pyramid. This building has tantalized explorers and scientists for centuries; they have puzzled over its meaning, the method of construction and whether it still conceals undiscovered chambers. In the latest examination of the pyramid French scientists have attempted to locate any secret chambers or passages by using a microgravimeter—a remote sensing device with which geologists and geophysicists identify hidden breaks and apertures in rocks. Information thus gained can then be transferred to a computer, which will produce a simula-

tion of the pyramid and its internal (but hidden) structure from these data, so that eventually it may be possible to identify previously unknown chambers.

In 1954, not far away from the Great Pyramid, in the southern section of the boundary wall, Kemal el-Malakh discovered the famous cedarwood ship built for King Cheops and then dismantled and buried here. It is the largest, oldest and best-preserved ancient ship in the world, but its exact purpose and function are disputed. In the Archaic period (c.3000 BC), single boat-pits are found associated with individual graves, but by the 4th Dynasty, the royal pyramids at Gizeh are flanked by several boat-pits. Five pits are known to be associated with the pyramid of Cheops, while the neighboring pyramid of his son, Chephren (Khafre), has six. Some archaeologists claim that these boats were placed near to the king's burial place to provide him with symbolic and mythological transport for his celestial journey with the gods after his ascension. Others maintain that the boats were actually used, perhaps several times or only once, on the occasion when the king's body and his funerary goods were finally transported by river from his capital city of Memphis to Gizeh.

The technological excellence and aesthetic appeal of Cheops' boat are, however, beyond dispute, and it provides a most important source of information about the design and construction of ancient ships. It can now be viewed in a glass-walled museum to the south of the Great Pyramid, built directly over the stone pit in which it was discovered. The boat was finally reassembled in its museum in 1970, after a painstaking program of restoration. Dr. Zaki Iskander was in charge of the chemical restoration of the boat, while Hag Ahmed Youssef Moustafa, Chief Restorer of the Egyptian Department of Antiquities, played a vital role in its conservation and restoration, reassembling some 1224 pieces over a period of 14 years. The first complete reconstruction was finished by 1968, but the boat was dismantled and reassembled five times before it was finally ready in its museum setting for public viewing. It now provides the visitor with a unique and awe-inspiring insight into ancient boat-building skills and modern restoration techniques. Other modern techniques also augment our knowledge about the Gizeh boat-pits; in 1987 remote sensing radar (which can differentiate between stone, sand, organic material and empty spaces) was used to confirm the presence of another wooden boat in its stone pit.

The tombs of Saqqara. The other great Old Kingdom necropolis—Saqqara—has also continued to provide major new discoveries, and the Egypt Exploration Society has gone on with its work here in recent years. Work on the temple enclosure, catacombs and surrounding area, discovered by the late Professor W.B.Emery, was completed in 1975/6, and the excavation of the temple-town of the Anubieion at the bottom of the Serapeum Way in the Memphite necropolis was finished in 1979/80. In 1974/5 a new venture was initiated when a joint expedition between the Egypt Exploration Society and the National Museum of Antiquities in Leiden came into existence. Its aim was to locate the few known tombs of the New Kingdom period in the area to the south of the Causeway of Unas at Saqqara. Most knowledge of this period has been derived from the southern capital of Thebes, so new information from the north regarding history, art, architecture and religion is of considerable interest and importance.

This area of Saqqara had been searched by travelers and collectors in the early 19th century, who sought objects for museums, and, although they have left no detailed records, it was obvious that the district was honeycombed with tombs. However, since no objects from these tombs had appeared since the last century, the excavators could hope that some of the tomb reliefs and even tomb contents might still be found in situ. The initial aim of the expedition was to relocate the tomb of Maya, the treasurer of Tutankhamun, whose statues are in the Leiden Museum. However, it was the magnificent tomb of Horemheb which they first discovered. This man became king of Egypt at the end of the 18th Dynasty and was actually buried at Thebes, but at an earlier stage of his career, when he was simply the military commander under Tutankhamun, he had prepared himself a tomb at Saqqara. After his elevation to the kingship, the Saqqara tomb became a place of worship, and in Ramesside times it may even have become a center where Horemheb's funerary cult was performed, to ensure his continued existence after death. The exact location of the tomb had been lost for many years, although, in the last century, some of its fine wall scenes had entered museum collections. A program to repair and ensure the tomb's safety has since been undertaken and where the original wall reliefs are missing, casts have been put in their place; this has been financed by the Dutch government as part of a cultural agreement.

Other important discoveries awaited the expedition. In the last century Lepsius recorded part of the superstructure of the tomb of Maya, but the underground complex had not been entered since the ancient tomb robbers plundered the tomb. The archaeologists have now rediscovered the tomb and have commenced their exploration of its chambers; any discoveries that provide additional historical evidence for the reign of Maya's king, Tutankhamun, would be welcome.

Other tombs which the expedition has uncovered have provided information about a range of Memphite families: the tomb of Tia (the daughter of King Sethos I) and her husband, also called Tia, is the first large tomb of the Ramesside period in the Memphite necropolis which has been located and planned in its entirety; the tomb of their steward, Iurudef, was found to contain a large number of coffins and mummies from later, intrusive burials; and

the tombs of a gold-washer, his son and a "Head of the Bowmen of the Army" are also under investigation. Thus, these tombs illustrate a range of burial styles for persons of different rank. The archaeologists will produce a complete photographic, epigraphic, architectural and descriptive record, and the expedition will have the opportunity at this site to study the typology, iconography, technology and dating of a specific group of coffins, as well as the incidence of disease in the human remains.

Surveys and settlement sites. In 1982 the Egypt Exploration Society celebrated its centenary. The range of current fieldwork which it undertakes demonstrates the breadth of interest in ancient Egypt. As well as the Saqqara expedition and the post-pharaonic excavation in the south at Qasr Ibrim, the Society has also been engaged in work on settlement sites. These are cities, towns or villages—"living" sites as distinct from burial places. They have become a focus of attention in the past decade, for, whereas the temples and tombs were built of stone, domestic dwellings were constructed mainly of mudbrick, and these sites are particularly vulnerable to environmental conditions. Various countries have turned their attention in this direction. A notable example is the current excavation of Tell ed-Dab in the Delta, where multidisciplinary studies have advanced knowledge of this site and elucidated problems associated with the supposed location of the ancient cities of Avaris (the Hyksos capital) and Pi-Ramesse. Another team (this time from the British Museum) is excavating the Greco-Roman city of Hermopolis Magna at Ashmunein; the site was surveyed in 1980 and the following year excavation began in an attempt to obtain a clearer picture of the central area of this city, and particularly of its main religious and public buildings.

To commemorate its centenary, the Egypt Exploration Society has commenced work on its own major contribution in this field, undertaking an archaeological survey of the ruin-fields of the northern capital city of Memphis. The Memphis Project was initiated in 1980; this site was selected because it is rare for one area to offer such a wealth of documentary and archaeological material, but also, because of its size, it had never been adequately mapped and there were no adequate records for much of the archaeological work which had previously been carried out there. Memphis was the capital city for some of Egypt's most important periods and, as such, provides a unique opportunity to study the continuous history of a major community and to look at different social and economic aspects. The study eventually aims to produce a detailed archaeological survey and maps of the city, with plans and elevations of all the standing monuments; all the reliefs and inscriptions will be copied and photographed. The archaeologists will also make use of contemporary documents as well as medieval and modern topographical sources. Other studies will concentrate on the stratigraphy and history of the city, and any details of previous archaeological or documentary work will be preserved. In addition, there will be investigations of the environmental evidence, and all the information from this comprehensive survey is constantly updated and computerized in London.

Another of the Society's excavations concentrates on a very different settlement site—the workmen's village at Tell el-Amarna. A new archaeological survey of the city of Amarna was started in 1977, to provide a detailed map of the site with more accurate information than previous records. The archaeologists also wished to determine which area should receive priority for future excavation. The workmen's village was chosen because it was compact and would provide the opportunity to study the houses and lifestyle of a particular community; it could also be compared with another royal workmen's village —Deir el-Medineh—which had accommodated the craftsmen (and their families) who were engaged in building and decorating the tombs in the Valley of the Kings at Thebes. There was also extensive documentary evidence from the Deir el-Medineh site.

The Society had in fact first excavated the Amarna village in 1921/22. The new venture began in 1979 and was completed in 1986; a limited excavation of the houses within the walled area was carried out, and an extensive study was made of the extramural locations, concentrating on the quarries and village rubbish heaps. The village was first established when Akhenaten founded his city of Akhetaten (the site usually known today as Amarna). It was abandoned during the reign of Tutankhamun, although it is possible that there may have been a brief reoccupation before it was completely deserted in the reign of Horemheb. The men who lived here with their families were engaged in work on the nearby city and the associated rock-cut tombs in the cliffs behind Akhetaten.

Some of the recent studies have concentrated on the village's domestic architecture; sufficiently well preserved, the houses provide information about building structures and fixtures for food preparation. Favorable conditions at the site have ensured the survival of organic remains, and an intensive study has been made of waste products and of the evidence for local farming. Large collections of bones indicate that oxen, goats and pigs were most numerous at the site, and researches in paleoethnobotany have sought to establish the range of cultivated plants that the villagers used. In addition to wooden and basketry objects, some 3500 pieces of textile have survived, thus providing a unique opportunity to study a wide range of domestic textiles from a pharaonic site. Also, pottery sherds from selected deposits are being registered for computer analysis, and from this it may be possible to determine any pattern of distribution of certain types of pottery in the different areas of the

village. There is a paucity of textual evidence to provide any written records of daily life, but archaeologists have been able to gather information relating to the economic basis of the community and the life-style of its inhabitants; the site is also of interest in terms of its wider historical and religious context. Once again, computers are used to store a series of databases, and the careful compilation of this kind of archaeological evidence will eventually assist us to understand the social and economic structures of ancient societies.

Kahun revisited. Many similar, purpose-built towns and villages, designed to house the pharaoh's work force, must have existed, but to date only three have been uncovered: Amarna, Deir el-Medineh and Kahun. Built about 1895 BC, primarily to accommodate the craftsmen and pyramid personnel employed in building, maintaining and servicing the pyramid and mortuary temple of Sesostris II at Lahun, the town of Kahun is the earliest example. It is situated in the Fayoum, a remarkably fertile and beautiful area, and lies on the edge of modern cultivation. William Flinders Petrie excavated the site in 1888/89, and it was one of his most significant discoveries, since this was the first time that a complete plan of an Egyptian town had been uncovered. Also, many of the houses were then still standing and contained property left behind by the owners. The wealth of objects of everyday use has contributed to our understanding of domestic conditions; most knowledge of ancient Egypt is based on the evidence of goods placed in the tombs, but

The excavation at Kahun in the 1880s: Flinders Petrie (with cap and stick), his wife and a visitor.

the Kahun material provides a different viewpoint and, in some cases, supplies new information because humble items from a domestic context were not always placed in the tombs. The Kahun objects include a wide range of tools and equipment which are uniquely important in illustrating technological developments of the period. In addition to this, papyri uncovered at the town have supplied records and details of civil and domestic life; they are particularly informative about the legal, medical, veterinary, educational and religious practices of the community which must have contained doctors, scribes, lawyers, craftsmen and tradesmen, in fact all the elements of a thriving small town.

The objects excavated from Kahun were ultimately distributed among various museums around the world, but the largest numbers went to Petrie's own collection, now housed at University College London, and to the Manchester University Museum. Manchester acquired these and many other major collections from Petrie's excavations largely through the generous patronage of a local textile manufacturer, Jesse Haworth. He provided substantial financial support for Petrie's excavations, and at Kahun, he and another businessman, Martyn Kennard, were the sole benefactors. In Manchester, Haworth's patronage of Egyptology is also evident in the considerable donations which he made to establish Egyptology galleries and suitable storage areas for the collections at the University Museum.

Since the 1970s, with the Mummy Research Project, the concept has been established at Manchester of subjecting parts of the Museum's collections to multidisciplinary scientific investigation, involving specialists from many areas of study. In the 1980s, it was decided to extend this scheme to the Kahun material and to reexamine and rework this collection. In particular, the team would consider the ancient technology at the site and it would reassess Petrie's claim that a proportion of the town's population was of non-Egyptian origin.

The Kahun objects provide fascinating information about the furnishings of the houses, building and carpentry techniques, metal casting, agriculture and fishing, makeup and jewelry, toys and games, and religious practices. In some cases, the Kahun objects have no parallels elsewhere, for the items were too mundane to be included among tomb goods; in other instances, items shown only in the painted or carved tomb wall scenes but not included among tomb goods were found at Kahun. There are mudbrick molds, firesticks, plasterers' floats (to one, there still adheres the lump of plaster that the owner forgot to clean off) and agricultural tools including hoes and sickles. In the recent study, it has been possible to identify a pottery tube as an ancient beehive.

Analysis of the botanical specimens has been undertaken, and there is a detailed and ongoing study of textile technology at the site. Because of the connection with Jesse Haworth, Manchester received the textile tools

Selection of objects from pyramid workmen's town of Kahun – butterfly clamps, mudbrick mold and plasterer's float.

Mirror with handle and copper torque also from Kahun. Torques are very rare in Egypt, but were produced for many years in Byblos.

from the site and, using these and the baskets, sandals, mats and other woven items, it is possible to study the processes of flax preparation, spinning, weaving and finishing of linen cloth, and also cording, netting, basketry, matting and sandal making. However, a puzzling feature is the apparently total absence of woven cloth or garments from the site.

At the time of excavation Petrie proposed the theory that part of Kahun's population was foreign, basing this on the stylistic evidence of some of the pottery which he designated as "foreign," on the presence of foreign weights and measures and on indications that certain religious practices at Kahun were not Egyptian. Subsequently, this theory has gained support from various quarters. Translation of the Kahun papyri has shown that in the legal, religious and household lists of the town, certain individuals were classified as foreigners, and there was apparently a sufficiently large number of them to require the presence of a special officer and a scribe who were in charge of them.

The current project has attempted to reexamine the pottery which Petrie described as "foreign" on stylistic grounds, but to use modern scientific techniques to determine if the clay fabric of these pots is different from that which occurs in Egyptian wares, or if the "foreign" pots were made at Kahun but following a different style. Neutron activation analysis was the method chosen for this, and it confirmed that the foreign group were indeed distinct, although it has not yet been possible to establish the exact provenance of these wares. Similarly, an analysis of 40 samples of metals from Kahun was undertaken, again using neutron activation analysis; here, no firm evidence emerged that the copper goods were imported, although the metal-working techniques may have been, but it was possible to gain an overall picture of the nature of the alloys and to see Kahun in the context of the general historical development of metallurgy.

At this stage, it can be tentatively concluded that the foreign residents may have come from a number of areas, including Syria, Palestine, the Aegean Islands and Cyprus, and that they may have come as traders, itinerant workers or perhaps originally as prisoners-of-war. The site may have declined gradually, and the population dwindled, due to local economic conditions. However, the quantity, range and type of articles left at the site seem to indicate a more sudden and unpremeditated evacuation. Petrie only excavated approximately two-thirds of the site, and further information may still be buried in the remainder of the town.

New disciplines, new technology. Archaeology, in its broadest sense, is therefore deriving considerable benefits from new technology. At the excavation sites, remote sensing devices and aerial surveys (as at Thebes and Amarna) can help the archaeologists to locate important traces and to establish which sites should be given priority.

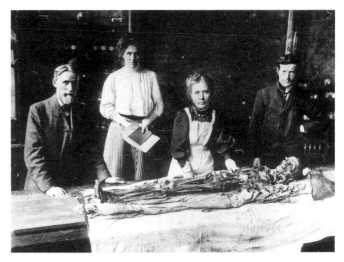

Dr Margaret Murray and team at the unwrapping of one of the Two Brothers at Manchester in 1908.

Once the material is removed from the ground, new techniques ensure that the objects are preserved and recorded, and data storage facilities enable researchers to assemble and assess the mass of facts more readily and accurately. Even objects which were taken from the ground decades ago can now be subjected to scientific scrutiny and can provide new facts about the history and socioeconomy of their original provenance. Modern technology has also advanced other areas of Egyptology: computers are used increasingly in language and textual studies, and also in such schemes as the Akhenaten Temple Project. In this project a computer was employed to match the scenes on decorated blocks originally from the Aten temples at Thebes which, when these buildings were dismantled in antiquity, had been recycled as infill in other buildings.

Other fascinating developments have taken place in the field of paleopathology (the study of diseases in the naturally or artificially preserved bodies of ancient man), and here Egyptian mummies provide the best opportunity for modern scientific investigations. Pioneering work was undertaken early in this century by Elliot Smith, Armand Ruffer, Wood Jones, Douglas Derry, Margaret Murray and others, and there has been a continuing, though intermittent, study of Egyptian mummies since then. Until recently this study concentrated on radiological surveys, but in the past 15 years major advances have occurred.

In 1968 the University of Michigan started a project to carry out an X-ray survey of the collection of royal mummies in the Cairo Museum. Lateral cephalometric X-rays of the skulls have enabled the researchers to compare the craniofacial morphologic variation of the mummies and to study the similarities and differences in members of the royal family; in the case of Queen Tiye, this evidence established the identification of her mummy. The professional interests of this team have

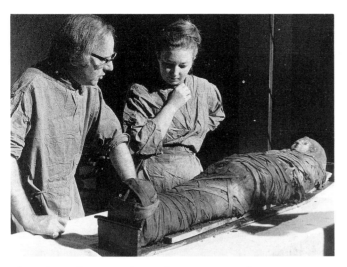

The author and Dr Tapp discuss the unwrapping of Mummy 1770 at Manchester in 1975.

been centered mainly on the dental history and disease of the mummies, and on the assessment of an individual's age at death from the interpretation of the X-rays.

Ramesses II has been the subject of another intensive medical study. In 1976/77 his mummy was taken to France to undergo conservation treatment; at the Atomic Energy Commission, the mummy was subjected to radiosterilization, using gamma rays from a cobalt-60 source, to clear it of the parasites which were attacking it. Further limited investigations were undertaken, and some results were obtained relating to the king's health; it was also shown that Ramesses was fair-skinned and that he probably had red hair.

A joint team from the USA and Canada has also undertaken a series of autopsies and scientific studies on a number of Egyptian and other preserved bodies. In 1973 the first of these autopsies was carried out in the USA on an Egyptian mummy from the University Museum of Pennsylvania in Philadelphia. Experts from various institutions collaborated on the research relating to this mummy and to three others also from Philadelphia, and indeed, the research project on the second Philadelphia mummy (PUM II) became the base from which the now international Palaeopathology Association developed. In 1974 the group was extended when the Canadian Royal Ontario Museum provided another mummy which was autopsied and studied by a joint American-Canadian team. These mummies are representative of a range of social classes and historical periods, and the team has utilized many techniques, including radiology, histology, electron microscopy, biochemical studies, neutron activation and atomic absorption techniques, carbon-14 dating and dental studies, and has produced extensive results, including interesting data on disease in these mummies.

Since 1973, a major program in England—the Manchester Mummy Research Project—has pursued certain aims in this field. First, it has sought to discover as much information as possible from the collection of 21 human and 34 animal mummies at the University Museum, relating to ancient living conditions, funerary and religious beliefs, disease and causes of death. Secondly, the Project has attempted to establish a methodology for the examination of mummies, using a wide range of scientific techniques under near-ideal conditions. The team of scientists has used such traditional and nondestructive techniques as radiology, but also, in 1975, unwrapped and autopsied one of the Manchester mummies, catalogued as number 1770. This was the first time that a mummy had been scientifically dissected in Britain since Margaret Murray and her team unwrapped the mummies of the Two Brothers at Manchester in 1908, and consequently the event attracted wide media coverage. The team has subsequently pioneered the use of virtually nondestructive methods of examination which combine radiology, endoscopy and histology, so that evidence can now be obtained without the need to unwrap or destroy a mummy.

The Manchester Project's work has been the subject of several books, a number of television and university teaching films and a major museum exhibition in 1979. Also, two international symposia on the theme of "Science in Egyptology" have been held in Manchester and have been attended by researchers in the field of Egyptian paleopathology from many countries. An outcome of one of these meetings was the establishment of an international mummy database at Manchester; this stores information on mummies in collections around the world, with emphasis on related scientific studies which have been carried out on the mummies and on examples of disease which have been thus discovered. The Manchester team has a longterm research program to develop the nondestructive approach and the related medical studies, and they have recently undertaken work in Egypt, examining excavated mummies at archaeological sites.

A paper presented by a Swedish scientist at the 1984 Manchester symposium heralded a remarkable development in paleopathology. This scientist had succeeded in cloning DNA (which contains an individual's genetic constitution) in tissue from the 2400-year-old mummy of an Egyptian child. From a sample of 23 mummies, this was the only one that had produced clonable DNA, but the possibilities for future work in this field are immense. Future studies may include research into the descent of Egypt's ancient population, and into the relationships between the rulers of different dynasties as well as between members of the same royal family. In the wider context, Egypt presents unique opportunities, with its well-preserved mummies, for studies relating to the genetic development of a population and to the evolution of DNA-containing viruses, over a considerable period of time.

Conservation and the future. Studies, however, have not only been concentrated on the incidence of disease in mummies. The conservation of mummies has become important, and correct environmental and display conditions for housing mummified remains, as well as a range of scientific techniques to combat the insect, fungal and microbiological attacks that cause the deterioration of mummies, are now being developed. In general, conservation, with regard both to the monuments in Egypt and to the objects at the excavation site or held in museum collections, has become an area of major significance in Egyptology over the past decade. In Egypt, the environmental problems have, for various reasons, been accelerated in recent times. The Aswan High Dam, beneficial in some ways, has ensured that the annual flood now no longer descends the Nile Valley, with the result that the water table in the Valley remains at a constant and relatively high level throughout the year. This has resulted in problems for some tombs and temples, for the damp now rises through the walls and is clearly visible in some buildings. Due to this problem, salt recrystallization occurs on the surface of these walls, causing the inscriptions, reliefs and paintings and, ultimately, the structure of the building to deteriorate.

In addition, the past decade has seen a marked increase in the number of tourists who visit Egypt to marvel at the monuments, but they also bring their own problems. Their presence in the tombs increases the ambient relative humidity, and also gradually wears away the wall surfaces and paintings. Many more sites are now open to the visitor, which, it is hoped, will ease the pressure on some of the best-known locations. However, conservation, in terms both of the preservation of the monuments and antiquities, and, where damage has already occurred, of the correct treatment of the problem, will continue to play a major role in securing this heritage.

One of the most exciting prospects in this field is the current study of the tomb of Queen Nefertari, a favorite wife of Ramesses II, in the Valley of the Queens at Thebes. This tomb, one of the most beautiful in Egypt, has been closed to the public for nearly 50 years. The walls, decorated with painted scenes showing the queen and her passage into the next world, are severely affected by moisture and salts, with the result that the scenes are flaking away. The latest attempt to deal with the problem, undertaken by Egyptian and American experts using a range of modern scientific techniques, will try to determine the routes by which the moisture and salts permeate the walls and will then devise means of blocking these and of protecting the tomb from further destruction.

There is no doubt that Egyptology faces many challenges, but there are also many positive aspects. Many countries now support excavations in Egypt and new facts are constantly emerging which encourage the reassessment of Egypt's historical background and social development. Language studies flourish in many centers, and a continually increasing knowledge of grammar and syntax enables scholars to produce more accurate and sympathetic translations of the ancient texts.

Perhaps Egypt, of all the ancient civilizations, appeals most vividly and directly to a wide public imagination. There is a growth in the support for Egyptology societies, and public lectures attract large audiences; Egypt is no longer a distant holiday location, and a Nile journey is now an experience enjoyed by many people. In museums in other countries, exhibitions of Egyptian antiquities draw large visitor attendances: the British Museum's "Treasures of Tutankhamun" exhibition in the early 1970s exceeded all expectations in the number of visitors it attracted, and a decade later, the Egypt Exploration Society celebrated its centenary of excavation in Egypt with two exhibitions, one at the British Museum and one in Manchester. The latter brought together, in some instances for the first time since excavation, objects which are in the collections at University College London and the Manchester Museum. Again in Manchester, the temporary exhibition featuring the work of the Mummy Research team attracted visitors from many areas, and other exhibitions elsewhere have encouraged public enthusiasm.

Museums around the world have also undertaken major renovations of their permanent Egyptian display galleries, among them the Metropolitan Museum in New York and the Museum of Fine Arts in Boston. Two large-scale installations in Britain are the new Sculpture Gallery at the British Museum and the completely refurbished galleries on Egyptian funerary beliefs and practices and daily life, at the Manchester University Museum, which received Britain's Museum of the Year Award in 1987. The Petrie Museum at University College London, which houses the famous archaeologist's significant research and teaching collection, has also been completely renovated and refurbished.

However, perhaps the single most important development in Egyptology over the past few years is the trend for Egyptologists themselves to become aware of the considerable potential offered to them by modern technology. If they will seize these opportunities and encourage specialists in other disciplines to work with them, a wealth of new information can be added to existing knowledge and the antiquities can be saved for the enjoyment of future generations.

A. Rosalie David

I
ANCIENT EGYPT

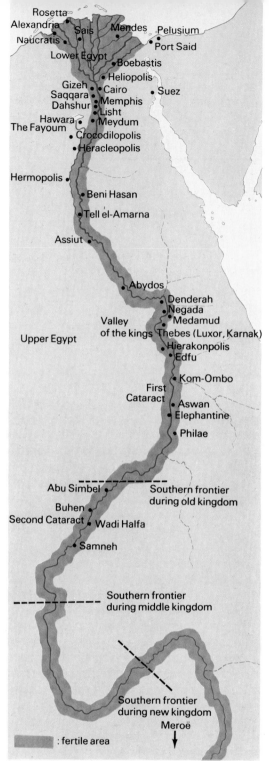

The land. The Egyptians called their land Kmt – "the Black Land" – referring to the rich black mud which the Nile annually deposited on the riverbanks and which enabled life to exist in this otherwise barren valley. They named the desert "the Red Land" (Dšrt). Today it is still possible to stand with one foot in the Black Land and the other in the Red Land, so clearly are the two areas defined. This contrast gave the ancient Egyptians a vivid realization of the juxtaposition of life and death; to them, nature clearly demonstrated the inevitable sequence of the death and rebirth of their land.

The Greek historian Herodotus aptly called Egypt "the gift of the Nile," and no one was more aware of this than the Egyptians themselves. With a very small annual rainfall, Egypt has always depended on the annual Nile floods for life, when the waters burst over the riverbanks and laid down rich black mud on the land. From earliest times irrigation was practised; banks were built to prevent over-flooding of the river and canals were cut to channel the water over otherwise barren ground. Agriculture was the chief occupation of the peasants, disrupted only during the months of late summer by the effects of the inundation, when alternative employment was provided for them. In ancient times a low Nile was disastrous and could result in starvation for many people.

A map of Egypt shows clearly that the country divides into north – the Delta – and south – the "tail" of the country – which winds up into Africa. The Delta, where the branches of the Nile run into the Mediterranean, is lush

Aerial view of the Nile showing the fertile Black Land beside the river and the desert Red Land beyond.

and green and today boasts the two great cities of Alexandria and Cairo; the antiquities here are less well preserved than the magnificent ruins of Upper Egypt which the dryness of the desert has saved. Upper Egypt, the southernmost part of the country, consists of an elongated stretch of cultivated land which extends for only a few miles on either side of the Nile.

In ancient times Egypt was the place where the cultures of Africa, Europe and Asia met, but it was nevertheless an isolated country, largely dependent on its own resources and the native genius of its people. It was protected from constant foreign invasion in the period of development by geographical factors and, unlike other parts of the ancient Near East, was off the direct route of advancing armies. This isolation helped the Egyptians to develop their civilization with little interruption, and although they made trading contacts with other countries from earliest times, they learned to rely to a large extent upon their own natural resources and to perfect the requisite skills.

The land was rich; domesticated animals, fish and poultry provided a varied diet, together with an abundance of vegetables and fruit. They grew flax and papyrus which provided them with linen for clothing and paper for writing; the land also provided them with hard and soft stone for building and carving statues and vessels, semiprecious jewels, such as turquoise and carnelian, copper and, above all, gold. For one commodity they were forced to look elsewhere. Wood, needed for so many aspects of life, was in short supply in Egypt, and cedarwood was imported throughout Egyptian history from Lebanon and Syria.

It is little wonder that the Egyptians considered themselves well-blessed by the gods; and their constant companion in all their activities – supplying their food, watering their land, providing a means of ready transport, linking the northern shores of the Delta where it bordered on the Mediterranean to the southernmost cataracts of Upper Egypt – was the Nile. Its power was only rivaled by the life-giving but destructive force of the sun.

Prehistoric Egypt (before 12,000 to 3100 BC). Men first arrived in Egypt in the Palaeolithic period (the Old Stone Age). Remains of their occupation have been found in the gravel terraces of the Nile Valley and in the surrounding desert. They were hunters and gatherers who fashioned stone implements – handaxes, choppers and fine flakes – often with great skill. They led a wandering life and hunted lions, goats, wild cattle, sheep and ibex and caught crocodiles, hippopotamuses, fish and fowl in the marshy swamps.

By the Neolithic period (the Late Stone Age) men had begun to settle in permanent villages and had acquired a knowledge of agriculture. The Neolithic came late to Egypt compared with the Near East, but there is plentiful evidence that by the second half of the 5th millennium BC animals were domesticated and men were cultivating

Predynastic figurine of the Negada culture (mid-4th millennium BC), found in a grave at Mamarija.

plants, building houses and making pottery and baskets.

Settlements have been found in the Fayoum and near Deir Tasa in Middle Egypt (the so-called "Tasian culture"). The burials of this period indicate that the Egyptians already believed in a continued existence after death. The dead were buried in shallow oval holes, near the desert and laid on one side in a contracted position, covered with a reed mat. They were supplied with pottery vessels, food, drink, palettes for grinding cosmetics, tools of stone and beads of bone, ivory and shell, for use in the hereafter.

The Chalcolithic period which followed was characterized by the occasional use of copper. Two main cultures developed in Egypt during this period. The southern culture has been named "Badarian" after the cemeteries in the neighborhood of the Middle Egyptian village of El-Badari; and other sites, scattered over Upper Egypt, have also produced "Badarian" material. The Badarians were peaceful farmers who produced easily recognizable, black-topped red or brown pottery, hollowed-out stone vases, slate palettes, carved ivory vases, combs and spoons, and necklaces of steatite beads which, for the first time, were glazed. Simple copper tools and beads have also been discovered. Near the human cemeteries, certain animals appear to have received sacred burials, perhaps indicating a religious belief.

The Amratian period, and the first stage of predynastic culture, developed out of the Badarian phase. Evidence for the Amratian exists in the cemetery at Hammamiya. Characteristic of this culture were the increasingly popular slate palettes, disk-shaped mace-heads, and polished red pottery with white line decoration.

In the meantime a different predynastic culture had developed in Lower Egypt, but the evidence for this has been partly destroyed by deposits of alluvium in the Delta which have probably covered the earliest levels. The cemeteries of the so-called "Gerzean" period (Middle and Late Predynastic) in this region are at Gerzeh, Abu Sir el Melek and Harageh. The dead were buried in graves – either oval or rectangular – which eventually housed the funerary equipment and food in separate adjoining compartments. These people made stone vases, flint implements, palettes in the shape of animals and birds, pear-shaped mace-heads, glazed vessels and jewelry; beads of iron, copper and gold have also been found. The characteristic pottery was of two kinds – the "wavy-handled" vases which may have had a Palestinian origin and the "decorated" ware – buff, pink or gray in color and decorated with red line-drawings of boats, landscapes, humans and animals. These northern products appear to have infiltrated into southern Egypt in some considerable numbers during the predynastic period.

The culture of Lower Egypt indicates association with foreign lands; the Mediterranean countries and Asia Minor were not far distant. During this period Egypt appears to have been transformed from an advanced Neolithic society, formed basically of many different localized tribes, into two well-defined and highly organized monarchies, situated in the north and south. At the same time a change becomes apparent in various aspects of the material culture – arts and crafts developed rapidly, and monumental brick buildings and writing appear – in short, the basic components of civilization. There seems to be no direct source within Egypt for these innovations, although some historians regard them as a natural development of

Late predynastic pottery vase of the Negada culture, with painted decoration, possibly used as a drinking vessel.

the earlier cultures found in Egypt. One suggestion is that a new race of people arrived in Egypt, either as a mass invasion or by gradual infiltration, bringing new ideas with them.

Indeed, a new physical type occurs in Egypt at this time. The skeletal remains of these people have shown them to be larger in build than the native inhabitants and to have had differently shaped skulls. Mesopotamia has been proposed as one place of origin for these intruders; in both Egypt and Mesopotamia writing developed at an early date. Mace-heads, cylinder seals and slate palettes displaying certain artistic affinities with their Mesopotamian counterparts now appear in Egypt, and were not known there before this time. The great recessed brick tomb structures of the earliest Egyptian dynasties may well have drawn inspiration from the brick temples of Mesopotamia. On the handle of a knife found in Egypt at Gebel el-Arak, and on tomb paintings at Hierakonpolis scenes of sea-battles were depicted in which ships of Egyptian and Mesopotamian type are in conflict.

It is unlikely that trade accounted for this outside influence on Egypt for there seems to have been no two-way flow of ideas or products. Quite possibly some of the immigrants came by sea, as shown on the Gebel el-Arak knife – through the Red Sea via the stream beds of either the Wadi el-Hammamat or the Wadi el-Tumilat; others doubtless made their way by land, perhaps through Syria and the Isthmus of Suez to the Delta. Some may have made a forceful entry; others perhaps came by peaceful infiltration. The whole process probably took many years and the effect on Egypt was short-lived – art-forms and architectural types cease to show continuous foreign influence after the 1st Dynasty. The different physical types eventually merged to form one nation.

This whole process is conjectural and the place of origin

of the new ideas is uncertain. One possibility which has been suggested is that perhaps immigrants may have come to both Egypt and Mesopotamia from a center as yet undiscovered. Perhaps we shall never know, but it is clear that a new factor inspired the already artistic inhabitants of the Nile Valley and set them firmly on the course they were to develop over the next few thousand years. For the first time we have an example of the ability of the Egyptians to make contact with, absorb, change and mold foreign ideas and people who entered their country. This "Egyptianization" process can be seen throughout Egypt's history.

In the Late Predynastic period (c. 3400 to 3100 BC) two independent kingdoms grew up. Both were similar in that they consisted of small independent districts, each of which had a main town, a local god and a chieftain. The northern kingdom in the Delta had its capital at Pe (the Greek "Buto") whose protective deity was the cobra-goddess, Edjo; the southern kingdom in Upper Egypt had its capital at Nekheb, near Hierakonpolis, under the care of the vulture-goddess, Nekhbet. Little is known of the rulers of these kingdoms, but fragments of a mace-head found at Hierakonpolis belonging to a king – Scorpion – are decorated with scenes showing his victory over enemies and his development of the irrigation of the land. It is likely that Scorpion paved the way for Narmer's later resounding success in unifying the country. The history of dynastic Egypt was born with the conquest of the north by a southern king, Narmer-Menes, who then proceeded to make himself king of a united Egypt. Menes is given as the name of the first king of the 1st Dynasty by the historian Manetho, and despite some controversy among modern historians, his identification with Narmer is generally accepted.

From this point onwards, until the end of their history, the kings of ancient Egypt never forgot the dualism of their kingship. In the royal titulary (or list of the five names of pharaoh) this was commemorated when the rulers were referred to as "King of Upper and Lower Egypt" and "Lord of the Two Lands." They also invoked the protection of the two ancient goddesses – vulture and cobra – of the two earliest capitals. The unification took place about 3100 BC and, by the chance of discovery, a slate palette, decorated with scenes on both sides, was uncovered by J. E. Quibell, an archaeologist who was digging at Kom el-Ahmar in 1898. This palette is thought to depict the unification of Egypt by the victorious King Narmer. On one side he is shown wearing the White Crown of the King of Upper Egypt, and on the other side he appears in the Red Crown of the Lower Egyptian king whose rule extended over the Delta and beyond.

The Archaic Period (1st and 2nd Dynasties, 3100 to 2686 BC). It is possible that Narmer married a princess of northern origin to consolidate his conquests. According to Herodotus, he moved his capital to the north where he founded as the residence city a site known as "White Walls" – the Memphis of later times. This was an ideal center from which to deal with the affairs of his much-expanded kingdom.

Seven other kings of the 1st Dynasty succeeded him and extended their authority from the Mediterranean to the first cataract, where they waged war against the Nubian tribes. They sent expeditions to Sinai to safeguard the importation of copper and malachite, and seem to have been victorious over some of the Libyans – tribes with distinctive red or blond hair and blue eyes who lived on

Below left: the crowns of Upper (*left*) and Lower Egypt.
Below right: the two faces of King Narmer's slate palette on which he is depicted wearing both the Egyptian crowns.

13

the edge of the western desert. A rock relief dating to the reign of Djer (the third king of the dynasty), found near Buhen in the Sudan, suggests that some attempt was also made to control this area.

The kings of the 2nd Dynasty (c. 2890 to 2686 BC) were from Thinis in the south. Little is known of them but this seems to have been a time of some internal dissension. The kings of the 1st and 2nd Dynasties were buried in great brick mastaba tombs. Petrie uncovered a series of structures at Abydos, belonging to the rulers of the 2nd Dynasty, and although they contained no human remains, they were believed to be the kings' tombs; there was also a large number of subsidiary tombs belonging to the royal entourage. Emery, excavating at Saqqara near Memphis from 1935 onwards, discovered a set of similar buildings which were twice as large as those at Abydos, were better preserved and contained some human remains. The structures were of mud-brick, with wood and stone used in their construction.

Much of our knowledge of this time is based on material found in the mastabas at Abydos and Saqqara. The structures at Abydos were individually identified by sealings and inscribed objects found within and also by the presence outside the tombs of stelae bearing the owners' names. At Saqqara inscribed material enabled a particular mastaba to be dated to a definite reign but did not establish the ownership. Emery believed that the tombs at Abydos were cenotaphs, never occupied by the kings, and that they were buried at Saqqara. The two sets of structures might then have represented the kings in their dual roles as kings of Upper and Lower Egypt. Not all Egyptologists subscribe to this theory but it cannot be denied that, whatever their purpose, the structures bear witness to the unity and consolidation achieved so shortly after Narmer's victory.

Egyptian craftsmen became increasingly skilled during the Archaic Period. They produced magnificent stone vessels and experimented in working with faience and blue glass. Copper tools and weapons were made as gold and copper working was developed. Statuary in stone, ivory and probably wood and copper was made, in addition to fine jewelry and furniture to be placed in tombs for the afterlife. Papyrus began to be used by the scribes for writing which was beginning to display elements of sentence structure by the end of the 1st Dynasty.

The Archaic Period, the time of experimentation, laid the foundations of later brilliance. The men of the Old Kingdom were to develop these skills and set their ineradicable stamp on ancient Egyptian civilization.

The Old Kingdom (3rd to 6th Dynasties, c. 2686 to 2181 BC). The Old Kingdom saw the establishment of a powerful state; the Egyptians were exhorted to practise modesty, discretion, honesty and respect for their elders and to know their places in the social hierarchy. At the top was the king; he was from the first regarded as divine, although a little below the gods, but by the 5th Dynasty he came to be thought of as the actual son of the sun god. In the early years there was a tremendous chasm between him and his subjects which lessened in time for a variety of reasons. At the beginning of the 3rd Dynasty Imhotep, the royal architect, designed for King Djoser the first great stone structure built by man – the Step Pyramid at Saqqara, which was surrounded by a complex of courts and buildings and enclosed within a girdle wall, measuring over a mile in perimeter. This was an experiment, using a new architectural form and new building materials and techniques, but the decorative elements found therein in many cases originated in the earliest mud and reed huts.

By the 4th Dynasty the kings were buried in true pyramids and the three at Gizeh, built for Cheops, Chephren and Mycerinus, were the peak of achievement in this field. The man responsible for the construction of the Great Pyramid was probably the Vizier, Prince Hemon, a son of King Sneferu and cousin to Cheops. By the 5th Dynasty pyramids were smaller and the construction was of a lower standard, with the result that, today, these pyramids are merely mounds of rubble. Separate pyramids were built for the kings and their queens and were intended to protect their bodies and funerary possessions – statuary, furniture, jewelry and other belongings for the afterlife.

Since the time of Menes the government of the country had been centered at the royal palace and the king delegated some of his duties to highborn officials. These were usually royal relatives who served him loyally in lifetime in return for a share in the king's eternity. They were often sons of minor queens. The capital was at Memphis where the nobility and the best artists gathered; other centers – all in the north – were at Gizeh, Heliopolis and Saqqara. In the 3rd and 4th Dynasties only the king was believed to have eternal life; by being buried near him the nobles hoped to share this life, in his service. Thus at Gizeh it is possible to see the rows of mastaba tombs belonging to these faithful officials stretching in lines at the bases of the royal pyramids, close to their masters in death as in life. The ultimate expression of royal favor was permission to prepare one's tomb in the shadow of the pyramid.

The peasants made up the largest part of the population and worked for most of the year on the land, which in theory belonged to the king. When the Nile inundation precluded work they were employed on the great state building projects, and were always liable for corvée (forced labor). They believed that, without pharaoh, their lives were of little value for he alone could give them some vicarious eternity. So they worked for him in the hope that their efforts would win them some chance of survival after death. Indeed, the whole economy of Egypt and most of the architectural and artistic efforts had this one aim – to ensure pharaoh's existence after death.

In the 4th Dynasty the material civilization and artforms reached a peak of excellence. After this there was a slow, inevitable decline and a final destruction of the system owing to social, economic and religious reasons.

Saqqara, necropolis of the Old Kingdom,
a complex of pyramids, chapels and tombs.
Below: entrance and view into the courtyard
of the pyramid complex.

Below left: the tomb room of the Pharaoh Unas. On the walls
are inscribed the "Pyramid Texts," designed to protect the
king and ease his passage into the hereafter.

Above right: a line of fluted columns in the pyramid complex.
The columns at Saqqara were an adaptation in stone of the
earlier reed forms.

Column with hieroglyphs in a mastaba next to the famous
step pyramid built by Djoser at Saqqara.

Painted reliefs in the tomb of Ti (5th Dynasty), an Old Kingdom nobleman, showing animals being driven out in rows.

Anarchy followed. The achievements of the Old Kingdom were partly regained and often imitated by later generations, but there was never again the same sense of direction and purpose and their art never recaptured the purity and severity of the early period. The reasons for this are complex.

In the 5th Dynasty the cult of the sun god became all-powerful, together with its priesthood at Heliopolis. A squat obelisk, whose gold-covered pyramidion (or peak) reflected the sun's rays, was the cult symbol, and worship took place in temples with courts open to the sky. The faith had a limited appeal. The kings adopted it as their religion for a time, but the worship was too intellectual and remote for the masses. However, it succeeded in promoting the power of the priesthood and in undermining the divinity of the king, who now became merely the "Son of Re'."

The king became less remote from his people, partly due to marriage with non-royal women, as in the case of Pepy I, instead of with members of his own family. The purity of the line and belief in the king's divinity were thus diluted. The royal family was also harassed by dynastic quarrels. Economically, the royal treasury became impoverished, partly through the need to maintain the pyramids and other funerary endowments of previous rulers, and partly through the practise of presenting gifts of royal land to nobles as endowments for the upkeep of their own family tombs and funerary rituals. Such gifts were often exempted from taxation. Temples, too, were presented with royal gifts of land and it was not long before the nobility and the priesthood rivaled their benefactor in wealth. The lands were hereditary and passed from father to son, and eventually great parcels of crown land were distributed among the children of former courtiers.

At the same time the nomarchs or governors of the provinces, who at one time had been royal relatives and dependent for their positions upon the king, began to establish their positions as hereditary. Their sons no longer felt obliged to the king for their power and came to consider themselves semi-independent minor kinglets, especially in the more remote areas. They no longer wanted to be buried in pharaoh's shadow but in rock tombs in their own provinces, far away from the capital. As the royal pyramids became smaller, there was less royal work for the artisans who took on the decoration of private tombs and the production of private statuary in the 5th and 6th Dynasties. Tomb-chapels like those of the nobles Ti (5th Dynasty) and Mereruka (6th Dynasty) at Saqqara are decorated with scenes of daily life which give a vivid impression of the Old Kingdom.

After the 90 years of Pepy II's reign the system finally collapsed, mainly due to internal pressures, but also aggravated by aggression on Egypt's eastern frontier. Egypt had no desire for expansion at this date; her enterprises were for purposes of trade, and there was not even a standing army. Expeditions were sent to Nubia and Upper Sudan from time to time, and Egypt was assured of trading access to the gold, diorite, ebony, ivory, panther skins and other exotic products of Nubia; Nubians also fought as mercenaries for Egypt. Towards the end of the Old Kingdom this southern frontier was guarded by "Governors of the South." Trading expeditions were also sent to the land of Punt (believed to be on the Somali coast) to obtain incense for the temple rituals. Copper and turquoise were mined in Sinai. From the 4th Dynasty onwards there was an active sea trade with Byblos, where cedarwood was obtained. Egypt came to wield great influence at Byblos and probably a number of Egyptians settled there and built a temple in the 4th Dynasty. The Libyans continued to cause trouble, and another threat appeared in the east. In the 6th Dynasty Weni led a military expedition as far as Carmel in Palestine and succeeded in reducing the danger – but only for a short time.

The Old Kingdom was the yardstick by which all later Egyptian achievements were measured. Magnificent results were attained in art, architecture and literature. There were medical and religious writings, such as the Memphite theology and the Pyramid Texts, designed to protect the royal body by magic when it became apparent that the plundered pyramids had failed, and moral treatises on conduct.

It is fitting that the Gizeh Pyramids and Chephren's Great Sphinx should have survived the ravages of time to remind the world of the achievements of this Golden Age.

The First Intermediate Period (7th to 11th Dynasties, c. 2181 to 1991 BC). At the end of the Old Kingdom Egypt fell into a state of rapid decline. According to the historian Manetho, in the 7th Dynasty "70 kings ruled for 70 days"; pharaohs of both the 7th and 8th Dynasties struggled ineffectively to maintain power from Memphis. Anarchy, violence and poverty were followed by famine, plague and utter depression. The old people who had lived through the peace and security of the Old Kingdom must surely have suffered most, but no one was safe from marauding thieves, hunger and fear. It was a topsy-turvy world. The loss of strong centralized power, firmly wielded by god's son, had resulted in this tragedy. Egypt returned to the state it had known before the country's unification by Menes. Separate localities, which had become neat administrative zones under Old Kingdom bureaucracy, now became independent states, often at war with each other. The internal chaos was worsened by the penetration of foreign nomads into the Delta region. The Egyptians bewailed their fate – their writings tell us that: "Every good thing has disappeared," and "not even the black of the fingernails is left." The departed fared little better it seemed: "The dead are thrown in the river . . . Laughter has perished. Grief walks the land." They began to question the purpose of their lives, and even to doubt their belief in survival after death, as the mortality of the pharaoh was emphasized by events.

The gloom was reflected in art. The self-examination had long-lasting effects, moreover; literary works show a depth of feeling quite absent from those composed in earlier, more secure times and religious thought underwent some profound changes. One of the most poignant pieces of Egyptian literature was the argument between a man, weary of his existence in strife-torn Egypt, and his soul, as he contemplates suicide. Death he views as an envied state, made clear in this verse:

Death is before me today,
As when a man longeth to see his home again,
After he has spent many years in captivity.

Various local governors sought to restore order and take power. The ruler of Heracleopolis, a town near the Fayoum, succeeded in uniting Middle Egypt and founded a line of rulers who were to make up the 9th and 10th Dynasties. Under their rule other provincial governors, such as those at Benihasan and Akhmim, were allowed to continue in a state of semi-independence.

New philosophies developed. "Instructions," such as those written by King Wa-ka-re' for his son Mery-ka-re', showed a new moral awareness of the need to care for others; life was not just a matter of following established codes of behavior in order to get on. The Egyptians had learned some valuable lessons from their troubles. Perhaps one most important result was the changed attitude towards death. Local governors were now held to be equal, if not superior, to pharaoh; they expected an eternal life comparable to his. The hereafter, too, underwent a process of democratization, and gradually everyone came to expect his individual survival after death. Those who could afford it equipped their tombs with model statues of wood – servants, bakers, butchers – to serve them after death. Beautiful painted wooden coffins were produced, and local dignitaries adopted the previously royal Pyramid Texts and had them inscribed with suitable additions in their coffins. These altered texts occur only at this period (during the Middle Kingdom) and much later, in the 26th Dynasty. Today, we know them as the "Coffin Texts."

Relief of the tomb owner (*right*) in a small mastaba tomb at Saqqara (Old Kingdom). The owner is seated in front of an altar of offerings that have been laid out for presentation to his Ka.

Art was also decentralized; Memphis was no longer the hub of the artisans' world and talent, vigorous if perhaps a little crude, flourished in the provinces. Religion, too, no longer centered on the capital, and men reverted to the worship of local deities as in earlier times.

While the Heracleopolitans held sway in the North, they had to contend with the princes of Thebes in the South whose rule extended fron Elephantine to south of Abydos. Fighting between them was intermittent until a Theban prince defeated the Heracleopolitans and, as King Mentuhotep I Nebhepet-re', ruled a united Egypt during the 11th Dynasty. He was king for 51 years, consolidating Egypt's borders, pacifying the land and restoring it to prosperity. He controlled his kingdom from Thebes and appointed a loyal Theban to every position of importance. His military activity was to launch punitive expeditions to ensure the safety of his borders and trading routes, mines and quarries. These were directed against the Libyans, the Bedouin of Sinai and the eastern desert, and Nubia. In Nubia he tried to restore Egyptian authority which had lapsed since the 6th Dynasty, and succeeded in levying tribute and ensuring a safe trading route. His was a defensive military policy to back up a far-reaching economic policy. Once again, Egyptian ships sailed the Red Sea to Punt.

He was buried in a unique tomb-temple – part pyramid, part temple – at Deir el-Bahri, Thebes, which is today overshadowed by the better-preserved temple of Queen Hatshepsut. Here a statue of the king was found in the burial chamber under the pyramid. Relatives and officials were buried in neighboring rock-cut tombs, and nearby was a chapel for his wife-sister, Neferu. Aerial photographs show the hollows in the sands where a garden once flourished in front of the tomb, planted with a grove of tamarisks and eight larger sycamore-figs which gave shade to the statues of the king.

Mentuhotep I was succeeded by his son, whose reign was peaceful, but when Mentuhotep III came to the throne the country again experienced difficulties and his brief reign ended with the usurpation of power by a certain Amenemmes, probably the Vizier and Governor of the South.

Perhaps the most marked and far-reaching development of this troubled period was the great increase in popularity of the god Osiris who was believed to have risen from the dead and promised his believers, whatever their status, a fair judgment of their earthly behavior and eternal life. The humblest man was given the hope of eternal life and could share in the resurrection of this god after death, because king and subjects alike were assimilated to Osiris after death.

The Middle Kingdom (12th Dynasty, 1991 to 1786 BC).

"A king shall come forth from Upper Egypt called Ameni, the son of a woman of the South . . . He shall receive the White Crown and wear the Red Crown . . ."

Thus states the Prophecy of Neferty, which was in fact composed after the accession of Amenemmes I. The new ruler, probably the former vizier of the last king of the 11th Dynasty, faced a difficult task in justifying his right to the throne and restoring the country. Jealous rivals must have threatened him from all sides. To secure the succession he made his eldest son, Sesostris, his co-regent so that the throne would pass smoothly to him. All the rulers of the 12th Dynasty were to adopt this policy. Although originally from Thebes, Amenemmes I moved his capital to the more central city of It-towe, near modern El-Lisht. With this move to the north, the leaders of the new dynasty abandoned the custom of burial in rock-cut tombs and reverted to pyramid-building, although they never attempted to raise such magnificent structures as the Old Kingdom had produced. Mastaba tombs were once again built near the pyramids for some of the high officials.

The land was gradually settled; an irrigation system was again established, and a great engineering feat was accomplished in the Fayoum, a large oasis in the western desert, by Sesostris II and Amenemmes III. The annual inflow into this great basin from the Nile, via the Bahr Yusuf, was reduced, the land reclaimed was encircled by a large semi-circular embankment and dykes and canals were built to prevent flooding. Altogether, 40 square miles of pastureland were reclaimed and the resulting lake also acted as a reservoir.

The administration of the country was also greatly reformed. The nomarchs had supported Amenemmes I in establishing his rule, encouraged by his restoration to them of many of their old privileges. By the reign of Sesostris III many were again abusing their privileges and he finally destroyed their power completely. We do not know how this was achieved, but certainly they never troubled the pharaoh again and their local tombs, law-courts, taxation and troop-raising were never again part of the Egyptian scene. A new middle class – small farmers, artisans and traders – came to power, all grateful to the king for their new status.

According to Manetho, Amenemmes I died at the hands of his own chamberlains. His successors – his direct descendents – continued to rule and carried out many of his policies. Foreign policy was administered on two main fronts – in Africa and in Asia. Nubia was reconquered as far as Semna, just south of the second cataract, and a string of sturdy fortresses was built between the first and third cataracts to subjugate this area. A new people had arrived in Nubia since the end of the Old Kingdom, and they were a good deal more aggressive towards the Egyptians. The fortresses became permanent bases with army families in residence, and the insurrections were again controlled. Egypt's access to the gold of Nubia was assured. In the north and northeast – Palestine, Syria and Sinai – trading and mining rights were protected by a defensive military policy.

Egyptian trade flourished. Cretan wares reached Egypt,

The Middle Kingdom produced fine jewelry like the pectoral of a princess (*above*), and powerful statues of royalty like that of Amenemmes III (*below left*) contrasted with a New Kingdom head of Akhenaten. Mentuhotep I (*right*) united Egypt in troubled times. Later troubles are charted *below*.

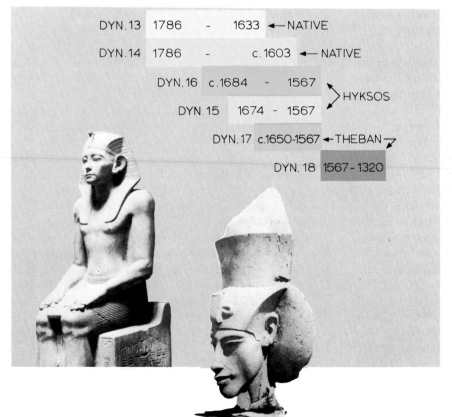

DYN. 13	1786	– 1633	←— NATIVE
DYN. 14	1786	– c. 1603	←— NATIVE
DYN. 16	c. 1684	– 1567	⎫ HYKSOS
DYN. 15	1674	– 1567	⎭
DYN. 17	c. 1650-1567		←— THEBAN ↗
DYN. 18	1567 – 1320		

and Aegean influence is apparent in certain decorative motifs on pottery and other objects, and in the shape and form of pottery. Kamares ware (Minoan pottery) has been found in Egypt at Lahun, Abydos and El-Harageh, and Egyptian objects have been found in Crete. Copper and bronze were imported from Cyprus, cedarwood from Lebanon and incense from Punt; Nubia supplied gold, copper, diorite, granite and amethyst. In Syria and Palestine the names of Egyptian kings have been found on objects which have come to light at Gaza, Ras Shamra, Tod, Megiddo and Byblos. At Byblos the native governors actually used Egyptian names and titles and Egyptian goods.

Middle Kingdom art reached a high standard. The royal portrait statuary is particularly striking, and in the features of these kings one sees something of the forcefulness, grim determination and also perhaps disillusionment of the men who had restored Egypt to power. By comparison, the private statuary is insipid; pharaoh was again supreme. The jewelry of this period was never surpassed in Egypt. The delicacy of the pectorals, crowns, armlets and collars of the royal princesses bears witness to the inspiration and skill of the craftsmen. Semi-precious stones – lapis lazuli, amethyst, carnelian and felspar – were mounted in gold. The jewelry found in the pit-tombs of the princesses at Dahshur and Illahun is today in the museums of Cairo and New York.

Architecture included the new pyramids at Lisht, Dahshur, El-Lahun and Hawara, and cultus-temples (for the worship of the gods), most of which were later dismantled and incorporated in the structure of other temples. Middle Kingdom temples do survive in part at Medinet Maadi and Tod. Private brick tombs were built around the pyramids and other tombs of the nobles continued to be built in the cliffs near the provincial centers until the reign of Sesostris III. Particularly ambitious building programs were carried out all over Egypt by Sesostris I and Amenemmes III. The latter is credited with the famous "Labyrinth" described by Greek historians as a wonder surpassing even the pyramids. It seems that this may be identified with the funerary complex of the Hawara pyramid, investigated by Petrie. The string of fortresses in Nubia was another innovation.

The Middle Kingdom was the Golden Age of Egyptian literature; the works of this age became classics, laboriously copied and thus preserved by later generations of schoolboys. The hieroglyphic language of the period is today regarded as the classical form, and "Middle Egyptian" is the first stage of the language which would-be Egyptologists learn.

The Old Kingdom had ended with a female ruler – Nitocris; the end of the Middle Kingdom is also marked by a similar unusual occurrence when Sobekneferu, daughter of Amenemmes III and probably sister of Amenemmes IV, became Queen regnant and the last ruler of the 12th Dynasty. This was probably due to the lack of a male heir.

Sphinx of Ramesses II at Memphis (19th Dynasty, New Kingdom). The sphinx at Gizeh was surely its precursor.

The Second Intermediate Period (13th to 17th Dynasties, 1786 to 1567 BC). Egypt again went through a period of slow decline in the 13th Dynasty when a series of "puppet" kings – Manetho's "60 kings of Diospolis" – ruled from Memphis and Lisht; they were dominated by a strong line of viziers. Despite this, an element of centralized control continued for over 100 years, and Egypt still exercised influence abroad. When the 12th Dynasty came to an end, a local dynasty broke away and ruled from Xois; this was the 14th Dynasty which continued to flourish after most of the country had submitted to the Hyksos (see below). In the reign of "Tutimaios" – believed to be King Djedneferre Dudimose – the Hyksos succeeded in gaining control of much of Egypt, and formed the 15th and 16th Dynasties. Memphis fell to the Hyksos ruler Salitis in 1674 BC, and the 13th Dynasty came to an end about 1633 BC. Meanwhile in about 1650 BC a new line of native rulers arose at Thebes; they formed a semi-independent state in the south and are known as the 17th Dynasty. Although they paid tribute to the Hyksos they preserved their independence, and it was these princes who eventually overthrew the Hyksos and drove them from Egypt. These Thebans then became the new native rulers of a united Egypt and founded the 18th Dynasty and, with it, the New Kingdom.

Who then were these foreign "invaders"? There is no evidence to suggest a vast ethnic invasion of Egypt, as was at one time believed by scholars, for the Hyksos do not appear to have had a common language, and there was no sudden change in burial customs as might have been expected to follow such an "invasion." The Hyksos generally showed great respect for Egyptian civilization; the new rulers adopted Egyptian titles and habits, and wrote their names in hieroglyphs. They worshiped the Egyptian god Seth, used Egyptian officials and maintained the general administrative system. Later statements that they burned cities and temples and created a period of anarchy are probably based on propaganda put out by their later Theban conquerors. Nevertheless, the fact that a non-Egyptian king sat on Egypt's throne gave the people a rude awakening.

The Hyksos spread certain ideas and techniques; they introduced both warlike and peaceful ideas into Egypt, including the use of bronze rather than copper, horses, chariots, new weapons, hump-backed cattle, the lyre and lute and the vertical loom. In our museums today, there are fine examples of the scarabs of this period, with their distinctive scroll designs.

Later generations regarded the Hyksos as one of Egypt's major disasters. Because they brought with them a new outlook, their presence cannot have been popular, and they changed ancient Egypt's attitudes to warfare and foreign conquest. From now on, Egypt would pursue an aggressive military policy and keep a fully-trained professional army. The one certain way to prevent a repetition of foreign rule was to attack and defeat the would-be conquerors in their own lands; and thus the concept of Egypt's Empire was born.

The princes of Thebes expelled the Hyksos from Egypt. Conflict began between the Hyksos ruler, Apophis, and Seqenenre' of Thebes. The body of the latter, which we still possess today, indicates by its terrible head wounds that the Theban died in battle. His son, Kamose, continued the fight; details of this war are recorded on two stelae, one of which was discovered in 1954 at Karnak. Apophis was driven from Middle Egypt, and Kamose was able to take the Hyksos capital of Avaris.

The younger brother of Kamose, Ahmosis, dealt the final blow. Having driven the Hyksos out of Egypt, he pursued them into Palestine, where he eliminated the danger in a series of campaigns. He then invaded the region of Kush, to the south of Egypt, which had allied with and supported the Hyksos. After a decade of fighting the supremacy of Egypt was assured. King Ahmosis I inaugurated the New Kingdom and the Empire.

The avenue of ram-headed sphinxes at the temple of Karnak (Middle to Late period). This was the way along which prisoners and booty were brought to be presented to the god Amun during the pharaoh's procession. *Inset:* head of Amenophis II from a sphinx, probably at Karnak (18th Dynasty).

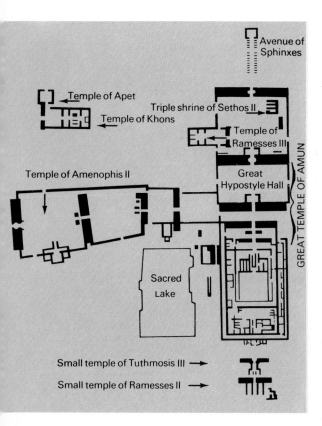

Karnak. *Left:* plan of the main part of the temple at Karnak. *Above:* general view showing the pylons and entrance to the temple and the column of King Taharqa. *Below left:* the obelisk of Queen Hatshepsut (18th Dynasty) carved from Aswan stone. The top was originally covered in gold. *Below:* column in the hypostyle hall showing the god Min.

The New Kingdom (18th to 20th Dynasties, 1567 to 1085 BC). The 18th Dynasty produced a series of active, able pharaohs who ensured by conquest of foreign lands that booty and tribute flowed into the Egyptian coffers. The wealth of Egypt had never been greater and enabled the building of magnificent temples and tombs at Thebes where the capital was now situated. Due to the dryness of the climate, many of these wonderful buildings, although partly ruined, remain today, and thus our knowledge of this period is greater than that of any other.

Nubia was again brought under Egypt's control. Some of the old Middle Kingdom fortresses were repaired and enlarged and a string of new ones built. Nubia became more "Egyptianized" than ever before and supplied Egypt with luxury goods – copper, gold, ivory, ebony, resins, African woods, carnelian and amethyst, leopard skins, ostrich plumes and domestic slaves.

In Asia Minor the pharaohs set out to conquer the loose confederations of city states which existed in Syria and Palestine. These city states, which ruled small areas of land beyond their gates, were constantly vying with each other. Sometimes one city ruler managed to gain the temporary allegiance of a few other city states, but it was generally a scene of shifting allegiances and intrigue. Tuthmosis I extended the boundaries of the new Egyptian Empire as far as Naharin, situated between two rivers – the Orontes and the Euphrates. Egypt set up native governors in charge of the newly-conquered areas in Syria and Palestine; in some city states, presumably those whose loyalty was in doubt, Egyptian garrisons were installed. Local chieftains were usually required to send tribute to Egypt and their sons were taken to Egypt as hostages, to be educated with the princes and later returned to their own cities, when fully-grown, as pro-Egyptian rulers. Thus Egypt increased her influence in Syria/Palestine.

By the time Tuthmosis III came to the throne, a new power – Mitanni – was beginning to cause difficulties for Egypt. The Mitannian Empire was made up of a large number of Hurrians, a people who had spread southwards into the Caspian Sea area, and its rulers were of Indo-Aryan stock. The Empire extended from the North Syrian coast to the River Tigris. Thus the small Syrian and Canaanite cities began to divide their allegiance between Egypt and Mitanni and gradually Egypt lost her former control. But Tuthmosis III succeeded in restoring Egypt's influence in Asia Minor in a series of 17 campaigns fought over 20 years. He pushed Egyptian rule as far as the Taurus mountains and the Euphrates, leaving garrisons at various points and reasserting Egyptian supremacy. Later in the dynasty Egypt and Mitanni made peace, cemented by marriages between Egyptian kings and Mitannian princesses.

But now a new power began to threaten the peace. Mitanni's neighbors were Assyria on one side and the Hittites, who occupied a large part of Anatolia, on the other. Towards the end of Amenophis III's reign a new

Hittite king, Shuppiluliuma, came to the throne and the Hittite Empire flourished. He sacked the capital of Mitanni and dominated Syria, having wooed away from Egypt many of her former satellite city states, causing dissension among them. Amenophis III, obese, world-weary and interested only in the luxurious life of his court, paid little heed; his son, the heretic Amenophis IV (Akhenaten), cared even less, so engrossed was he in his great religious revolution. The letters from the city states, begging for Egyptian aid, went unanswered. Ignored by her ally, Mitanni fell under Hittite domination and when Shuppiluliuma died, eventually became part of the Assyrian domains. The Egyptian Empire disintegrated, to be restored years later by the pharaohs of the 19th Dynasty.

The diplomatic correspondence of the latter part of the 18th Dynasty between Amenophis III's court, that of his son and the kings and princelings of other Near Eastern states is preserved in the Tell el-Amarna letters found at Akhenaten's capital, and in the Boghaz Keui tablets from the Hittite Record Office. Both sets are written in Akkadian, the diplomatic language of the time. From these it appears that the city states of Syria/Palestine were either subdued or went over to the Hittites, and in the south the governor of Jerusalem had to contend with the raiding nomads – the Khabiru – who are believed by some scholars to have had links with the Hebrews.

At its height the Egyptian Empire, governed by strong pharaohs, was a success. Although its organization was less sophisticated than that of the later Assyrian and Persian empires, and it was smaller, it was the first large imperial power to be established in the Middle East.

During the Empire more Asiatic peoples entered Egypt, bringing new fashions in clothing, and new customs, vocabulary and deities. The cities of Egypt at this time must have reflected the brilliance and wealth of the period, with their cosmopolitan crowds made up of all the races with whom the Empire came into contact. Trade between Egypt and other lands flourished. In addition to a lively exchange in goods between Egypt and Asia, Egyptian ships still sailed to Punt to barter for incense, and for myrrh trees which were eventually planted in temple gardens in Egypt. Scenes in the Temple of Hatshepsut at Deir el-Bahri show an expedition to Punt, and give interesting glimpses of Puntite houses, built on stilts, and of their portly queen.

The monarchs of the 18th Dynasty were all-powerful. The practise of the king marrying the Great Royal Daughter, often his own full or half-sister, was frequent in the early 18th Dynasty; the system of co-regency between a king and his son was also used by several rulers. From the reign of Amenophis I onwards the kings built rock-cut tombs near Thebes, on the west bank of the Nile, in the so-called Valley of the Kings. Although these burials must have contained sumptuous treasures, the only intact burial to have been discovered is that of the minor ruler, Tutankhamun. The mummies of many of the 18th-Dynasty pharaohs, however, were removed by priests to a safe hiding place and have been discovered and placed in a special room in the Cairo Museum. These pharaohs built mortuary temples at Thebes where the cult of these dead rulers could be performed. In neighboring valleys some of the queens and princes were buried. The tombs of the nobles, also nearby, are famous for their decoration which shows delightful scenes of everyday life, unlike the royal tombs.

Although we can still gaze on the mummified features of the rulers, what do we actually know of the personalities of these great monarchs? Among the monuments and literary works, the chronological tables and official documents, we can perhaps discern some of the feelings and emotions of pharaoh and his court. For example, we know that Tuthmosis III was a lover of nature. On his campaigns in Syria he found time to collect unusual plants and animals and send them to Egypt for a botanical garden at Thebes. Most of the pharaohs also enjoyed such active pursuits as lion and elephant hunts, as well as target-shooting.

Occasionally, behind the facade of protocol, we can glimpse the quarrels and intrigues, the jealousies and rivalries of the royal family. Hatshepsut, daughter of Tuthmosis I by his Great Royal Wife, was married to another of her father's children by a secondary wife – Tuthmosis II. He died, having fathered only daughters by Hatshepsut but leaving a son, born to a royal concubine. Hatshepsut, who it seems could not tolerate being ousted by the child of a non-royal favorite of her husband, claimed the throne for herself. With full pharaonic powers, titles and regalia, she ruled Egypt as Queen Regnant, and justified her actions in scenes painted in her temple at Deir el-Bahri of her fictitious divine birth and appointment and coronation as rightful ruler by her own father. This building, which blends so well with its setting at the foot of the Theban cliffs, was designed by the royal architect and favorite, Senenmut. Eventually, Senenmut and Hatshepsut fell from power and Tuthmosis III, now full-grown, seized his rightful throne. Apart from a notable lack of military endeavor, Hatshepsut appears to have ruled Egypt as well as any of her male counterparts.

Another court where the known facts present a vivid picture of a luxurious way of life was that of Amenophis III. Young Tiye, the daughter of a commoner (her father was Yuya, overseer of horses) was chosen as the wife of Amenophis III. This unprecedented event was proclaimed on a series of commemorative scarabs. Amenophis married many other women, including princesses from Mitanni, but Tiye remained his Great Royal Wife. He grew increasingly indolent, whiling away his time in his great palace at Malkata with its beautiful pleasure lake. His mortuary temple has not survived but today, on the Theban plain, the visitor can see two enormous statues – the Colossi of Memnon – which once stood before the temple pylons (gateway buildings).

At the end of the 18th Dynasty Akhenaten came to the throne, known at first as Amenophis IV. With his queen, Nefertiti, he founded a new capital where he could pursue his worship of the strange, featureless god, Aten. After some years his religion became exclusive and the monuments of other deities were destroyed and defaced, and their priesthoods and worship terminated. At Akhetaten, his capital (the modern Tell el-Amarna) this monotheistic revolution in religion was pursued by the royal family and the court; a simultaneous revolution occurred

Hathor-headed capital from the New Kingdom temple of Queen Hatshepsut at Deir el-Bahri. The goddess Hathor is shown with the face of a woman and the ears of a cow.

justify his claim to the throne. But Ankhesenamun wrote a letter to the king of the Hittites, Egypt's old enemy, begging him to send one of his sons to Egypt to marry her. Apparently, she was desparate to avoid whatever fate awaited her at home, for this invitation, if accepted would have resulted in a new Hittite king for Egypt. However, the Hittite king delayed, and when he eventually sent a prince the young man was murdered en route to Egypt. Ay finally married Ankhesenamun and neither she nor her younger sisters are heard of again. None of Akhenaten's daughters had apparently provided a male heir – children born to Meritaten and Ankhesenpaaten by their own father died at birth – and the mummified foetuses discovered in Tutankhamun's tomb are probably the only pathetic remains of his offspring.

Ay was succeeded by Horemheb, the last ruler of the 18th Dynasty, who had formerly been Commander of the Army and Chief Administrator. Perhaps he had been the power behind the throne since the return of the court to Thebes, using Tutankhamun and Ay as figureheads. This

Temple of Queen Hatshepsut. *Left:* column with hieroglyphs describing the queen as the "son" of god. *Below:* the Birth Colonnade, whose austere columns show scenes of Hatshepsut's birth.

in art, where emphasis was placed on true representation, unlike the earlier "idealized" style of art.

Nefertiti bore her husband six daughters and no sons. After some years she disappeared from the scene – perhaps through death or banishment – and Akhenaten married his eldest daughter, Meritaten. As he had no sons, his chosen successor was Smenkhkare, probably a son of Amenophis III by a secondary wife, perhaps Sitamun, Amenophis III's own daughter by Queen Tiye. Tests carried out in the 1960s on the mummies of Smenkhkare and Tutankhamun have indicated that the two boys were probably full brothers, and sons of Amenophis III. Akhenaten now gave Smenkhkare the royal heiress – his own daughter-wife, Meritaten – and himself married his third daughter, Ankhesenpaaten (the second, Maketaten, had died as a child). Akhenaten and Meritaten both died and Smenkhkare married the widowed Ankhesenpaaten. Upon his early death, the throne and Ankhesenpaaten passed to Tutankhamun, in the absence of any other male heir. A restoration of the old religion and the multitude of deities now took place. Amun, in particular, was reinstated, and the capital returned to Thebes with Tutankhamun, Ankhesenpaaten (now re-named Ankhesenamun) and the remaining three daughters of Akhenaten. As Tutankhamun was only a child at his accession, one must assume that the policy was not his but that of an older, experienced man.

The boy-king died in his late teens and the throne passed to a non-royal adviser, the elderly Ay. It was arranged that Ay should now marry the royal widow and heiress, to

non-royal ruler devoted his reign to the restoration of the old order and to the attempted destruction of all traces of the hated heretic pharaoh and his family.

Ramesses I, the first king of the 19th Dynasty, was the son of a low-ranking military officer. Horemheb raised Ramesses to the rank of vizier and named him as his successor. After Ramesses' brief reign Egypt's might was restored under his son Sethos I who, despite his lack of royal lineage, set out to confirm by his actions his right to rule Egypt. The family was connected with Tanis in the

25

Delta but Sethos retained Thebes as his capital. Though Egypt was still recovering from the Amarna heresy, she now experienced a restoration of the temples and traditional religion – a continuance of Horemheb's policy. The priesthood again became powerful and Amun was worshiped as state god. Sethos professed his religious zeal in his building projects – the great Hypostyle Hall at the Temple of Karnak and his temples at Qurneh, Thebes and at Abydos where six chief deities as well as Sethos himself, as a dead, deified ruler, were accommodated. As a commoner, the king could not afford to displease any state deity.

Nubia was still in Egypt's possession, and the turquoise mines of Sinai continued to be worked. Sethos, who with his son was to carry out a policy of restoring former glory, now set out to reconquer Egypt's lost Asiatic empire. His campaigns are depicted in the Hypostyle Hall at Karnak, in a series of wall reliefs. The Empire had probably not been entirely abandoned at the end of the 18th Dynasty but the loyal states were menaced by an increased number of Egypt's enemies. Sethos fought one campaign against the Libyans and three against other troublemakers. In a final campaign against the Hittites, Sethos won the day and restored Egyptian control over part of Syria. Local governors were used, as previously, to administer Egypt's conquests.

Ramesses II, Sethos' son, continued the reconquest of Asia Minor. He advanced into Syria, and at Kadesh on the Orontes a battle took place between Egypt, with her allied city states, and the Hittites with their satellites. Despite the glowing accounts recorded on various buildings in Egypt, both sides were doubtless glad to withdraw and in the 21st year of Ramesses' reign an Egyptian-Hittite alliance brought peace. This was welcomed by the Hittites who faced domestic troubles. Both Egyptian and Hittite versions of the treaty have been found – the two states were to be considered equals; they promised eternal peace, and mutual aid if either was attacked by an outsider; there was also provision for the extradition of political refugees. The gods of both states were invoked to guarantee the treaty and it was cemented by the marriage of Ramesses II to a Hittite princess.

At home, Ramesses II became famous for his monumental and impressive buildings, though they show little refinement. These include the Ramesseum at Thebes – his mortuary temple, the famous rock-cut temple at Abu Simbel and monuments at Tanis. He moved the capital to the northern city of Pi-Ramesse. He had many wives, including his favorite, Nefertari, whose tomb is particularly beautiful and he had over a hundred children. Like his father, Sethos I, he was buried in the Valley of the Kings.

With Ramesses' death, Egypt entered upon her long period of decline. A new world would now face the pharaohs of Egypt. Hittite power waned with the rise of Assyria; Knossos, the center of Minoan culture on Crete, was destroyed about 1400 BC and a new people from the

Entrance to the rock-cut temple of Abu Simbel. The colossal statues have been resited up the cliff to save them from the waters of the Nile, swollen by the Aswan dam.

mainland came to Crete. Migrations in central Europe caused a displacement of population in the regions of the Balkans and the Black Sea, and this created a population movement in western Asia which put pressure on those peoples who occupied the islands and coasts of the western Mediterranean. These in turn were driven to find new homes, and these "Sea Peoples" finally reached the shores of North Africa, where they joined up with Egypt's old enemies – the Libyan tribes. Soon Egypt was to face several determined attempts by this coalition to enter and settle in Egypt. Famine probably aggravated the situation, driving the Libyans and the Sea Peoples to attack Egypt early in the reign of Merenptah. They were repulsed, and over 9,000 were taken prisoner. Egypt enjoyed a temporary peace as some of the Sea Peoples made their way to other Mediterranean shores where they perhaps later became the Lycians and Etruscans.

Merenptah was the last memorable ruler of the 19th Dynasty. Some believe that it was during his reign that the Exodus of the Children of Israel took place. The rulers at the end of the 19th Dynasty reigned briefly, and even the order of their succession is confused. Egypt never again achieved greatness. Perhaps weakened irretrievably by the incursion of the Sea Peoples, the country lacked both faith in old beliefs and inspiration for new ideas. The large numbers of Asiatic peoples who had been present in Egypt since the 18th Dynasty had perhaps affected the Egyptian way of life; certainly they rose to positions of eminence at court and in the army, and perhaps influenced ideas about the afterlife, for Ramesside funerary practises and tomb decoration lack the conviction of eternal happiness which is such a feature of earlier dynasties. Or perhaps Egypt never recovered fully from the Amarna revolution, when faith in pharaoh and worship of the traditional deities was irretrievably shaken.

Our main sources for the 20th Dynasty are the so-called Great Papyrus Harris, which gives a general picture of conditions at this period including the increasing wealth of the priesthood of Amun; and the scenes and inscriptions on the walls of the Temple of Ramesses III at Medinet Habu, which show the renewed conflicts with the Sea Peoples and Libyans.

A new wave of Sea Peoples swept down through Syria and Palestine in about 1200 BC with their families, possessions and cattle. The Hittite Empire disintegrated, Byblos and Ugarit fell. Troy was also defeated, an event which is remembered in Homer's *Iliad*. Finally, Ramesses III was forced to face two attempted invasions of Egypt by the Libyans, led by the Meshwesh tribe and supported by the Sea Peoples, whose aim was to settle in the fertile Delta lands and in Syria/Palestine. Ramesses III eventually repulsed them in a battle fought both on land and at sea. Some fled to Asia Minor and Syria; the Sheklesh and Sherden people quite possibly eventually reached Sicily and Sardinia; the Philistines settled down in Palestine. The whole appearance of the Near East was changed.

Although Egypt had defeated the invaders, her prestige gradually declined in the final years of the 20th Dynasty. This is made clear in the "Story of Wenamun," written at the end of the 20th Dynasty. Gradually the Libyans – especially the Meshwesh – filtered into Egypt; they became mercenaries in the Egyptian army and eventually achieved considerable power. Their descendents later founded the 22nd Dynasty.

Ramesses III built his temple at Medinet Habu. The royal tombs were still splendid. However, increasing lawlessness menaced the peace. An attempt was made by members of the royal harem and army officers to assas-

Tomb of Nefertari, favorite queen of Ramesses II, in the Valley of the Queens at Thebes.

Part of the mortuary temple of Ramesses III at Medinet Habu. The sculptures show the pharaoh striking his enemies.

sinate the king and to place the son of one of the secondary queens on the throne. It seems that corruption was rife among officials and judges.

The last Ramesside rulers – Ramesses IV to XI – presided over a declining state. Bad harvests led to famine, which in turn encouraged widespread tomb-robbing. Troubles flared up in the royal necropolis, and the workmen appear, according to contemporary accounts, to have had reason to fear the continuing incursions of Libyans which caused them to stay away from work. With the decline in pharaoh's power, the importance of Amun's priesthood at Thebes grew, and the office of high priest became hereditary. Eventually a high priest – Herihor – ruled Upper Egypt from Thebes, under the nominal authority of a pharaoh who resided at Tanis. The wheel had turned full circle and the king's deputy and servant of the god now wielded kingly power.

Column before the entrance to the mortuary temple of Ramesses III. It is a late (Ptolemaic) addition with leaf-shaped capital.

Hypostyle hall of Ramesses III's mortuary temple at Medinet Habu. This corresponded to a reception hall in a royal palace.

The Late Period (21st to 31st Dynasties, 1085 to 332 BC). In the 21st Dynasty Egypt was split into two halves, with the legitimate line of kings ruling from Tanis, and the high priests of Amun forming their own "dynasty" at Thebes. Ties of friendship and even marriage existed between the two lines, but separate rule existed again in the two halves.

Egypt had by now lost any pretensions to supremacy abroad; Syria/Palestine was dominated on land and sea by the Philistines and the Phoenicians. A new super-state, Assyria, was growing in the north. From now on the pharaohs were forced to rely very heavily upon mercenaries, and the days of the great campaigns in Asia were over. Egypt had to be content with armed raids, political interference and intrigue, and whenever the Egyptian forces came into contact with the new powers it became sadly apparent that Egyptian arms and equipment were inferior. Iron – a commodity not abundant in Egypt but which the new states possessed – had replaced bronze as the foremost metal for weapons. Gradually the Egyptians lost the ability to assert themselves, and the fiction of a powerful, supreme pharaoh was mocked by the existence of the dual "kingship" of Tanis and Thebes.

The tombs of the kings of the 18th to 20th Dynasties had been constantly plundered. The golden funerary equipment had long since been carried off, but the priests of the 21st Dynasty made an attempt to prevent further desecration of the royal remains by reburying the mummified bodies of their former kings and queens, with their remaining coffins and funerary equipment, in a deep tomb near Deir el-Bahri. In the late 19th century AD this cache was brought to light, and ten years later another tomb, containing many coffins, ushabti (human figurines) and papyri, was discovered to the north of Deir el-Bahri.

Many of the Libyan mercenaries, descendents of the earlier Libyans who had infiltrated into Egypt, had settled down at Heracleopolis. They achieved positions of great influence and, as close confederates of the Tanite rulers, they achieved power and founded the Dynasty which Manetho calls "Bubastite" – the 22nd Dynasty. Contemporary with their rule, a portion of Egypt probably broke away and continued as the 23rd Dynasty. Sheshonk, the first king of the 22nd Dynasty, who appears in the Bible as "Shishak," invaded Palestine, attacked Jerusalem, and plundered the temple of Solomon. But the upsurge of vigor was only temporary.

During this and the previous dynasty a new practise arose. The King's daughter (and not his wife, as in earlier times) was now known as "God's Wife of Amun." Under Osorkon III the absolute power of the High Priest of Amun at Thebes was curtailed by the installation of the king's daughter as consort of the god. She was henceforth used to ensure pharaonic control over Thebes and Upper Egypt, but although she possessed considerable power, and vast estates and officials, her authority was limited to Thebes and she was not allowed to marry.

In about 730 BC an event occurred which had far-reaching effects on Egypt. The Biblical "Ethiopia" – geographically the regions of Nubia and Kush – had separated from Egypt at the end of the 20th Dynasty. They governed themselves from the capital of Napata, and continued to worship fervently the Egyptian deity Amen-Re'. Like many outposts, this area was more "Egyptian" than Egypt. Under their ruler Piankhy the Ethiopians (or Kushites) marched from Napata to Thebes and easily subdued the whole of Egypt, which was again in a state of confusion, setting up a new line of vigorous rulers which held out some hope for the future. It is possible that the 24th Dynasty, under King Bochchoris of Sais, continued to rule a small section of Lower Egypt.

The Kushites set out to organize Egypt. Building projects were carried out and art, although not realizing earlier standards, nevertheless flourished. The Kushites ensured that the danger of a division of the country was minimized by forcing the Divine Consort of Amun to adopt Piankhy's sister, Amenirdas I, as her successor; in turn, Amenirdas adopted Piankhy's daughter. Thus the process of adoption ensured that the position was not hereditary, but could be manipulated by the king. The Divine Consort had considerable power at Thebes only, where she was assisted by her steward.

The Kushites set out to challenge Assyria over Egypt's one-time possessions in Syria and Palestine. Outright force was impossible, but the Kushites employed various indirect methods – political intrigue, subsidies of Nubian gold and

promises of aid to states which showed signs of rebellion against Assyria. An Egyptian contingent was sent to help King Hezekiah of Judah in his struggle against the Assyrians, but the Egyptian army was defeated resoundingly by Sennacherib, the Assyrian ruler. Inevitably, Assyria was forced to take firm action against Egypt to put a stop to her meddlesome policies. Esarhaddon and Ashurbanipal both attacked Egypt, and Memphis and Thebes were temporarily occupied. Eventually, Tanutamon, the Kushite king, reoccupied Memphis, and power was regained at Thebes by the Divine Consort, Shepenopet II, and the fourth prophet of Amun, Mentuemhet. A second Assyrian attack eventually persuaded Tanutamon to flee from Egypt to Napata, never to return. This brief and unusual experiment of Nubian supremacy over their erstwhile lords thus ended, and was never repeated.

The Kushites established a new capital at Meroë and all contact, except by trade, between Egypt and the far south ceased. The Kushites continued with their own version of pharaonic culture – they built pyramid-shaped tombs, they worshiped the gods of Egypt in temples, and they continued to write the classical form of the hieroglyphic language.

Egyptian material remains from the 21st to the 25th Dynasties are comparatively poor and sparse, partly due to the decline in political and military power, but perhaps also because many of the finest antiquities of the period have perished through flooding and silting, since the capital cities were frequently situated in the Delta. Certainly some of the works of art which have been found, such as the mask of Psusennes I of the 21st Dynasty from the royal burials at Tanis, and the bronze statue of Queen Karomama dating to the 22nd Dynasty, provide evidence of continuing skill. Generally, however, the works which do remain indicate imitation of earlier designs, in an attempt perhaps to recapture the spirit of happier times.

After attacking Egypt, trouble in another part of his empire (Elam) caused Ashurbanipal to return to Assyria, leaving only a few of his troops behind. Twelve native princes were placed in control during his absence; one of these, Psammetichus of Sais, was not slow to seize this opportunity and with the aid of Greek mercenaries and military assistance from Gyges, king of Lydia, he established himself as King of Upper and Lower Egypt. At Thebes the Divine Consort of Amun, Shepenopet II, was instructed to adopt the daughter of Psammetichus as her successor, and the prophet of Amun (Mentuemhet), who had wielded such power under the Kushites, was replaced by one of the Saite supporters. Psammetichus appointed his own men to key positions and discontinued the payment of tribute to Assyria. The power of Assyria in any case was waning and, having thrown off its yoke, Psam-

Late-period art. *Far left:* bronze statue of Queen Karomama of the 22nd Dynasty. *Left:* gold figurine of the god Amun carrying a ceremonial sword (probably from Karnak).

metichus set about restoring Egypt's military power by building up an army containing many foreign mercenaries – Ionians, Carians and Lydians. As the Libyans, whom Egypt had previously employed as mercenaries, had gained too much independence and power the Saites were anxious to curb it by introducing other foreign mercenaries.

Psammetichus I and his successors built up a fine navy and merchant fleet and, with the aid of Phoenician sailors, dominated the Mediterranean. They encouraged foreign traders and communities to settle in Egypt and showed them favor. Although this commercial enterprise expanded Egypt's wealth, the privileges granted to the foreign communities angered the native Egyptians and eventually their antagonism resulted in the confinement of the foreigners to their own special cities. At Naukratis, for example, a self-governing, independent community of

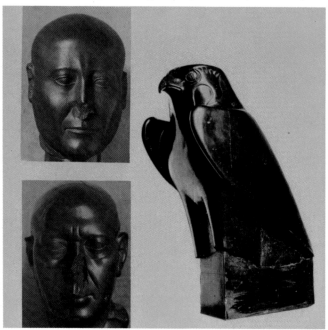

Art of the 26th Dynasty. Two heads of priests (above: the "green head" from Memphis), and the hawk-god Horus.

Greek traders flourished, while a Jewish community, worshiping Yahweh, grew up at Elephantine.

The Saite rulers were interested in all commercial enterprises which were likely to increase their wealth and influence. The export of corn from Egypt was begun. And in Roman times the provision of grain for the Roman Empire was to become one of the main reasons for Egypt's importance. The Saites also initiated the project to build a canal from the Nile to the Red Sea, and Phoenician sailors were commissioned to attempt the circumnavigation of Africa.

This period is sometimes regarded as a time of nationalism when the kings, having driven out the Assyrian oppressors, attempted to revive earlier glories. Although the kings doubtless made use of this feeling of nationalism

to enable them to acquire the throne, they actually showed a strong bias later on in favor of the foreigners, who were encouraged to settle in Egypt. Indeed they owed their actual seizure of power to foreign military aid and mercenaries. The Egyptians, perhaps realizing this, never gave the Saite kings the support which truly "native" rulers might have received.

Egyptian dissatisfaction with the large groups of foreigners now resident in the country was expressed in a nostalgia for the former "pure" Egyptian civilization. This archaism took various forms – ancient titles of the nobility were revived, art forms from previous periods were imitated, reliefs and sculptures from the Old Kingdom in particular were copied, and there was a revival of animal worship. Even the styles of dress and writing were influenced, and the study of their own past was eagerly taken up. Art forms show great precision and attention to detail, and their very perfection gives them a certain beauty; fine sculptured portraits were produced and carefully carved ushabti figures. However, the works usually copied from or inspired by earlier pieces lack the dynamism which characterizes the originals.

In 612 BC a coalition of Babylonian and Persian armies had captured and sacked Nineveh, the Assyrian capital, and Saite foreign policy consisted mainly of attempting to maintain the balance of power by supporting first the Assyrians against the Babylonians and Persians, then allying themselves with Babylonia against Persia. Ultimately, however, the Persians established a great empire, while Egypt was torn by a civil war between its Saite pharaoh and "a man of the people," Amasis, who won the struggle. A few months after Amasis' death Egypt fell to Cambyses, King of the Persians.

In 525 BC Egypt became part of the Persian Empire. (This was the 27th Dynasty in Manetho's list.) According to some contemporary reports, Cambyses proved to be a hard taskmaster who did little to help Egypt and attacked some of its religious practises. On his return to Asia, Egypt was placed in the charge of a satrap, as it was now a Persian province or satrapy. This was the usual custom in the Persian Empire. Although based to some extent on the earlier Assyrian Empire, it was more efficient and was highly organized. For nearly two centuries Egypt was a well-managed province except for a period when native princes gained a brief independence for the country.

Darius I succeeded Cambyses as ruler and, unlike his predecessor, showed an active interest in the ancient civilization of Egypt. He sent a satrap to Egypt with instructions to make a detailed account of the history of Egyptian law from the knowledge of Egyptian scribes, priests and soldiers. He also ordered the completion of the canal which the Saites had started, and built temples for the Egyptians. He appears to have shown a genuine interest in their welfare, and attempted to gain their acceptance of him as their rightful pharaoh by using the royal pharaonic title.

But in 486 BC the Egyptians rebelled against their Persian overlords; they were promptly subdued by Xerxes, the new Persian king, and their condition grew worse. Temple building ceased and Egypt was made to realize that it was now just one of many Persian provinces.

A final breath of freedom came when native princes gained a brief independence from Persia during the 28th to 30th Dynasties; but in 343 BC, under King Artaxerxes III, Egypt was once again reduced to the status of a Persian province. This time the gold and silver were carried off from the temples and a satrap was again installed. This second Persian domination (the 31st Dynasty) consisted of three Persian kings. But the end of Persia itself was now in sight.

Philip of Macedon had already put his country on the map as a coming world power. His son, Alexander the Great, now started on his amazing career of unprecedented conquest of the known world. In 332 BC he reached Egypt, where the Persian satrap surrendered to him without a struggle. Alexander was accepted as pharaoh, and laid the foundations of the future great city of Alexandria. During his famous visit to the oracle of Amun at

Anubis, god of embalming, wearing the double crown and holding the Ankh sign and the scepter.

Siwa he became convinced of his own divinity. Then, having made provision for the government of Egypt – the appointment of native governors, suitable arrangements for tax collection and the stationing of a small army under the general Ptolemy – Alexander left Egypt to pursue his world conquest.

The Ptolemaic Period (332 to 30 BC). The youthful Alexander the Great died, leaving a four-year-old son as his heir. The child was promptly murdered, and Alexander's empire was divided among his generals. In 305 BC Egypt became the property of the general Ptolemy, and was ruled successively by 15 Ptolemies, as well as the famous Queen Cleopatra, before Octavius conquered the land in 30 BC and made Egypt a part of the Roman Empire.

The Ptolemaic period was a time of great intellectual achievement in Egypt, yet also one of severe deprivation and humiliation for the native Egyptians. On the one hand, the Ptolemies created the beautiful city of Alexandria on the shores of the Mediterranean which became an intellectual center, attracting the most eminent scholars of the ancient world. A museum and the largest library in the world were built there, and branches of learning such as mathematics, medicine and geography flourished. On the other hand, the Ptolemies, by using to their own advantage the divine power of pharaoh, brutally exploited the land and the native inhabitants of Egypt. Previously, all land and property had theoretically belonged to the king, and the Egyptians were pharaoh's loyal subjects; however, this absolute authority had never been exercised, and in practise private ownership of land and property had been common from the earliest times. The concept of pharaoh's divinity and authority was closely bound up with Egyptian religious beliefs.

The Ptolemaic Greeks, whose acceptance of the Egyptian deities and beliefs was nominal, saw in this theory an excellent opportunity to exploit the country and its people for their own ends. Deliberately, they conceived a policy which would cripple the Egyptians. Landowners were forced to become tenants, leasing their land from the state, embodied in the person of pharaoh. They were restricted to one area, and their land could be taken away from them without recourse. Private ownership no longer existed, and every facet of the farmer's livelihood was subject to crippling conditions. His animals could be taken away, and each year the type and amount of crops he could grow were regulated by the state. He was expected to maintain the canals on his land and to pay heavy taxes in corn. The state then insisted upon buying a certain amount of his crop at a fixed price.

The industries of Egypt were similarly under state control and certain commodities were state monopolies. Many officials were employed to operate this system and to ensure that the state exacted its heavy taxes. The Egyptians could do little to alleviate their troubles; strikes were not uncommon, but when they broke out they were cruelly

Roman-period jewelry from the grave of a queen at Meroë in the Sudan, about 25–10 BC. Ring, showing the sun disk, bracelet and armband, in gold inset with glass. Meroë, excavated by Garstang, was the last outpost of Egyptian civilization, keeping alive ancient Egyptian traditions until the Christian era.

Roman mummy portrait of a woman from a Fayoum tomb. This practise of painting a naturalistic portrait of the deceased stems from Late-period mummy art.

subdued and the leaders massacred, so these outbursts were doomed to failure. Some Egyptians, desperately weary of their lot, disappeared into the deserts where they became the first hermits and forerunners of the Christian monastic communities, or they sought refuge in the temples. The situation worsened when Octavius became the Roman ruler of Egypt. A Prefect was left in charge, and the Ptolemaic system was continued, the taxes now being used to supplement the private Imperial income. Under an absentee Roman landlord, the lives of the Egyptians became even more difficult.

Under Ptolemaic rule many Greeks, Macedonians, Persians, Jews, Lydians, Thracians and others were encouraged to settle in Egypt. Ptolemy offered the Greeks the opportunity of high government posts and gifts of land. They, and not the Egyptians, served in the army and navy and flourished as traders and artisans. The Ptolemies showed marked favor to their non-Egyptian subjects, who repaid them with loyalty. In predominantly Greek cities, such as Alexandria and Naukratis, the Egyptians were considered as "foreigners," and throughout the land two distinct communities existed – the downtrodden natives and the favored foreigners.

Under the earliest Ptolemies marriage between Greeks and Egyptians was unacceptable, and throughout Egypt a Greek birthright, education and upbringing were the only means of gaining entry to the highest intellectual, social and artistic circles. Towards the end of the 3rd century BC a small number of native Egyptians began to become "hellenized" by receiving a Greek education and accepting, at least superficially, Greek ideas and values; some Egyptian women even married Greek men. The old Egyptian aristocracy had been abolished, and the new "hellenized" Egyptians formed a new native elite. However, the majority of the Egyptians and Greeks, divided by such alien backgrounds and circumstances, never really intermingled. This is borne out by the differences preserved in their art forms, religious beliefs and burial customs. Greeks and Egyptians retained their own distinctive

The temple of Philae, Roman period. *Top:* 19th-century drawing. *Above:* the "Birth-house," also known as pharaoh's bed. All temples of the Ptolemaic period had "birth-houses" reserved for the worship of the mother goddess Isis.

tombs; the only known exception is the tomb of Petosiris in which scenes and inscriptions of Egyptian type – showing metal-working, carpentry, agriculture and the offering of food – are arranged in registers, as in traditional Egyptian tombs, although many of the details in the scenes show Greek influence.

The Egyptian coffins of the period differ from earlier styles in that wood had become scarce and was replaced by cartonage – coarse canvas stiffened with stucco. The face and head, molded in plaster on canvas, painted with bright colors and inlaid with glass or stone eyes, were attached to the actual head of the mummy by bandaging. Sometimes the whole of the upper part of the figure was modeled in plaster, and the women's jewelry was imitated in inlaid

glass and gilding. Later, during the Roman period, the earliest known painted portraits were produced. The face was painted on a wooden panel (probably during the lifetime of the deceased) and attached to the bandaged head of the mummy. Most of these portraits have been found in the Fayoum district, and some are strikingly beautiful. The features are delicately modeled, using light and shade – a practise not found in traditional Egyptian art. Both the faces portrayed and the techniques used are more Greek than Egyptian, and here we have a brief glimpse of the type of painting which was later to be associated with Europe. Beneath the portraits and the bandaging, the deceased were mummified exactly as in earlier times.

In sculpture, although there were some attempts to unite Greek and Egyptian concepts, as in the statue of Alexander IV, the two art forms continue to reflect two separate societies and traditions. The reliefs on the walls of the Egyptian temples show figures of deities that are fuller than those of the past, with exaggerated curves, and executed with a clumsiness unknown in pharaonic reliefs. There is no doubt, however, that the purpose of the reliefs and the traditional pose of the figures remained unchanged. While Greek was used as the official script, and Demotic – a cursive form of hieroglyphs – was used by native Egyptians for business purposes, the Egyptian hieroglyphic script continued to adorn the walls of temples and was used for sacred purposes, although by now probably few understood its meaning.

One section of the Egyptian community which the Ptolemies did attempt to placate was the priesthood, perhaps because the priests wielded considerable power, and also because the ancient religion, based on the concept that pharaoh was the divine son who possessed Egypt, was

33

an essential prop to the Ptolemies' economic and political rule. To this end the Ptolemies, anxious to appear as rulers accepted by the gods, repaired, restored and made additions to older temples such as those at Karnak and Luxor, and erected new temples at Edfu, Denderah, Esneh, Kom Ombo and Philae. These were built on the same general plan as earlier temples, but incorporated some new elements. There were, however, no Greek characteristics in the basic design or purpose. No important remains of Greek temples in Egypt, built for the Greeks, have come to light, although they undoubtedly existed.

In religious belief the Egyptians and Greeks remained separate, although there were some attempts to produce an accepted "State triad" such as Isis, Serapis and Harpocrates, Egyptian deities in Greek form. An official Greek cult of Alexander the Great was established in Alexandria, and the Ptolemies paid great attention to the idea of pharaoh's divinity; they were themselves worshiped in life and in death, and showed great respect for Egyptian religious beliefs. They assumed pharaonic titles, dress,

regalia and customs, and perhaps even to a greater extent than the Egyptian pharaohs they practised consanguineous marriages. This custom now became acceptable for commoners as well.

Under the Greeks, unlike earlier conquerors, the native Egyptians lost all freedom; they became second-class citizens, not only subject to foreign rulers but also subservient to foreign settlers. The resources of their country and their manpower were used by unscrupulous rulers who manipulated time-honored religious beliefs for their own ends. It is ironic that the one queen whom most people associate with Egypt – Cleopatra – was of this line of foreign oppressors. Only in their art and their religious and funerary beliefs could the Egyptians cling tenaciously to their ancient ideals and the memories of a great past. With this final assertion of national pride, the civilization of pharaonic Egypt died forever. It would be many hundreds of years before travelers and scholars would rediscover Egypt's past; then once again the world would marvel at the achievements of the ancient Egyptians.

A secondary temple in the complex at Karnak, built when the Egyptian empire had reached the highest point of its

achievement. On either side of the entrance there are inscribed scenes showing the king making offerings to Min.

THE EGYPTIAN PYRAMID

From Mastaba Tomb to Step Pyramid

The earliest method of burial was to place the body in a contracted position in a pit in the sand; this pit was either oval or rectangular in shape (*below left*). The body was wrapped in a reed mat, and a few possessions were placed in the pit, such as necklaces, bangles, and vessels containing food and drink. These would satisfy the needs of the deceased in the next world, it was hoped. This method of burial probably continued to be used for the poor throughout Egyptian history.

At the beginning of the dynastic period (c. 3100 BC), for the burial of kings, the royal family and the nobility, it became the custom to build a superstructure in mud-brick over the burial pit in the sand. This resembles a bench in shape, and has become known by the Arabic word for bench – "mastaba." This superstructure prevented the sand from being blown away from the tomb and thus exposing the body, and so assisted in preserving the body from destruction and provided a safe storage place for the dead man's possessions – the main functions of the tomb.

At the beginning of the 1st Dynasty, the tomb has a simple design, and is an enlarged version of the pit-burial, with the body probably placed in the central compartment, with possessions in adjoining chambers. A brick superstructure, above these chambers, was divided into interior compartments where equipment for the afterlife was stored (*below middle*).

The exterior of the superstructure was decorated with mud-brick paneling, painted in bright colors, imitating the matting found outside the houses of the living. This kind of tomb probably closely resembled the palaces and houses of the time, for the dead were believed to "dwell" in their tombs for eternity.

Outside the enclosure wall of some tombs, there were rows of subsidiary tombs for the owner's servants, buried to care for him in the afterlife.

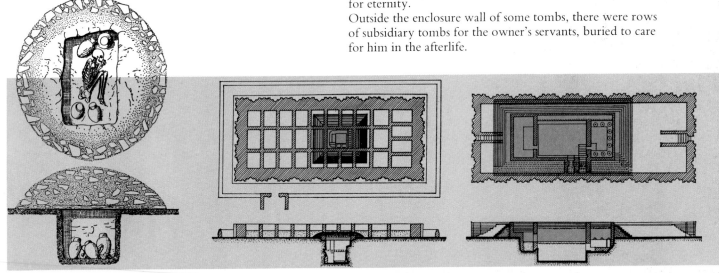

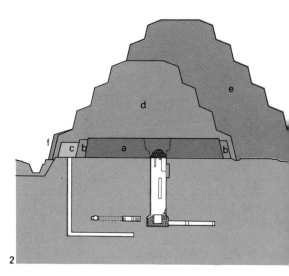

From Step Pyramid to True Pyramid

The kings and nobles of early Egypt were buried in modest tombs of sun-dried brick. At the beginning of the 3rd Dynasty Imhotep, prime minister to King Djoser and a gifted architect, designed a new kind of stone tomb for his master. This was the first step pyramid (*figure 1, above*) which rose in six unequal stages to a height of 204 feet. The original building stood only 26 feet high (*figure 2a*). This was then extended about 14 feet on all four sides, and a second facing of limestone was added (*b*). A step mastaba had now been formed, and a further enlargement of about 28 feet was made on the east side (*c*). At this point a new design was adopted: the mastaba was again extended by

$9\frac{1}{2}$ feet on the east side, this time making it the lowest stage of a four-step pyramid (*d*). Finally, the pyramid was extended to north and west (*e*), the design was changed from four steps to six, a little was added to each side, the steps were completed, and the whole encased in dressed Tura limestone (*f*). Other pyramids make it possible to trace the gradual transition from a step pyramid to a true pyramid. For instance the 4th-Dynasty pyramid at Meydum (*figure 4, below*), which probably started off as a mastaba or a small step pyramid, shows one stage in this transition. The original form of the building cannot now be discerned. However, the tomb was later increased in height to make it a

seven-step pyramid, to which was added still another step (*a*). Finally, the steps were filled in with local stone and cased with Tura limestone (*b*) to make a smooth surface. An entrance to the pyramid was made in the north face. Another transitional feature is illustrated by the northern stone pyramid of Dahshur (*figure 3, below*). Earlier, stones had been laid in inclined courses, according to the tilt of the walls, as in the inner casings used for reinforcement inside the Dahshur pyramid. It will be noted, however, that the stone courses behind the outer facings are laid flat, which shows that these facings were added later.

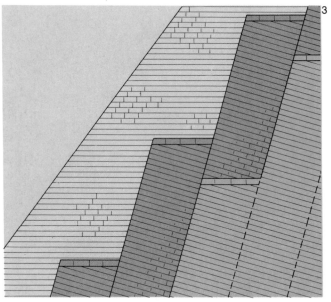

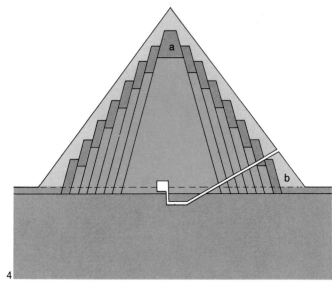

The famous Bent Pyramid at Dahshur (*figures 5 and 7*), was built by Sneferu of the 4th Dynasty. It is peculiar in its profile, being steeper in the lower part than in the upper, thus producing a "bent" look. The Bent Pyramid was unique in possessing a corridor that ran from the north. The entrance to this corridor was to one side of the west face, and it led to the upper chamber. From it a roughly hewn passage ran to the roof of the lower chamber, which was also served by the customary passage from the north (*figure 7a*). The mouth of the passage was blocked to each side by an unusual portcullis (*b*), which slid sideways instead of dropping perpendicularly into the passage (*figure 6*).

5

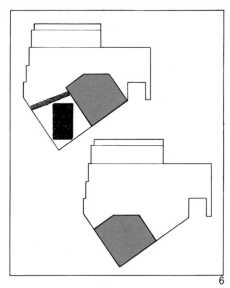

6

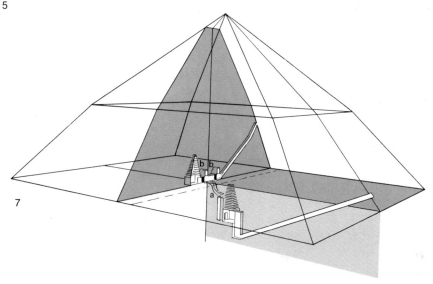

7

The northern stone pyramid at Dahshur (*figure 8*), thought also to have been erected by Sneferu, is the earliest known tomb which was designed as a true pyramid. However, the sides incline at an angle of 43° 36′ instead of the 52°, which was customary in the other true pyramids such as those at Gizeh. Moreover, for the first time in the history of the pyramid, the stones beneath the outer casing, as we have seen, are laid in level courses. With this pyramid we are close to the acme of the age of pyramid-building represented by the great pyramids at Gizeh. The pyramids of Egypt as a whole were built from the earliest dynasties of the Old Kingdom to the time of the Middle Kingdom, but the great age of pyramid-building covered only the 400 years from the 3rd to the 6th Dynasty, when the pyramid was the recognized type of tomb for royalty.

8

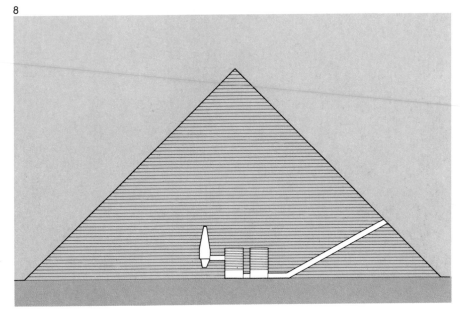

The Pyramids of Gizeh Group

The three famous pyramids of Gizeh, situated near modern Cairo, dominate the wide reaches of the Nile Valley for many miles around. The monuments rise into the sky like isolated mountains. Built on a wide plateau, each pyramid is surrounded by a complex of buildings of its own.

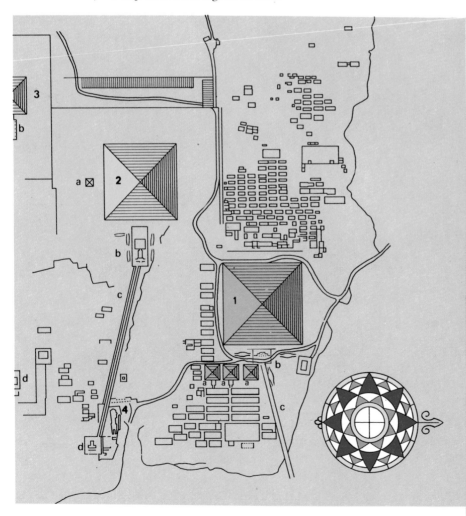

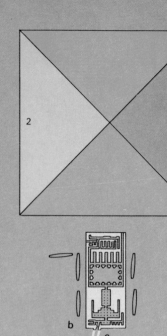

The pyramid of King Khafre (Chephren) appears to be much taller than the Great Pyramid of Khufu since it was built on higher ground. However, when both were intact it was about ten feet lower in height. Its casing, made of Tura limestone quarried in the hills across the Nile from Gizeh and ferried over by boat, remains intact at the top. The standard elements of a pyramid complex appear for the first time in a complete form in connection with the Khafre pyramid – a mortuary temple, causeway, a valley building where part of the funerary rituals were performed and five boat pits. The function of the latter is obscure. The Great Sphinx (4), carved from an outcrop of rock, has the body of a lion and the face of Khafre.

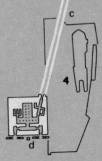

A plan (*left*) of the three pyramids of Gizeh shows how each lies within a complex of associated buildings. The plan shows: 1. Pyramid of Khufu (Cheops); 2. Pyramid of Khafre (Chephren); 3. Pyramid of Menkure (Mycerinus); *a*. subsidiary pyramids; *b*. mortuary temple; *c*. causeway; *d*. valley building; 4. Sphinx.

g Khufu (Cheops) built his great
amid, the largest of the three, at the
northwest corner of a plateau five miles
west of Gizeh. The entrance is in the
north face, above ground level. The
so-called "Queen's chamber" (x), an
Arab misnomer, was probably first
intended to be the burial chamber but
was soon abandoned. The Grand Gallery
(y) was then continued upwards from
the original ascending passage to give
access to the King's Chamber (z). A
granite sarcophagus, lidless and empty,
still rests in the King's Chamber, which
has a flat ceiling composed of nine slabs
of stone weighing approximately
400 tons.

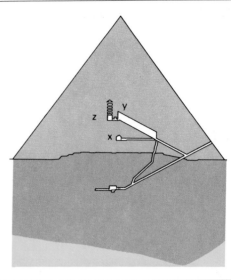

lion's body of the Great Sphinx is.
feet long, and its face, thought to be
of King Khafre, is over 13 feet wide.
monuments have aroused such awe
speculation over the ages as the
inx.

The pyramid of Khafre had two
entrances. Originally another chamber
(y) was intended for the royal burial but
was abandoned. In the actual tomb
chamber (x) a granite sarcophagus was
found.

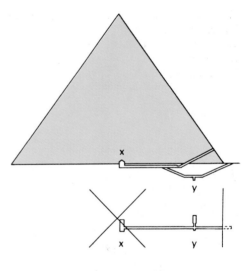

plans for the pyramid of King
nkure (Mycerinus) at Gizeh never
seem to have been fully carried out,
perhaps owing to the unexpected death
of the king. At some point a decision
seems to have been made to enlarge the
superstructure, requiring the abandon-
ment of the sloping corridor (v), the
deepening of the floor of the burial
chamber (w) and the cutting of a new
sloping corridor (x) beneath the first one.
Two other chambers were also added
(y and z). A basalt sarcophagus was
found in the second chamber (y), but
this was later lost at sea near Spain when
it was being transported to England.
Three smaller pyramids with mortuary
temples surround the main pyramid.

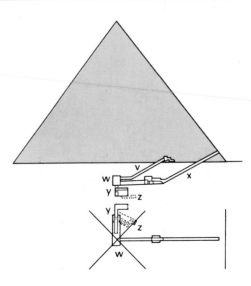

The great pyramids of Gizeh were built over 4,500 years ago as tombs for Old Kingdom pharaohs. Grouped at the edge of the desert near Cairo (*left*), they were built by three pharaohs of the 4th Dynasty, Khufu (Cheops), Khafre (Chephren) and Menkure (Mycerinus). The largest is the Great Pyramid of Khufu (*at back, above*). That of Menkure (*foreground*) is less than half the size of the other two. The Great Pyramid, which covers about 13 acres, was originally about 480 feet high, and contains over 2 million stones, each weighing an average of 2½ tons. Originally the pyramids were cased in polished limestone, now mostly gone (see *below*, and Khafre's pyramid *above*).

Pyramids of the Later Dynasties

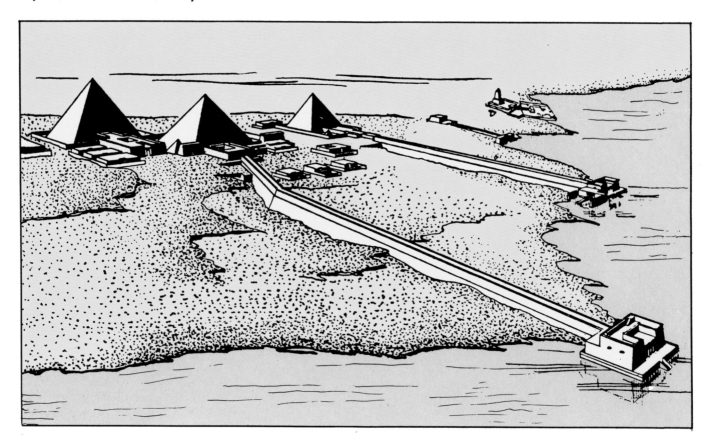

Although the peak of pyramid-building
was reached in the 4th Dynasty and
never surpassed, this method of burial
continued to be used intermittently
throughout Egyptian history. Selected
examples are:
The sun pyramids of Abu-Sir (5th
Dynasty). See *above* reconstruction.
The kings of the 5th Dynasty were
mainly concerned with the worship of
the sun-god, and restored the practise of
pyramid-building. Here are the
pyramids of kings Sahure (*right*),
Neferirkare (*left*) and Niuserre (*middle*),
now reduced to mounds of rubble. The
pyramids of this dynasty were inferior
to those of the previous one, and are not
well preserved, although originally they
must have been magnificent buildings.
They were constructed of small stones
and cased with Tura limestone, instead
of the earlier practise of building
completely with solid blocks of stone.
The pyramid of Neb-hepet-Re
Mentuhotep (11th Dynasty) at Thebes
(see reconstruction *below*). This complex
is unique and contains many innovations,
including the construction of a cenotaph
and the king's tomb within the temple
building.

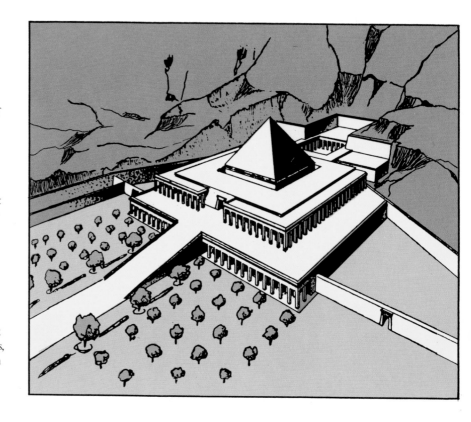

II
EXPLORERS
AND
TRAVELERS

Before the decipherment of hieroglyphs in 1822 by Champollion the modern world knew little about ancient Egypt, and there were few sources to which the student of Egyptian civilization could refer. These included Biblical writings, Classical authors and some later accounts written by early explorers and travelers who had visited Egypt. Some of these accounts were well-informed in part, but generally the early information, though fascinating, was inaccurate.

The first explorers of Egypt were the Greeks. The civilization of ancient Egypt, with its weird religious beliefs, magnificent buildings and fund of wisdom and learning already exerted a powerful spell over foreign tourists. During the Greco-Roman occupation of Egypt, Greek visitors were welcome to visit the country and pursue their studies, and the earliest accounts of Egypt's customs and geography were being written by a handful of observant tourists. Herodotus was among these visitors; blessed with a keen and inquisitive mind, this loquacious Greek busily gathered snippets of information on a variety of topics. Native interpreters and dragomen were probably pleased to supply this rather gullible gentleman with information and anecdotes and, if necessary, to embroider the facts for him – for a fee. Herodotus appears to have found his travels in Egypt exhilarating; he even managed to reach the First Cataract, shortly after 450 BC. Wherever he went he made detailed notes of all he saw and was told.

Eventually, Herodotus set about writing his comprehensive history of Egypt. As he wrote, he did not know that his work would survive for many hundreds of years, and would be acclaimed by scholars of the 20th century AD as the earliest comprehensive study of Egypt which they possess. He wrote of the landscape of Egypt and its geography with delight; but it was the people and their customs which intrigued Herodotus rather than their monuments. He was a superb story-teller, recounting amusing anecdotes related to him by the native guides. He covered a wide range of subjects – hieroglyphs, mummies and the Egyptians' peculiar love of animals. Their reverence for cats he notes particularly:

"When a fire breaks out, the cats behave as though divinely possessed. The Egyptians stand around trying to restrain the cats rather than to quench the flames; but the cats dart between or leap over the men and jump into the fire. At this, great grief overcomes the Egyptians."

He gave a meticulous account of the processes of mummification, listing the stages involved, and morbid customs, such as the following, did not escape his notice:

"At their rich men's banquets, when they have done eating, a man carries around a wooden corpse in a coffin, made and painted to look exactly like a real corpse, about a cubit or two cubits long. This he shows to each of the company and says:— 'Look upon this and drink and be merry; for thou shalt die and such shalt thou be'."

Other Greek authors, less colorful than Herodotus, also found that Egypt was worth their attention. Hecateus of Miletus wrote of the formation of the Delta, the annual flooding of the Nile and the fauna of the Nile Valley. Strabo, a Greek-speaking native of Pontus, took up temporary residence in Alexandria, which was at the center of the intellectual world. Driven by curiosity, Strabo set out to explore the region of Upper Egypt with a companion. For these two friends, the years 24 and 25 BC were exciting ones; they visited many Egyptian sites – vast temple complexes, tombs and the pyramids, those mysterious structures, already so ancient, which stretch out along the edge of the western desert like so many wheaten cakes. (The Greek word "pyramis" means a wheaten cake.) The explorers reached the First Cataract, and gathered a wealth of information. Strabo was able to draw on his experiences to write a book about Egypt – number 17 in his geographical series.

The interest in Egypt was now quite widespread among scholars. In 59 BC Diodorus Siculus visited Egypt, and the resulting work – the *Bibliotheca* – contained details of his journey and the information he had gathered on education, animal worship and medicine in Egypt. There is little doubt, however, that his writings had been influenced by Herodotus. Plutarch, on the other hand, had a very original approach to Egypt; his interest lay in the religion of the Egyptians and he gives a worthy account of the legend of Osiris and Isis. Pliny the Elder discusses the geography and some of the monuments of Egypt, and those obelisks which the Roman emperor had had removed to Rome. The pyramids, which have fascinated visitors for so long, are declared to be royal treasure houses of the pharaohs:

"Indeed it is asserted by most persons that the only motive for constructing them was either a determination not to leave their treasures to their successors or to rivals that might be plotting to supplant them, or to prevent the lower classes from remaining unemployed. . . ."

The Classical authors who mentioned Egypt also include Claudius Ptolemaeus, Juvenal, Tacitus, Plato, Ammianus Marcellinus, Josephus, Eusebius, Julius Africanus and Clement of Alexandria. They had one thing in common – a fascination for the ancient Nile civilization. Different aspects interested them – obelisks, antiquities, geography, flora and fauna, mummification and hieroglyphs.

Let us now turn to one of the most important sources for Egyptian history. Pharaoh Ptolemy II Philadelphus commissioned Manetho to write a History of Egypt. Manetho was High Priest in the Temple of Heliopolis and a native Egyptian. He was trained in all aspects of Egyptian religion and could read the sacred hieroglyphic script – a rare ability – in addition to Greek, the language in which he wrote his books. Like all Egyptians, he was a keen student of his country's illustrious past and, as a priest, he revered its traditions. He had access to the records of past events which were kept in the secret safety of the temple libraries as well as to the King Lists which adorned the temple walls. His lifetime (323 to 245 BC) coincided with a

time when most native Egyptians were under foreign domination; as a priest, he had a particular responsibility to record the events of Egypt's past.

Manetho gathered enough information to fill eight volumes; as he worked, he was unaware that his writings would be the only native source written by an Egyptian historian to survive from the Classical period; indeed, they would only survive in part, edited and preserved in the works of Josephus, a Jewish historian of the 1st century AD, of Eusebius (c. 320 AD), of Julius Africanus (c. 220 AD) and of Syncellus (c. 800 AD). (These are the approximate dates of their histories.) The priestly historian could not foresee that many of the sources to which he had access would shortly be destroyed by the Greeks – the temples burnt, the priesthood destroyed and many of the sacred records lost for ever. Certainly he did not know that later scholars would come to value his writings as one of the best original sources for the history of ancient Egypt. His Chronicle of Kings, listing Egyptian rulers from the accession of Menes (c. 3100 BC) to the conquest of Egypt by Alexander the Great (332 BC), with estimates of the lengths of the rulers' reigns, subdivided into 31 dynasties, would be preserved

The "Colossi of Memnon" (Amenophis III) on the Nile at Thebes. *Left:* a 19th-century print. *Below:* as they are today.

by later writers. With some caution and certain scholarly reservations, the historians of the 20th century AD still use Manetho's list as the basic source for the construction of an Egyptian chronology.

But the Classical era was fading; Europe was passing through the Dark Ages and Egypt was invaded and conquered by the Arabs. Visitors to Egypt ceased to visit Alexandria and Upper Egypt; at Gizeh, the Sphinx slept. The years between the 7th century AD and the Renaissance brought few European travelers to Egypt. But the Arabs who spread Islam throughout much of the East were themselves taking a renewed interest in the exploration of Egypt and her monuments.

These early Arab travelers included men such as Magrizi, Ibn Battuta and Ibn Jubair. In the middle of the 8th century AD a certain Abou Ma'sher Ja'fer Ben Mohammed Balkhi visited the pyramids at Gizeh and recorded his experiences. At the end of the 12th century Abou Abd Allah Mohammed Ben Abdurakim Alkaisi paid a visit to Gizeh; he relates that the Great Pyramid had been entered by the Caliph Mahmoud, who used a battering ram and forced a passage through the north side. Future generations would know this passage as "Mahmoud's hole." This writer bravely entered the pyramid where he saw a "human body in golden armor, decorated with precious stones." Many Arab travelers visited the ruins of Egypt, marveled at them and described them in colorful terms for posterity.

Far away in Europe men were beginning to turn their attention to the East. In England, the Elizabethan era was dawning, with all its lust for travel and exploration. The European writers began to show curiosity about the civilization of ancient Egypt, and to produce historical works based as usual on the only available sources – the Bible and the Classical authors. There are no firsthand accounts and many errors occur in these books. English, French and Italian writers made their contributions, the most popular subjects being the pyramids, hieroglyphs and mummification. During medieval times, the native Christian Egyptians – the Copts – continued to produce literature written in the Coptic language and from the beginning of the 17th century these manuscripts began to appear in Europe. Athanasius Kircher, a Jesuit, made a study of the Coptic and hieroglyphic texts; all knowledge of the ancient hieroglyphs of Egypt had been lost and many believed that the rows of animals, birds and figures were merely magical symbols. No one realized that the script was a language which, when deciphered, can be read as easily as Greek or Latin. In 1643 Kircher produced a fundamental study of the Coptic language – *Lingua Aegyptiaca restituta*. It was the first step towards the understanding of Egyptian scripts.

Let us now turn to those men who opened up Egypt to the West. From the 15th century onwards European travelers began to visit Egypt; new travel accounts were written, based now on firsthand information. Tourists arrived at the pyramids, guided perhaps by the distant ancestors of some of the guides whom the parties of visitors encounter in the 20th century. There, however, the similarity ends. The 15th-century tourist passed through Egypt bound for the Holy Land; his visit included Cairo and the Gizeh pyramids and perhaps Alexandria. A few scholars and business agents of trading companies were also among the early travelers. Germans, Frenchmen, Italians and Englishmen braved the dangers and difficulties of the journey; theirs was a true adventure – the sands still partly covered the ruined monuments, and the Sphinx lay buried.

In the 17th century a new type of traveler, the nobleman, began to include Egypt in his grand tour. He was suave, well-educated, with a particular interest in the Classics and considerable private means. Such travelers visited Gizeh, Saqqara, Thebes and even Aswan, and avidly noted down details of the monuments and produced fair sketches of all they saw. On returning to Europe, a few published books on their travels in the East.

In the year 1610 an enterprising gentleman traveler, George Sandys, visited Gizeh. He was a skilful artist and produced the first realistic drawings of the pyramids and later published a popular version of his travels. In 1638 John Greaves visited Egypt, and set about making the first really scientific study of the Gizeh pyramids, taking careful measurements of the Great Pyramid and making various other observations. He entered the pyramid, and from firsthand information was able to contradict the Classical writers who, basing their evidence on hearsay, stated that the interior walls of the pyramid were decorated with hieroglyphs. Greaves finally published his findings in his *Pyramidographia*, based on his firsthand knowledge of 20 pyramids apart from the Gizeh group. Of the King's

The Great Sphinx and the Gizeh pyramids as they appeared to travelers in 1847. This print is taken from *The Holy Land*, a travelogue by David Roberts, Rev. G. Croly and W. Brockendon published in 1855.

A colossal statue of Ramesses II at the entrance to the temple of Luxor. The sketch, made in the 19th century, shows it half-buried in the sand, while the modern photograph reveals a similar statue excavated and restored.

Chamber in the Great Pyramid he wrote:

"Within this glorious room (for so I may justly call it) as within some consecrated oratory, stands the monument of Cheops or Chemmis, of one piece of marble, hollow within, and uncovered at the top and sounding like a bell . . ."

Greaves' experiments included opening the skull of a mummy to examine the materials used for embalming, and he also pondered the meaning of the hieroglyphic script, to little effect.

In the meantime, other travelers – French, Italian and German – continued to explore Egypt in the 16th century. A Jesuit, Père Sicard, reached Aswan. A scholar as well as a traveler, he visited 24 temples and many decorated rock-cut tombs, and to him fell the exciting task of rediscovering the site of ancient Thebes.

In the 18th century the travelers developed new aims – they began to collect small antiquities in Egypt and brought them back to Europe, where they formed the basis of small museum collections. They began to clear the sand from some of the monuments, and to make copies of some of the hieroglyphic inscriptions. They traveled up the Nile to Upper Egypt and Nubia where they encountered considerable difficulties. There were no "organized tours," and many physical dangers and hardships were involved. Thomas Shaw visited Alexandria and Gizeh, sometime between 1720 and 1733, and wrote:

"In our journeys between Kairo and Mount Sinai, the

heavens were every night our covering; the sand, with a carpet spread over it, was our bed; and a change of raiment made up into a bundle was our pillow."

If we could look back in time to the years 1737 and 1738 we should see two dahibeyehs – the sailing vessels used in Egypt – moving gracefully up the Nile. On board one was Richard Pococke; he had already visited the sites of Lower Egypt – Gizeh, Saqqara, Dahshur and the Fayoum, and he was now traveling to Aswan, visiting many places en route – Philae, Karnak, Luxor, Abydos, Denderah and Edfu. This Anglican clergyman eagerly sketched the magnificent monuments which he saw, and his drawings were enthusiastically received in England. In the meantime, in the other boat, a Danish sea captain, Frederick Lewis Norden, followed a similar course. He was the first European to examine and describe in some detail the temples of Nubia. Two years later yet another traveler – a doctor, Charles Perry – also took this route, pausing to make some detailed notes of the carved reliefs on the walls of the great Temple of Karnak.

James Bruce, a wealthy Scottish landowner, arrived in Alexandria in 1768, intent upon finding the source of the Nile. He started his African trip in Egypt, using the Nile as the quickest means of transport available. He visited Karnak and Luxor and the Valley of the Kings and the site of Meroë in the Sudan, one of the last outposts of Egyptian civilization.

In the meantime, Egyptology was becoming a serious discipline in Europe. Private and public collections of antiquities were growing, and there was a considerable demand for more antiquities. Societies for scientific and antiquarian study were formed – some of these even published their own learned journals. Historians continued to produce works on Egypt, but now they had access to

A 19th-century sketch of the interior of the temple of Abu Simbel, from Roberts' *The Holy Land.*

contemporary travel accounts on which to base their assumptions. Mummies were dissected in an attempt to discover how the embalming process was carried out, but surgical methods added little to the knowledge of embalming techniques described by the Classical authors. Some new theories gained popularity – it was the age of the pyramid cultists and cultural diffusionists, men who exaggerated the importance of Egyptian culture and placed Egypt at the center of ancient civilization. Egyptology was exerting an influence on many classes of society, and the layman as well as the scholar eagerly awaited new developments in this field. As the 18th century faded, the histories still contained many inaccuracies, and only the privileged few could actually visit the sites of Egypt. But the key to ancient Egyptian civilization was the Egyptian scripts, which were soon to be deciphered.

Northwest view of the temple of Philae as it appeared to French travelers in the early 19th century. From a drawing in the *Description de l'Égypte* commissioned by Napoleon after his successful invasion of Egypt in 1798.

III
PIONEERS OF EGYPTOLOGY

By 1798 Napoleon Bonaparte had carried out his successful invasion of Egypt and a new era began which had far-reaching effects upon Egyptology. Napoleon's interest in Egypt extended beyond the purely military and among his entourage he included a couple of hundred scholars whose task was defined as the exploration and description of various aspects of the country, including its ancient monuments. A series of volumes was produced by this scientific mission in which the monuments are well illustrated, and the series was acclaimed as a great success and brought prestige to France. A precedent was set for future scientific missions.

In digging a trench at Rosetta in 1799 a French officer unearthed a large black basalt stone inscribed in three different scripts. When the British invaded Egypt in 1801 and Alexandria capitulated, one of the prizes which they seized was the large black stone, which eventually reached the British Museum in London. Future generations were to know it as the Rosetta Stone; the inscriptions on the surface are in Greek, and also in Demotic and hieroglyphs – the two scripts used to write the language of ancient Egypt.

In 1822 a Frenchman, J. F. Champollion, deciphered the ancient hieroglyphic script. His discovery was the culmination of centuries of speculation. As early as the 5th century AD an Egyptian scholar, Horapollo, had attempted to analyze the possible meaning of these pictographs. He, and many people after him, were unsuccessful, because the erroneous belief persisted that the hieroglyphs were individual "pictures" representing things or ideas, and not sounds. Some headway was made by Kircher with his study of Coptic, and towards the end of the 18th century it became apparent that Coptic, with certain modifications, was the most recent form of the ancient Egyptian language,

Opposite: detail of colossal statue of Ramesses II, at Abu Simbel. *Above:* fallen statue of the king at Memphis, near the temple of Ptah. *Inset:* view of the ruins of Memphis from the *Description de l'Égypte*, with French officers measuring the hand of another statue of Ramesses II.

49

written in Greek and using a few additional letters. At about this time Bishop William Warburton recognized that the hieroglyphs were not mystical symbols with a deep inner meaning but were simply a method of writing; they had been used by the Egyptians to write letters, business accounts, literature and legal documents in addition to sacred texts. The hieroglyphs had indeed originally been pictographs but had evolved into a practical script, no more mysterious or obscure than Greek or Hebrew.

The Rosetta Stone, originally the text of a decree dating to 196 BC in the reign of Ptolemy V Epiphanes, was bilingual; the Greek text was easily translatable and provided a key from which the parallel Egyptian scripts could be deciphered. But progress was not easy. In the Demotic script a group of characters was identified which corresponded to the Greek name of Ptolemy (this was the work of a French orientalist, de Sacy, and a Swedish diplomat, Akerblad). Six examples of this name also occurred in the hieroglyphic portion. More than ten years later, in 1814, an Englishman, Thomas Young, took up the task and

achieved further results. He soon realized that the hieroglyphs and the Demotic script were very similar, and by comparing these with the Greek version, and using an earlier idea that in the hieroglyphs the names of kings and queens were encircled by "cartouches," he was able to identify the names of Queen Berenice and Tuthmosis. He made various other discoveries before breaking off his studies.

And so we reach 1822 when a young schoolteacher from Grenoble, Jean François Champollion, produced his famous *Lettre à M. Dacier*. Champollion had prepared himself for his task by learning to master ancient languages and Coptic. After much deliberation, he worked out a valid system for the decipherment of hieroglyphs, based originally on his analysis of the cartouches of Berenice, Cleopatra, Alexander, Tiberius, Domitian, Trajan and some other titles and epithets. On 29 September 1822 his famous letter was delivered at the Paris Academy. Two years passed and in his *Précis du système hiéroglyphique*, Champollion was able to expand his ideas further, to demonstrate the significance of many signs and to prove

Incised and painted hieroglyphs, probably from a New Kingdom tomb. The two cartouches contain the name of the pharaoh, Tuthmosis II.

The Rosetta Stone, found in 1799, carrying a decree of Ptolemy V (196 BC) in hieroglyphs, Demotic and Greek. By distinguishing the name of Ptolemy in all three scripts, the first hieroglyphs were deciphered.

that a close association existed between hieroglyphs and the Demotic and Hieratic scripts. More material was needed to work on, and in 1828–1829 Champollion and Rosellini, an Italian professor, set off for Egypt to make copies of monuments and inscriptions. The first chair of Egyptology was set up in 1831, founded for Champollion at the Collège de France. But he was unable to complete his work and died at the early age of 41.

Other scholars continued Champollion's great work; his own grammar was published posthumously and he left notes for a dictionary. His worthy successors included Lepsius, who led a Prussian expedition to Egypt in 1842 to 1845 and produced a 12-volume collection of inscriptional material from Egypt and the Sudan; Robert Hay (1799–1863) and others, who made several visits to copy the monuments, paintings and inscriptions. Other philologists of the 19th century included Birch, Goodwin, Hincks, Chabas, de Rougé, Maspero, Brugsch, who published a grammar of Demotic in 1855, and Erman who, with Sethe, laid the basis for the scientific study of Egyptian grammar. In the 20th century further advances in

knowledge were made by Möller, Griffith, Gunn, Sethe, Gardiner and others.

And so, gradually, an understanding of the Egyptian language in all its stages was built up. At present, one can only speculate about its origin, but it is accepted that it has affinities with Semitic languages, such as Hebrew and Arabic, and also with North African dialects. In this it probably reflects Egypt's role as meeting place of Asia and Africa from earliest times. Hieroglyphs, already developed as a script, occur on Egyptian remains as early as the 1st Dynasty. Today, when we refer to "hieroglyphs" we mean the "sacred carvings" or "writings" which retain their pictorial form; these occur carved on temple walls, where they were indeed sacred in purpose, and are also written on papyri and sherds where their use was practical – poems, texts, business documents. Hieroglyphs can be read in one of three directions – from top to bottom, from right to left and from left to right; they must be read in the opposite direction to which the human figures, animals and birds in the script are facing. They consist of signs with phonetic values – a number of alphabetic letters, each

Painted hieroglyphs on Queen Nefertari's tomb in the Valley of the Queens at Thebes (New Kingdom). Nefertari, wearing typical 19th-Dynasty dress, is playing a game, seated on her throne and holding the scepter. The hieroglyphs include a cartouche of her name and say that she is "The King's Great Wife, Lady of the Two Lands, Nefertari, beloved of Mut."

standing for one sound, and bilateral and trilateral sounds, and also determinatives (picture-signs which indicate the meaning of the word but have no sound value). The two types of sign are used in conjunction with each other in all Egyptian texts. This form of writing was used at least as early as 3100 BC, and the last example of it which has been found occurs on the island of Philae, dating to 394 AD.

During the later centuries other scripts were more widely used for the language, in non-religious contexts. Hieratic, a cursive script derived from hieroglyphs and written with a pen, was obviously much easier for daily usage and probably originated almost as early as hiero-glyphs. It was used for religious texts written on papyri, for business correspondence and literature, and also on ostraka, or pottery sherds. From Hieratic a popular script developed, known as Demotic. From about 700 BC onwards, and throughout the Greco-Roman period, Demotic was used by the literate Egyptian population for their business, literary and private correspondence. It was cursive and was written with pen and ink.

But let us turn back again to the years after Napoleon's invasion of Egypt. European travelers now visited Egypt in greater numbers. Egyptology became increasingly popular among the upper classes of Europe who eagerly awaited publications of drawings such as those of David Roberts, which were published in his work *The Holy Land*. Today these drawings are evocative of a past age, when there was time to sit and sketch the temples, often covered in drifts of sand, or to catch the glory of a sunset over the Theban ruins. Another work which captured the popular imagination and became a "bestseller" was Wilkinson's *Manners and Customs of the Ancient Egyptians* (1837). In the meantime, explorers continued to come to Egypt, includding men such as Johann Ludwig Burckhardt, who explored Nubia and discovered the temples of Abu Simbel.

By the middle 19th century Egypt, under the rule of Mohammed Ali, was becoming more easily accessible to the West. Mohammed Ali's aim was to introduce modern innovations into his country, and the Suez Canal and new railways, making transport easier, encouraged visitors to come to the Nile Valley. In addition to travelers, government officials, consuls and merchants in Egypt began to collect antiquities; a new field of enterprise had opened up and there were some who were more than ready to jump on the bandwagon. Only spectacular objects, such as statuary, jewelry and mummies with their trappings were considered valuable, and often the dealers' main aim was to acquire "treasures" which would fetch good prices. The methods by which the "treasure-seekers" worked ignored smaller objects, such as beads, amulets and pottery, and much irreparable damage was done. Archaeological methods were unknown.

However, conditions were soon to improve. In 1854 a young French official of the Louvre arrived in Egypt; his mission was to collect Coptic manuscripts. The young

Old Kingdom hieroglyphs carved into a mastaba column at Saqqara. They are less garish than those of the New Kingdom.

Mariette, during his stay in Cairo and Alexandria, noticed in the gardens of two houses a number of sphinxes of a similar type. He had read the Classical account of Strabo, who mentions "a temple of Serapis" at Memphis where he had seen a number of sphinxes, some partly and some entirely covered in the drifting sands. Later, Mariette made his way to Saqqara near Memphis where, he tells us:

"I perceived the head of one of these same sphinxes obtruding itself from the sand. This one had never been touched, and was certainly in its original position. Close by lay an oblation table on which was engraved in hieroglyphs an inscription to Osiris-Apis. The passage in Strabo suddenly occurred to my mind. The avenue which lay at my feet must be the one which led up to that Serapeum so long and so vainly sought for. But I had been sent to Egypt to make an inventory of manuscripts, not to search for temples. My mind, however, was soon made up. Regardless of all risks, without saying a word, and almost furtively, I gathered together a few workmen, and the excavation began! The first of the Grecian statues of the *dromos*, together with the monumental tables or stelae of the temple of Nectanebo, were drawn out of the sand, and I was able to announce my success to the French Government, informing them, at the same time, that the funds placed at my disposal for the researches after the manuscripts were entirely exhausted and that a further grant was indispensable. Thus was begun the discovery of the Serapeum."

In four years the Serapeum was uncovered, and the

tomb of the Apis bulls was found to contain long galleries, huge sarcophagi, stelae and offerings. Mariette was appointed Conservator of Monuments in Egypt in 1858, and under his directorship the Antiquities Service was developed. The two main aims of this organization were systematic excavation of sites and the establishment of a museum in Cairo where the Egyptian monuments and treasures could be displayed. This dream was realized with the foundation in Cairo of the Boulaq Museum. Mariette spread his energies widely over a number of sites; these included Abydos, Tabis, Memphis and Thebes and Saqqara, and some spectacular discoveries were made. However, very little of the work was published, and the continuation of Mariette's task fell to another Frenchman, Maspero, who arrived in Egypt in 1881 to assist the already ailing Mariette.

Maspero was Director General of the Antiquities Service until 1914. During his period of office the French Mission was set up; this permanent establishment was intended as a base where the publication of monuments could continue and where students could receive further training in Egyptology. From 1881 onwards excavation permits were granted to foreign excavators by the Service of Antiquities, and they were allowed to keep a proportion of their finds. Scientific scholars now began to come to Egypt in order to excavate and to obtain further knowledge rather than to acquire elaborate exhibits for museums or private collections – although their discoveries often provided new items for the great museums of the world. The days of the treasure hunter and plunderer were numbered. And so the Antiquities Service in Egypt was created. It continued under foreign direction until more recent times, when it began to be staffed by the Egyptians themselves.

In the meantime, the 19th century had witnessed developments in the techniques and attitudes to pyramid exploration. The story starts with men such as Giovanni

Below: wall with four rows of painted hieroglyphs in the tomb of Ramesses VI, Valley of the Kings.

Above: hieroglyphic examples from the Egyptian alphabet, which contained 24 basic signs. They illustrate how the signs derived from original representational pictures of the object described. *Right:* Painted hieroglyphs on a sarcophagus at Toena el-Gebel. They are read according to the direction in which the birds, animals or people face.

Belzoni, who entered the second of the Gizeh pyramids – belonging to Chephren (Khafre) – in 1818. Further exploration of the Great Pyramid was carried out in the next few years by a sea captain, Caviglia; he also cleared the sand from the Great Sphinx and explored some of the Gizeh mastaba tombs. At this time, 1836, Colonel Richard Vyse arrived in Egypt. He met Caviglia, and when Vyse set out on a tour of Upper Egypt he was sufficiently interested in pyramid exploration to hire Caviglia to organize work on the second and third pyramids at Gizeh during his absence. But, when Vyse returned, he wrote:

"I set out early in the morning, and went immediately to the Great, and to the Second Pyramids, where I expected to find M. Caviglia, and his men, but I did not find a single person, and afterwards I discovered the people at work on three mummy-pits behind the Sphinx, and the Second Pyramid . . ."

The mummy-hunting caused some disagreement between the two men, and although peace was made and the men continued to work together for some time, Vyse eventually found a new assistant – a civil engineer named Perring. Together Vyse and Perring undertook the first comprehensive survey of the three Gizeh pyramids and also those at Saqqara, Dahshur, Lisht, Meydum and

Below: drawing of Abu Simbel, discovered by the 19th-century traveler Johann Ludwig Burckhardt in 1812, before the site was cleared of sand and the temple cleaned and restored. *Right:* the two tombs at Abu Simbel dedicated to Hathor and Nefertari.

Hawara. Vyse's methods would be unacceptable today – he used gunpowder in his exploration of the Great Pyramid – but useful notes were kept and his assistant, Perring, carried out some excellent work. He made copies of the hieroglyphic inscriptions inside the pyramids (known today as the Pyramid Texts) which were placed inside the royal burial place to assist the king in his journey after death. (Internal decoration of the pyramids began again in the 5th Dynasty.) From this record it was eventually possible for scholars to identify the names of the kings who had built the pyramids.

During the latter half of the 19th century men from many nations contributed to a knowledge of the pyramids – Americans, Germans, French, Swiss, Italians and British. Gradually they forced the pyramids to give up some of their well-kept secrets, and exploration, excavation, copying and translation of inscriptions continued. The earliest explorers, with their vivid descriptions of their adventures, were soon joined by men such as Champollion, Erman, Lepsius, Maspero, Mariette, Burckhardt, Hoelscher, Jequier, Junker, Naville and Petrie, who produced a mass of scholarly literature. Although Gizeh was the site where pyramid exploration continued for the longest period, exploration was also undertaken at other places. As well as Saqqara, where work was done initially by Firth, Quibell and Lauer, other Old Kingdom sites excavated were the funerary temple of Abu Gurob and the necropolis at Abusir where German archaeologists revealed the whole funerary complex of this period. At Hawara Petrie opened one of the 12th-Dynasty pyramids built by Amenemmes III and at Lisht, the expedition of the Metropolitan Museum of Art, New York, excavated another pyramid of this period belonging to Sesostris I, together with the surrounding funerary complex.

The burial sites of the Middle Kingdom revealed other treasures to the archaeologists; at Dahshur, de Morgan discovered the jewelry of Princess Hathor-Sat, daughter of Sesostris III, while at Lahun, in a small tomb near to that of Sesostris II, Brunton, who had been trained by Petrie, found the treasure of another royal princess. The crowns and jewelry have been acclaimed ever since as superb examples of craftsmanship. At the sites of Nuri, Napata and Meroë, in the south, the American archaeologist Reisner devoted the years between 1900 and 1914 to the excavation of the sites and the pyramids which these Ethiopian kings had built for themselves. And so, pyramid exploration slowly became more scientific as well as widespread, and some idea gradually emerged of the development of pyramid building.

Apart from the "true" pyramids, the burial site of Mentuhotep I of the 11th Dynasty at Deir el-Bahri, which combined pyramid and temple in one structure, was also excavated, first by Naville and Hall for the Egypt Exploration Fund in 1903–1907, and then by Winlock for the Metropolitan Museum of Art, New York. In the 1930s excavations were carried out at Gizeh by Selim Bey

Hassan, and at Saqqara by Abdessalam Hussein and Selim Bey Hassan for the Egyptian Antiquities Service. In more recent times, a pyramid of the 3rd Dynasty at Saqqara, attributed to Sekhemhet, was excavated by Zakaria Goneim, for the Antiquities Service, and the Valley Building of the Bent Pyramid at Meydum has been excavated by A. Fakhry. In the 1950s the remains of the so-called "solar boats" or funerary barques were discovered by Kemal el Malakh near the Great Pyramid at Gizeh.

Parallel with the scientific interest in the pyramids of the 19th century, other developments occurred. In Britain and America the ideas of the Great Pyramid theorists aroused great interest. The most famous of these was Charles Piazzi Smyth, Professor of Astronomy at Edinburgh. The theory was based on the idea that in the measurements used in the construction of the Great Pyramid were hidden secrets of knowledge which were vitally important to mankind. It was at this time that Egyptology became popular with the middle classes on both sides of the Atlantic. Learned societies sprang up whose aim was to produce journals which dealt with new information and to raise funds for excavations in Egypt. Travel to Egypt became a very real possibility, and the first organized tours were arranged for intrepid visitors, who were transported up the Nile in steamboats or sailing craft. Field expeditions were sent out regularly from America and Europe, and many sites were scientifically excavated.

It is impossible to list the achievements of distinguished scholars from many lands, whose work was untiring. At Thebes in Upper Egypt the royal tombs were discovered by men such as Belzoni, Loret and Winlock, and in the late 19th century, during Maspero's directorship of the Antiquities Service, a cache of royal mummies – kings

Excavation in progress on a site at Karnak between the Sacred Lake area and the temple complex.

Restoration work at the Temple of Queen Hatshepsut, Deir el-Bahri. Transportation has not changed since antiquity.

and queens of the New Kingdom – was found at Deir el-Bahri. They had been secreted there, in a safe hiding place, by the priests of the 21st Dynasty. Ten years after this discovery another cache was found, not far away, containing funerary equipment and mummy-cases. So by the early 20th century it was believed that no more royal tombs awaited discovery in the Valley of the Kings. However, Lord Carnarvon and Howard Carter thought otherwise, and in 1922 their faith was rewarded by the famous discovery of the tomb of Tutankhamun, complete with the king's mummy and most of his funerary equipment, including the famous gold mask. The world marveled at the treasures uncovered. In 1929 the necropolis of the Tanite kings of the Late Period was discovered by Montet at Tanis, and here another magnificent gold mask – belonging to King Psusennes I – was found.

And so the story goes on. Many sites have been excavated, more in Upper Egypt than in the Delta; the pyramids have yielded more of their secrets; knowledge of predynastic Egypt has been expanded by men such as Petrie, Quibell and de Morgan; and considerable light has been thrown on the Archaic Period by Emery's excavations at Abydos and Saqqara. Excavation continues to provide new answers as well as new problems, more texts are translated and grammars and dictionaries are written to enable the student to grapple with the ancient Egyptian language. All this fresh knowledge necessitates constant revision of ideas relating to history, religion, art and social conditions.

Perhaps a turning point for Egyptology was the arrival on the scene of a young man whose ideas were to revolutionize the technique of excavation in Egypt, as well as elsewhere. In 1884 an unknown surveyor – William Flinders Petrie – was asked to undertake work at Tanis for the Egypt Exploration Fund (founded a couple of years previously) on Egyptology and its links with the Old Testament. Petrie had come to Egypt at the age of 26. His father, interested in the theories of Piazzi Smyth, had been anxious to make accurate measurements of the Great Pyramid, but eventually only his son made the journey and, setting up camp in a tomb near the Great Pyramid, began his survey of the monument. It was to be the most

thorough and accurate study to date, and Petrie continued to contribute to Egyptology for the rest of his life. Margaret Murray, in her *The Splendour that was Egypt*, later wrote of him:

"When Petrie began his career, Herodotus was our only guide to the history of Egypt; when he ended that career, the whole of Egyptian prehistory and history had been mapped out and settled."

Petrie did a vast amount of work, excavating during the winter and publishing the results in a series of reports in the summer months. His sites included Daphnae, Naukratis, Hierakonpolis, Naqada, Kahun, Tell el-Amarna, Abydos, Diospolis Parva and Tell el-Yehudiyeh.

But it was his methods of excavation which distinguished his work. Previously, only large monuments and buildings had been considered worthy of notice, and small finds as well as the levels of soil in which they were found had been ignored, thus destroying evidence vital to the reconstruction of any historical sequence. Petrie was one of the first to be concerned with the context of small finds – whether amulets, potsherds, beads or even domestic rubbish – and he recognized the importance of their relation to each other and to the levels of occupation on the site. He established a typology of weapons, stone vessels, pottery and so forth, and thus created a viable system of historical dating for Egyptology. He also laid the foundations for future work on Egypt's prehistory, a subject previously unrecognized. His methods were taught and used widely and have formed the basis of systematic, scientific excavation ever since. In 1894 a Chair of Egyptology – the first in Britain – was established for him at University College, London, by Amelia B. Edwards, to promote the teaching of Egyptian archaeology and training in field methods.

And so we turn to the present day. Much remains to be done in all fields – excavation, translation and further analysis of new knowledge. As in earlier times, many nations are contributing to the knowledge of and interest in Egyptology. In addition to excavations by the Department of Antiquities in Egypt, various countries continue their work at certain sites. Despite a very limited number of professional openings available on completion of their training, students all over the world continue to pursue university courses in Egyptology; tourists still flock to visit the great monuments as eagerly as the travelers of old; adult education centers give popular classes in Egyptology, and exhibitions of Egyptian antiquities continue to draw the crowds. The success of projects such as the removal of the Temple of Abu Simbel to a new site (made necessary by the new High Dam at Aswan) indicates how greatly the world prizes such ancient monuments. The subject continues, as it has done for so long, to hold wide popular appeal, and to attract scholars prepared to devote their lives to its furtherance. This is a healthy situation, and as far as the 20th century is concerned, the ancient Egyptians can rest assured. They are not being forgotten.

TUTANKHAMUN'S TOMB

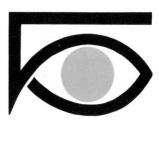

The finding of the tomb and treasure of the "boy king" Tutankhamun in 1922 (he is shown as a harpooner, *opposite*) is one of the most exciting episodes in the history of archaeology. Fortunately the discovery was recorded in photographs of exceptional quality, some of which have been used to recreate the story on these pages. At that time it was known that all the pharaohs of the 18th Dynasty – except the "heretic" king Akhenaten – had been buried in the desolate Valley of the Kings near the New Kingdom capital of Thebes, and the sites of most of their tombs had been found – except that of Tutankhamun. Indeed, the American archaeologist, Theodore Davis, stumbling upon a cache of funerary equipment from Tutankhamun's tomb, decided that he had discovered the tomb itself and wrote, "I fear that the Valley of the Kings is now exhausted." But Howard Carter, an English Egyptologist, thought otherwise. Enlisting the backing of a wealthy Englishman, Lord Carnarvon, who was in Egypt for his health, Carter searched for the tomb in the Valley of the Kings, season after season, both before and after World War I, but all in vain. In 1922, when almost ready to give up, Carter and Carnarvon decided to explore the one remaining area around the tomb of Ramesses VI beneath the towering "Peak" (*below*) whose pyramid shape may have been one of the reasons why the New Kingdom rulers selected this valley as a burial site. At last their patience was rewarded when a rock-cut step was revealed, and then more steps.

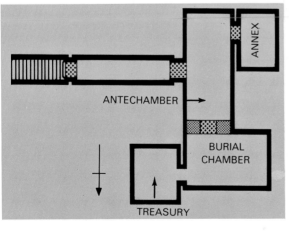

Carter, noting the gold and silver everywhere, the dazzling jewelry (like the vulture pendant to the *left*), the chests, animal-shaped beds and gilded chariots, was overwhelmed by "the gorgeousness of the sight." Twice, it seems, thieves had entered the antechamber, leaving it in confusion but getting away with very little. In fact it took Carter and his men two years to clear out, repair and preserve this vast accumulation. A final door between the antechamber and the burial chamber revealed an immense shrine of gilded wood. Thus far the thieves had gone, but no further. Three more gilded shrines, one within another, were carefully opened. Finally, Carter and Carnarvon opened the doors of the last shrine (*below*) to reveal a magnificent red sandstone sarcophagus.

The entrance to Tutankhamun's tomb had been concealed beneath the remains of ancient workmens' huts near the tomb of Ramesses VI (*above*). Fifteen steps led down to a plastered door with traces of seals, including that of Tutankhamun, which showed that the tomb had been robbed in antiquity. Behind this door a passage led to a second door, behind which Carter saw for the first time (*above right*) the jumbled treasures within – food, chariots, flowers, a throne, beds, all thrown together in indescribable confusion.

Tutankhamun and his young wife, Ankhesenamun, depicted on the side of a small chest found in the tomb. The elegant drawing and informal poses of the royal couple reflect the recent "Amarna revolution" in Egyptian art.

Howard Carter carefully dusts the king's nose. The gilded shrines have now been cleared away and the massive sandstone sarcophagus opened to reveal the first of three mummified coffins, nested one within the other. On the first lay a small wreath of flowers, perhaps placed there as a final farewell by Tutankhamun's young widow.

Tackle had to be used to lift the inner coffin from the outer ones, heavily anointed with unguents. The first two coffins were of gilded wood. The features of the second (*below*) were painted to reveal the suffering of death. The third coffin (*opposite page*) was made of thick 22-carat gold.

On the backrest of the gold-plated wooden throne, found in the antechamber, the young pharaoh and his wife are touchingly revealed in affectionate attitudes. Gold and silver, with inlays of colored glass paste, calcite and ceramics, were used to create this splendid scene. Tutankhamun, who was only 19 when he died, was a very minor pharaoh, his tomb was far less elaborate than those of wealthier kings, and it is clear that his burial was hastily arranged and the grave goods assembled in a most haphazard manner. Yet of all the tombs in the Valley of the Kings, only Tutankhamun's has survived virtually intact.

60

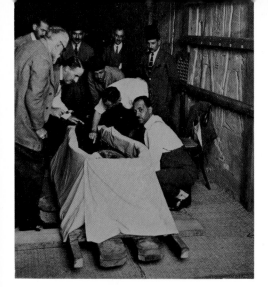

Howard Carter (*to the left*, bending) helps unwrap the mummy, which was found intact inside the innermost coffin with a magnificent gold mask over its face.

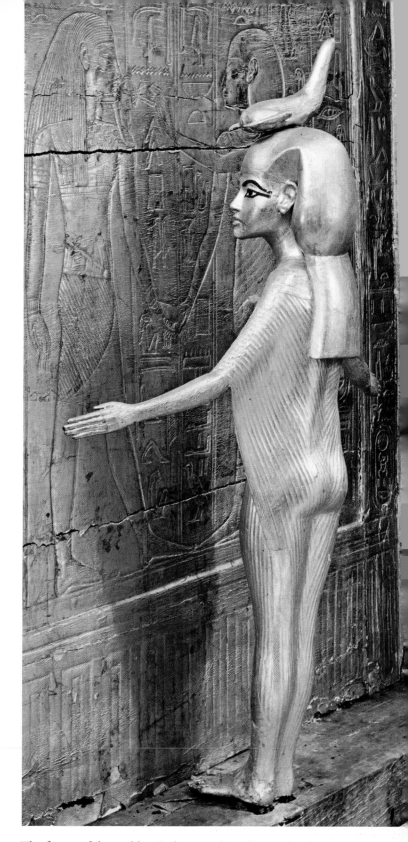

The figure of the goddess Serket, standing about 3 feet high, guards the shrine of wood covered in gold leaf which held the mummified viscera of the king. Isis, Nephthys and Neith protected the other three sides of the shrine. Inside it, within a linen-covered alabaster chest, four compartments held the viscera of the king in miniature gold coffins. This was but one of the many precious objects found in the so-called treasury behind the burial chamber.

61

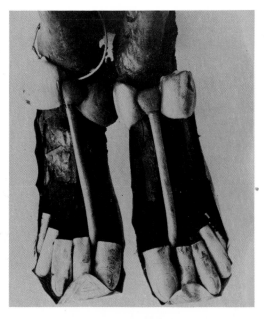

When first revealed, the third coffin (*left*), of solid gold, was wrapped in a red linen shroud folded back to reveal the face alone. A necklace of flowers lay across the breast. The features showed great serenity, symbolizing the fortitude of the pharaoh as he awaited his resurrection from death, just as those of the second coffin had indicated the suffering of death. Elaborate symbolism and ancient ritual had governed the choice of equipment, decoration and the layout in Tutankhamun's tomb.

The purpose of the funeral ritual and its intricate symbolism was to bring the dead king safely into the afterlife with his body intact and all his worldly possessions about him. Unfortunately, the king's mummy, when unwrapped (*left*), turned out to be badly damaged by over-lavish use of unguents. However the feet (*above*), partially encased in golden sheaths and sandals, and the hands were well preserved. On the mummy's head lay the golden death mask, a masterpiece of portraiture.

Among the innumerable treasures discovered in the various chambers of the tomb, including the annex (a small room opening off the antechamber), were several ornate fans, originally holding ostrich feather whisks. The decoration on the example to the left shows the young king in his chariot, with his hounds, shooting an ostrict (*bottom*), and the return from the hunt (*top*) with bearers carrying the game before the pharaoh. The king's actual chariots and bows and arrows were found in the tomb.

The gold death mask of Tutankhamun, surely a close portrait of the dead king. "The youthful Pharaoh was before us at last. . . . Here was the climax of our long researches!" wrote Carter, recalling the moment of discovery in 1925. The solid gold is inlaid with glass and semi-precious stones.

63

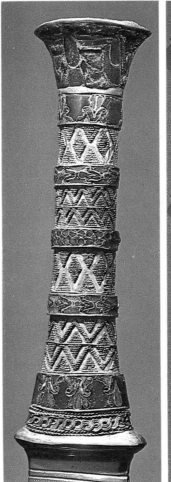

A first view of the treasury, beyond the burial chamber, which contained some of the most precious of the funeral furnishings. Prominent is a gilded chest with carrying poles, and on it a statue of the dog-headed Anubis, wrapped in linen. At the back is the canopic shrine with its guardian goddesses. The thieves entered here, but took only a few jewels.

A royal dagger, with decorated sheath and pommel, and (*below left*) a lotus-flower triple lamp of alabaster. If this makeshift tomb was so rich in treasures, those of the great pharaohs must have been splendid beyond belief. It took ten years (1922–1932) to clear Tutankhamun's tomb of its treasures, which are now permanently displayed in the Egyptian Museum, Cairo.

A detail from the painted decoration on the walls of the burial chamber. Its walls alone were decorated with paintings.

IV
ART AND RELIGION

We are separated from the Egyptians not only by several thousands of years but also by a different approach to life. This difference in outlook is perhaps most apparent in the art and religion of Egypt, which were closely linked. Together they manifest the most basic beliefs which lay behind one of the world's greatest civilizations.

ART

Egyptian art took several forms, including sculpture in the round, bas-relief and painting. Because of the belief in an afterlife, great care was taken to provide the deceased with material possessions; these were made to last "for eternity," whereas the everyday articles of use were designed for a more temporary purpose. Thus the art which is preserved today is, to a great extent, funerary.

We can assume, however, that domestic dwellings, especially the palaces, were also decorated with brightly-colored wall paintings. This is indicated by fragments from the royal palaces of Amenophis III at Thebes and of his son at Amarna, as well as the reproductions of the facades of palaces on Old Kingdom sarcophagi. But most domestic buildings, being constructed of mud-brick, have perished, whereas the tombs were built of stone.

One of the most outstanding and perhaps most characteristic achievements of the Egyptians was the painting found in the tombs of royalty and of the nobles. The walls of these tombs are covered with scenes; in the tombs of noblemen there are scenes from the everyday life of the owner, depicting his profession, family life and the pursuits which he enjoyed – hunting, fishing, banqueting. There are also scenes of agricultural life – the sowing and reaping of crops, wine-making, baking and brewing – in addition to those showing craftsmen, such as goldsmiths, potters and brickmakers plying their trades. Today, along the banks of the Nile, many such activities can still be seen. However, although the tomb scenes show glimpses of daily life thousands of years ago, the way the tomb owner and his companions are presented seems strange to modern eyes, for the concept of the human figure in Egyptian art was quite different from our own.

We have become accustomed to regard most works of

Painted relief in the tomb of Nefertari. The figure on the far left is Osiris while the main figure represents Horus "protector of his father" in the costume of a Sem priest. The stars painted on the ceiling were a popular funerary motif.

today either as a form of decoration (in churches, public buildings or homes), or in some cases as imparting a belief or message, or relating a story. To comprehend Egyptian art it is essential to understand its basic principles. To the Egyptians, funerary and religious art was utilitarian; it was not regarded as a method of tomb decoration, although it effectively performed this function as well; neither were these paintings designed to inspire the beholder with religious fervor, nor were they an attempt to commemorate great deeds and preserve them for posterity, for the subject matter is homely and down-to-earth. The purpose of Egyptian tomb-painting was to serve the owner of the tomb; it was closely linked with the magical and religious beliefs of the people. The tomb was regarded as the "house" of the deceased where he would spend eternity, and the paintings represented the activities which the tomb owner hoped he would continue to enjoy in the next world. So the Egyptians, by a process of sympathetic magic, sought to secure for themselves a prosperous and pleasant hereafter.

This process, it was thought, could be achieved in two ways. First, great attention was paid to representing in minute detail the situation they desired. The tomb owner and his family are shown as idealized humans, with slender bodies and youthful beauty, free from physical defects, and enjoying the blessings of life. Their individual features show little variation, for these figures are not intended to be portraits of the deceased; they are symbolic representations of a "perfect man" and his family. Other figures in the scenes, those of lesser importance, included to ensure the well-being of the tomb owner – the servants, dancing girls, musicians, laborers, brewers, bakers, etc. – are more realistically depicted. Here, the inevitable signs of old age – graying hair, baldness and excess weight – are shown, as well as infirmities such as blindness. Whereas the facial expressions of the noble and his class are bland, free from emotion or passion, the other figures often exhibit gaiety or bad temper, and considerable humor.

Accompanying most of the scenes are hieroglyphic texts, often providing a title for the scene, naming the noble and giving a brief account of his activity, as well as the requisite magical formulas. These inscriptions were intended to identify the scene and thus ensure its existence for eternity, for to the Egyptians, names were not only a means of describing people, objects, events, but were essentially part of them; knowledge of the name and its magical repetition gave power over the object or man. The paintings and their accompanying inscriptions in the tomb were "brought to life" by the priest, who recited the required formula on the day when the tomb, enclosing all the funerary equipment and the mummified body of the deceased, was finally sealed. Once the paintings had undergone this magical ceremony, they were believed to "come to life" and to exist in reality for eternity. If the mummified body of the tomb owner suffered damage at any time, his representation on the tomb wall, together with his statue

However, the statues of the gods were for the most part simply produced to increase the power of the god and, with the smaller models, to afford protection to the possessor. The statuettes placed in the temples and dedicated by ordinary people were intended to represent the giver so that he could then take part in the rituals which were carried out in the temple and thus ensure his eternity.

Statuary may be divided into two main groups – royalty and commoner – but the general principles governing the art form apply in both cases. As in tomb-painting, there was rarely any attempt to produce likenesses of patrons. Indeed, the traditional canons were applied to sculpture as to painting. The main aim was to produce an idealized figure, free from physical defects, and according to a prescribed set of rules. The patron was assured of eternal life by the simple device of adding his name to the statue, thus establishing the identification of the statue with him.

Certain devices were employed which gave the statues an overall similarity, although over the years and even in the same period many details differ. Often the same conventional group is used – the popular family unit of man, wife and children. In some statues, especially of the Old Kingdom, the pupils are not shown in the eyes, giving the face a contemplative expression as if gazing on some eternal, far-distant scene from which the spectator is excluded. In actuality, the two halves of the human face are never identical and often differ quite considerably, but the Egyptian artist attempted to show them as similar as possible; this had the effect of giving the features an unnatural regularity.

The modern tourist who enters an Egyptian temple or a tomb is immediately aware that the ancient Egyptians preferred to cover vast areas of wall space in their sacred buildings with sculptured reliefs. In the temples, the walls, ceilings and columns are decorated with closely-worked scenes in bas-relief or relief en-creux (engraved), sometimes still bearing rich traces of the painted plaster, for in some of the tombs (particularly of the Old Kingdom) it was the practise to carve the walls with scenes which were then enhanced with paint.

Again, stelae – rectangular stone slabs – were executed in this manner and often bore scenes showing the deceased making offerings to the gods, along with formal inscriptions, sometimes giving details of his life and career.

The conventions governing this art form were the same as those for painting; these two forms are more closely related to each other than to statuary, although bas-relief is closer to statuary in its rendering of the actual features – for it is, in effect, a series of "statues" projected onto a flat surface. Incised relief and bas-relief were often used together; usually the outside walls of the monument were executed in incised relief, and the inner walls in bas-relief, though sometimes this process was reversed.

The artist. Before discussing the techniques employed in Egyptian painting and sculpture we should spare a thought for the artist. The man who performed a duty so vital in Egyptian society, who could by withholding his services jeopardize the eternal bliss of countless wealthy and influential people, was in fact regarded simply as an official of the state with particular skills. He was a technician, classified together with metalsmiths, carpenters and quarrymen, who created the tomb with him.

The decoration of a tomb was a united effort, in which several artists or relief-sculptors would work together under the general guidance of the Master. Each man was responsible for a part of the work, and did not seek individual recognition. Indeed the art is anonymous, except in a few instances. It was never intended that scholars and tourists (who have visited the monuments from the Roman period onwards) should enter the sacred temples and tombs, gaze upon the artist's work and pass judgment upon its aesthetic merits. The Egyptian artist himself would have found our attitude to artists in society quite incomprehensible. He performed a service, in the same way as any other skilled craftsman or minor clerical official, and certainly neither had nor would have expected any particular "mystique" or fame in posterity through his work.

It was customary for boys to follow their fathers' professions and young artists were apprenticed to master craftsmen. They learned to copy designs and there was no pressure on them to produce new or original ideas. Technical perfection was the ultimate aim, and an ability to reproduce as closely as possible the traditional forms.

Sculptured wooden head from Saqqara (5th Dynasty), with inlaid eyes, a good example of sculpture in the round.

The workshops were attached to the residence of the king, to one of the temples or to a noble establishment, and the artists' work was closely supervised. It was probably necessary to obtain the permission of the king before embarking on any private work, perhaps even for the decoration of the nobles' tombs, although they appear to have found time and energy to produce sidelines, such as trinkets, toilet ware, amulets and so forth. These found a ready market among the sophisticated and fashion-conscious ladies of Egypt.

The craftsmen who lived at Deir el-Medineh have already been mentioned; they were lively, humorous people, well able to take care of their own affairs – by forceful methods if necessary – and determined to gain a place on the social ladder. They must be considered fairly typical of the Egyptian artist-craftsman.

Techniques of the artist. The Theban tombs of the New Kingdom, nestling in the barren wastes beyond the cultivated land, today provide the best examples of

Painted ceiling in the tomb of Sennefer, the royal gardener, in the Valley of the Nobles at Thebes (New Kingdom). The whole ceiling is covered with these colorfully painted vines, illustrating Egyptian expertise in secular design, contrasting with their mastery of religious themes. It is known as the "Tomb of the vines."

Egyptian painting, for although the scenes in the temples were originally painted in vivid hues, the plaster has fallen off many of the walls, leaving only the carved reliefs behind. Many of the statues of stone and wood have also lost their original colors.

In the necropolis at Thebes there are fine examples not only of completed scenes, but also of the various stages leading up to completion, for it was the custom to leave a tomb unfinished. This was probably due to some religious convention or superstition rather than to the unexpected and premature demise of the patron, although this must have happened occasionally.

Color was the main feature in these tombs; today the hues are almost as fresh as the day when they were first applied. The use of color was symbolic; certain colors are always used in certain places – a reddish-brown for the skin of a man, a pale yellow for that of a woman, dark brown for Nubians, certain colors for specific deities, and so forth. The Egyptians used a limited color range – red, yellow, blue, green, black and white; it was used in powdery cakes, and made of red oxide or ocher, yellow ocher or orpiment, powdered azurite or blue frit, powdered malachite, chrysocolla or green frit, carbon black and gypsum or whiting. Variations and graded or muted tones were rare, but they were achieved by mixing the primary substances. Gray and pink can both be seen in use during the Amarna period. The materials used by the artist were simple. Often a shell or broken potsherd sufficed for his palette, although some palettes were purpose-made; and chewed reeds and little palm fiber brushes, together with a small water pot, made up his equipment.

The type of stone which existed in the area where the tomb was sited determined whether the walls were first carved with reliefs and then painted or whether they were simply painted. In the Old Kingdom, when some of the most important tombs were situated at Saqqara (an area where there was good stone) it was the custom to decorate the tombs with carved reliefs. During the New Kingdom, however, the valleys of the kings, queens and nobles at Thebes did not possess sufficiently hard stone, and the walls were merely plastered and painted.

A factor which was common to both painting and bas-relief was, of course, the preliminary drawing of the scene. Once the architect of the tomb had provided the correct dimensions and necessary details, the Master Artist was able to produce scale drawings of the scenes which were to decorate the walls of the tomb. These were then submitted to the patron who would perhaps suggest changes. The walls would then be prepared; some tombs had natural rock-hewn walls, and in this case any holes would be filled in with plaster and the walls coated with plaster or stucco. In other tombs, the walls might be of composition – clay mixed with straw – and several layers of plaster would be applied.

Once there was a smooth plaster surface on which to

Detail from the great ceiling painting in the hall of the sarcophagus in the tomb of Pharaoh Sethos I. It depicts the passage of the sun at night. The crocodile and the hippopotamus goddess Tauert are shown here.

work, the Master was able to transfer his sketches, drawn to scale, on to the walls. The sketches were drawn at first on a grid, with geometric divisions, and thus very little deviation would occur between the figures; the whole could be increased in size according to wish, but the proportions of the figures would remain the same. This grid, devised according to traditional principles and strictly followed, facilitated the transfer of the sketches to the wall. Once the Master had completed the sketches, using either black or red ink, the assistants completed the work under close supervision. There was little opportunity for individualism or originality, since they were governed rigidly by traditional principles. The actual application of the colors now took place; the paints were dissolved with water and applied with a gum-like substance to the walls. Probably a sealing was finally added to the surface, perhaps bees-wax.

With bas-relief and relief en-creux, the process was only slightly different; once the surface had been smoothed and the preliminary sketches transferred onto the walls, the carving was carried out. Incised relief – usually employed on outside walls subject to weathering – consisted of cutting the silhouettes of the figures deeply into the wall, and then superimposing the details on the basic shape. With bas-relief the background itself was chiseled away, leaving the figures, half in the round, to stand out from the wall. Details were added and the paint was superimposed.

One puzzling question remains. How were the tombs lit, to enable the artists to carry out their intricate work? There would have been insufficient light from the open entrance, and the lamps available at that time would have been inadequate; torches and flares, used to light the temples and probably the palaces, would have produced traces of smoke on the walls and ceilings of the tombs – and this is absent. Today large mirrors are often used to illuminate the tombs, but the problem of how they were lit in antiquity has not yet been solved.

In discussing the techniques employed by the Egyptians we are constantly faced with the enigma of how their limited range of tools and instruments enabled them to achieve such high levels of craftsmanship. This is true of their sculpture no less than of their painting. Various materials were used for statuary – wood, ivory, slate, gold, faience and certain types of stone. Hard rocks such as diorite and porphyry were carved without difficulty, and yet only simple copper tools with wooden handles appear

Wall painting from a 12th-Dynasty tomb, showing a woman with a lotus flower. The artist's grid technique is illustrated in the drawing (*right*). Where the paint has worn thin on the original, the red grid lines from which he worked are visible.

to have been available. Chisels, small axes, knives, drills, picks and saws were the sculptor's equipment. There has been much speculation as to how the Egyptians cut their stone, both for statuary and for building, but no really convincing theory has been put forward to explain many of the technical problems. Abrasion was the method used to polish the stone, an arduous process but one which produced spectacular results.

To make a statue, a block of stone was squared off, and on the side and front an outline was made in ink of the required subject. This outline was then incised on to the two planes; a rough figure was chiseled out of the block, and the delicate work of carving the statue began.

The Amarna Period. The art of this period must be discussed separately, for it constitutes a break – the only significant one – in the history of Egyptian art. As we have noted, religion and art were closely interwoven. When Amenophis IV introduced new religious beliefs and ideas, changed his name to Akhenaten and established a monotheistic religion, symbolized by the Aten or sun's disk, he broke down the conventions which had dictated the basis of Egyptian art for centuries. He built a new capital city – Akhetaten – at a place where there had previously been no habitation; in more recent times this site has been known as Tell el-Amarna and from this both the period of history and the style of art have taken their name.

Akhenaten's beliefs were bound up with the concept of "ma'at," which is loosely translated as "truth." Whereas previously the pharaoh, his family and those who were noble or wealthy enough to buy the privilege had been portrayed on the walls of their tombs and on monuments with a perfect, idealized physique, now the pharaoh

himself set an example by being shown with his physical deformities. Indeed, the deformities were quite possibly accentuated on purpose, for members of the royal family were also frequently shown with distorted limbs and elongated skulls, and in some cases it is difficult to determine whether these are realistic portraits, or whether the deformities of the king have become an "art-form," applied at random to other figures.

With Amarna royal statuary, two changes are immediately apparent. First, the members of the royal family usually display these peculiar physical characteristics (although some sculpture is free from the more exaggerated forms) and secondly, the traditional postures for royal figures are relaxed to the extent that in both statues and reliefs the curtain is lifted on private life at the

Unfinished sketch from the tomb of Amenophis II. The primary drawing was completed, but it was never painted.

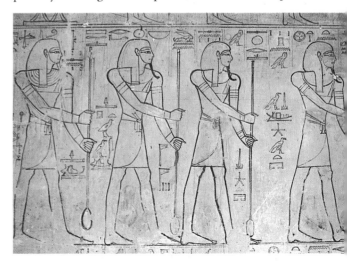

palace, and Akhenaten and his family appear informally, with the king kissing a small daughter, the royal couple embracing their children and the family taking meals.

The large numbers of private statues which were previously placed in the tombs and the temples are no longer found in the Amarna period. Divine statues of the state deities, once the focal points of temple worship, are replaced by representations of the Aten as the sun-disk from which rays descend, ending in hands which symbolize the bounty bestowed on the royal family by the divine power and, by the agency of Akhenaten, on the land of Egypt. It is worth noting that this representation of the Aten occurs both before and after the Amarna period, on the back of the gilded wooden throne of Tutankhamun, and also in the tomb of Ramose where the decoration forms a bridge between the Amarna period and the reign of Amenophis III immediately preceding it.

Funerary art also underwent radical changes. The tombs at Amarna, intended for the royal family and the nobility who had followed and served them, display distinct differences from, for example, the Theban tombs. The life which the Egyptian noble hoped to enjoy after death is no longer depicted on the walls, but instead events in his career are shown, emphasizing in particular the role which the king has played in his life and his advancement. This, of course, reflected the doctrine, supported by Akhenaten, that he alone, as the divine son, could mediate between the Aten and the people; it also emphasizes how much less importance was attached to life after death and the attendant funerary beliefs which had been such features of the worship of Osiris. In the Amarna tombs the figures no longer appear in the traditional horizontal rows. Basically, however, the idea is retained of showing the human figure partly in profile.

Painting was still used in the tombs, the temples, the palaces and on statuary, but the artist could now experiment more freely with the use of color, and blended his pigments to break away from the flat, primary colors previously used. Subjects included details observed from the surrounding landscape – birds soaring in flight and clumps of the papyrus plant – painted in delicate, muted tones. A palace mural from Amarna shows two little princesses (originally part of a larger family scene) with characteristic full hips and thighs and elongated skulls.

During the Amarna interlude the purpose and structure of the temple underwent considerable change. In the temple built by Akhenaten at Thebes (later destroyed, but of which thousands of blocks remain) the reliefs symbolized the worship of the Aten.

And what of the artist, who must have flourished in the environment to which he was transferred? At Akhetaten he certainly enjoyed a freedom which he had never possessed in the other capital cities. He probably received his instructions directly from the king – this strange young man with his revolutionary concepts – but for the first time, the artist found himself granted official permission to

Akhenaten and his family, from a relief at Tell el-Amarna. Behind the pharaoh is his wife, Nefertiti, and behind her, Merytaten. The scene depicts worship of the sun.

Queen Tiye (*above*), mother of the heretic king Akhenaten. *Below:* an unfinished head of Nefertiti, Akhenaten's queen. Both heads show the sophisticated realism of Amarna art.

Head of a king, probably that of Smenkhkare, co-pharaoh with Akhenaten in his later years. The sensitive portraiture of an individual rather than a type is typical of Amarna art.

experiment. He was requested to ignore the strict religious canons which had limited his fathers, and to base his work on the concept of "ma'at."

There can be no doubt that the artists at Akhetaten achieved a high standard, both in painting and statuary. Perhaps this is nowhere more apparent than in the famous limestone portrait head of Nefertiti which was found in the workshop of the sculptor Thutmose. The sculptured head is coated with plaster and painted, except for the eye sockets and the blank shoulder ends; the colors and fine modeling of the features have together created a superb example of craftsmanship with none of the exaggerated indications of the art of this period. Other unfinished pieces, clearly intended to represent this queen, testify to her beauty as well as to the skill of the artist.

The Amarna artists are not entirely anonymous; the names of some of them – Bek, Iuty and the afore-mentioned Thutmose – are known to us, and clearly some of the workshops had a certain degree of independence and were under the direct control of the master artist himself.

Artists from Crete who had fled from their homeland when catastrophe overtook them in the reign of the previous king, Amenophis III, had settled down in Egypt, and doubtless they continued to exert their influence on the art forms developing at the new capital of Akhetaten, which they may well have made their home.

In Amarna art there is a conscious attempt to break with traditional ideas. To some people, these art forms appear grotesque and repulsive, carrying this break with tradition to extremes of ugliness and destroying the "perfection" of the traditional art. To others, the art expresses freedom and originality, the informal family scenes are endearing, and this interlude is seen as the peak of creative artistic ability in Egypt's long history.

Until the last days of Egyptian civilization, when most of the art forms had changed under the pressure of new ideas, the temples alone remained virtually the same as in earlier times. New temples were established in the Greco-Roman era, and the overall design of these buildings and the style of the reliefs which decorated the walls were similar to those of the New Kingdom. The figures in the wall reliefs are more voluptuous and perhaps a little coarser than the slender figures of the Empire buildings but, designed to last for eternity, they still testify to the glory and power of the gods of Egypt and the everlasting majesty of pharaoh, their son.

RELIGION

To the general reader, the religious beliefs of the ancient Egyptians seem to be one of the more baffling aspects of this ancient civilization. Many doctrines, often contradictory, and a vast array of deities confuse the issue, and from classical times down to the present the subject has inspired much speculation and scholarly thought. It is beyond the scope of this chapter to give more than the briefest outline of some of the most basic elements of religion in order to show how the Egyptian explained the existence of the universe, his own existence, and his life after death.

A multitude of gods. Religion was a unifying force in the lives of the Egyptians. Together with death it was one of the main concerns of their society, involving both the king and the poorest of his subjects, and pervading every aspect of life. Religion never deteriorated into a hollow state worship and every man valued his individual relationship with his gods. The long narrow strip of cultivation on either side of the Nile was geographically

Ma'at, goddess of truth, wearing her distinctive feather, the symbol of justice. She receives the adoration of Ramesses VI whose hand appears on the right. The painting is in the tomb of Ramesses VI in the Valley of the Kings.

difficult to rule. Yet throughout the centuries, despite disasters and invasions, Egypt remained a state, governed for most of the time by one supreme ruler who was considered to be the divine son. Towards the end of her civilization, despite a succession of foreign invaders, Egypt still retained her religious beliefs and to some extent imposed them on her conquerors. Religion was the cornerstone of Egyptian civilization.

To the casual observer, the Egyptians seemed to worship countless deities. The deification of living creatures was commonplace – cows, crocodiles, rams, dogs, lionesses, ibises, monkeys, bulls, vultures, serpents, falcons and many others – and animal cults retained popularity from the earliest to Greco-Roman times. Even certain inanimate objects and forms of vegetation were venerated. To other nations of the ancient world, the worship of animals was considered characteristic of Egypt and not a little shocking. There were of course also anthropomorphic deities, some with mummified forms, and many of the models of these gods and goddesses appear so similar that they can only be identified by the signs which they often wear on their heads and by qualities attributed to them.

The functions of the deities were as varied as their appearance. These functions often overlapped or were interchangeable, due to the process of syncretism, which had taken place throughout Egypt's history.

To simplify the situation, we can loosely divide the gods into two main categories. In the first group are the local and state gods; these occur in legends and myths and usually possessed their own temples. Local gods continued to command great authority in their own regions from earliest times, but seldom achieved national importance. Often they were animal gods, like Bastet, the cat goddess, whose center was at Bubastis where hundreds of bronze cats were dedicated to her, and Sobek, the crocodile god whose worship was centered at Crocodilopolis in the Fayoum and also at Kom Ombo.

From the ranks of the local deities arose the great state gods. Originally each locality had worshiped a particular god or group of gods, and when the tribal leader of that area succeeded in making himself a ruler of Egypt, it was natural that his local god, who had thus blessed his ambitions, should be elevated to the status of a national god.

However, with the exception of the Amarna period, the great gods were never exclusive and tolerated the existence of other deities. Indeed this was one of the reasons why the Egyptian pantheon was so vast, for no god was ever entirely eliminated, although the attributes of two deities might often be united under the name of one.

The first of the gods to receive royal approval and general acceptance was the sun god Re', not a surprising choice in a land where the "god" is usually visible in the sky. Re' began his steady rise to power as early as the 2nd Dynasty when he became closely associated with the king. The pyramids built throughout the Old Kingdom are connected with this belief, and by the 5th Dynasty Re' had become the chief god of the state. The king took the epithet "son of Re'" and it was believed that after death the king alone joined his father Re' in the heavens. With the collapse of royal power at the end of the Old Kingdom and the ensuing troubled years of the First Intermediate Period, the supreme power of Re' was undermined and he never regained such prominence. By the Middle Kingdom his worship was replaced by that of the popular god Osiris, who promised a democratic hereafter, although Re' retained his official power. In the New Kingdom Re' was united with the new state god Amun, under the name of Amen-Re'. The center of the worship of Re' was one of the foremost religious towns in the Old Kingdom – Heliopolis – now a select suburb of modern Cairo.

A striking example of the rapid rise to glory of a provincial deity is that of Amun. Originally an obscure god

Black granite statue of Sekhmet, the lion-headed goddess of the desert and destruction, protectress of the pharaoh. From the mortuary temple of Ramesses III at Medinet Habu.

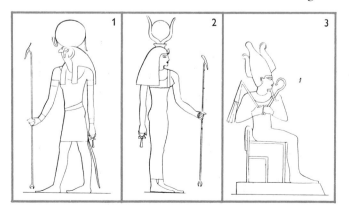

who was worshiped in the region of Thebes, Amun rose to be one of the most famous of all Egyptian deities and was certainly the most wealthy. The pharaohs of this period built up an unrecognized threat to the supremacy of their successors, for other cults became jealous of Amun, and it was not long before the priesthood of the god became a threat to the very pharaohs whose forebears had established his power. It is possible that this was one of the reasons which forced Amenophis III and, to a much greater extent, Akhenaten to disband the priesthood and introduce a new form of worship. Again, in later dynasties, the interests of pharaoh and the priesthood of Amun were to conflict.

The second major group of gods were the gods of the people, or the "household" deities. They protected the poor, who worshiped them in their own humble surroundings. These deities possessed no temples of their own and had no place in the religious doctrines, but it was to these gods that the people offered up their prayers rather than to the remote gods of the state. They took a variety of forms. Deceased kings or outstandingly brilliant officials, such as Imhotep, the architect of the first stone pyramid and god of healing, were occasionally deified. However, the two most popular of these minor deities were the homely, ugly, deformed dwarf Bes, god of marriage, bringer of joy and protector against evil, and the goddess Tauert, who symbolized fecundity and protected all women in childbirth. Portrayed as a pregnant hippopotamus, Tauert was used as a subject for countless amulets, doubtless worn by women of all classes.

Isis and Osiris. Only one god not only gained a place in the hearts of the ordinary Egyptians, but also exerted a considerable influence on the state religion and funerary beliefs and, with his wife, was adopted by other peoples as a deity. This was Osiris, god of vegetation, judge of the underworld and king of the dead. There are various versions of the Osiris myth, including that handed down by the Greek writer Plutarch. It was believed that Osiris had originally been a human king who had established order and brought the elements of civilization to his people. The myth is concerned with this king, his jealous and evil brother Seth who murdered him, and Isis, his

Statue of the household god Bes. He is represented as an ugly dwarf but was very popular, especially among the common people, being the god of marriage and domestic happiness.

Drawings of some Egyptian gods. *Left to right:* 1 and 7. Re', the sun-god. 2. Hathor, goddess of dancing and music. 3. Osiris, god of the underworld. 4. Amen-Re', the great state god and chief god of the New Kingdom. 5. Isis, mother goddess and wife of Osiris. 6. Ptah, god of handicrafts. 8. Anubis, god of embalming. 9. Khnum, the potter god.

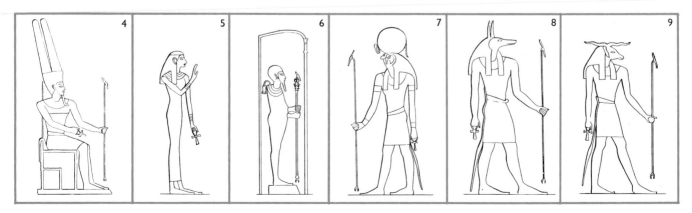

Funerary wall painting in a tomb at Deir el-Medinah, Thebes. The deceased (*left*) accept offerings from the family.

devoted wife and mother of his posthumously conceived son, Horus, who fought Seth and avenged his father's death. Eventually Osiris was restored to life, not as a human king but as king of the dead and judge of the underworld. Various significant elements emerge in this story – the suffering, destruction and final triumph of a good man, the ultimate defeat of his wicked enemy, the devotion of Osiris' wife and son, the judgment of the dead, with the promise of eternal reward. The similarity to certain aspects of the Christian faith is apparent.

Osiris was also a vegetation god, perhaps his original role; he embodied the annual process of the renewal of the land, symbolizing the rebirth of Egypt each year after the floods. His resurrection as a king of the dead and his renewal as a vegetation god were closely linked.

What could Osiris offer his followers that the other gods could not? As a human king, he had experienced death and had triumphed over it; thus he could assure his followers an eternal life and the continuous rebirth of Egypt. His appeal was irresistible, and gradually he replaced the other gods in the affections of the pharaoh and the people. By the end of the Old Kingdom his cult was gaining popularity and by the First Intermediate Period he had replaced Re'. Upon death, every king was believed to become an Osiris, while the living ruler, his successor, was the embodiment of Horus, his son. Not only the kings were given assurance of eternal life; by the Middle Kingdom every person in Egypt who worshiped Osiris could look forward himself to becoming an "Osiris" upon death and enjoying the benefits of the hereafter.

The worship of Osiris profoundly affected the Egyptians. Though he claimed no single locality as his own, his main centers were at Busiris and Abydos. To these every worshiper hoped to make a pilgrimage at least once during his lifetime. Neither did the god possess any temple of his own. He was worshiped at the temples of other gods, although it is probable that he never received the usual rituals accorded to these other deities in their temples. However, if any god received general acceptance throughout Egypt, it was Osiris, and his worship affected temple ritual, funerary cults and moral precepts. Similarly, his consort, Isis, the perfect example of a devoted wife and loving mother, received wide acclaim right down into Roman times. Seth, however, became the symbol of wickedness.

There were attempts from time to time to simplify the structure of the Egyptian pantheon. Deities were grouped into triads, usually representing family units of father, mother and son – or enneads, groups of nine gods who were associated with a particular religious center or town. The first ennead originated at Heliopolis; other groups were formed elsewhere, and the term "ennead" was still applied to them although they sometimes consisted of a varying number of gods.

The Egyptian's concept of the creation and what lay beyond it profoundly affected his attitude to all aspects of life. In this time of darkness and chaos there were no laws or institutions; together with the physical creation of the earth, mankind and the gods, there emerged on this "First Occasion" abstract concepts such as law, religion, ethics and kingship, whose principles were established for eternity. All the elements which were required to ensure a stable society were provided. To the Egyptian mind, there was no change; the universe worked according to a certain pattern governed by principles laid down in primeval times. Egyptians did not question the beliefs which had been handed down to them; they did not desire to change their society. Their main aim throughout their history was to emulate the conditions which they believed had existed at the dawn of creation.

In this belief, they differed widely from ourselves, who accept the idea of a constantly changing society with new sets of values, new solutions to fresh problems, and advances in many aspects of learning. It is not surprising that the Egyptians should cling to such beliefs, for their surroundings – the yearly renewal of the seasons which is so apparent in Egypt – must have suggested to them that life was a cyclical process, whose pattern had been established at some far distant date and which would never change. Nor is it surprising that such beliefs should produce a society which was stable for so many centuries.

Throughout their history the Egyptians endured famine, disaster, foreign invasion, the collapse of the established order – religious, social and economic. Yet despite everything they never abandoned their native gods. When disaster struck the land, it was generally believed that neglect of the gods and of the principles of their forefathers had brought about the general collapse. On a personal level, illness of body and mind was regarded as the result of ungodliness, and the repentance of sins was thought to restore the sick man to health. Right up to the end of their history a belief in their gods gave the Egyptians a sense of national unity and, until the arrival of Christianity, helped them to preserve their uniquely Egyptian consciousness throughout successive foreign occupations.

Hypostyle hall with Hathor-headed columns in the temple of Denderah, from a 19th-century sketch in *The Holy Land*. The temple dates from the Ptolemaic period.

Temple of Denderah, as it was in the 19th century. View of the northern gate looking towards the main temple.

Mansions of the gods. The temple of the god, either state or local, was known as the hwt-ntr, or "mansion of the god." This was the main function of the temple – to be the home of the deity.

The temples were never centers of regular community worship, although they played an important role in the social, economic and administrative life of the Egyptians. Their immediate influence was more secular than religious. They possessed great estates and employed large numbers of personnel. Moreover the king bestowed vast wealth on them, particularly on the temple of Amun at Karnak during the New Kingdom. Much of the booty from his victorious military campaigns was donated to the temples, in thanks for the god's protection. In addition to this source of wealth, revenues also came from the taxes which the provinces were expected to pay and from some of the gold mines, and the economic powers of the temples were protected by royal decrees. Since money was not used in Egypt until the end of the Late Period, the temple revenues were paid in kind – grain, oil, beer, wine and metal, among other commodities. This necessitated a complex administrative system, employing many officials who recorded the temple revenues and expenditure. It also required large storehouses where the goods could be kept.

Each temple employed both priests and lay personnel. The main function of the priesthood was to minister to the needs of the god; the priest was the "servant of the god" and he performed his duties in the "mansion" of the deity. He appears to have had no pastoral duties nor to have attempted to impose the worship of his deity on others. There was no "congregation" belonging to an Egyptian temple and the priest's principal task was to care for the god's welfare. The office of priest was usually hereditary and remained in certain families as a secondary profession; for example, the priesthood of Ma'at, the goddess of justice and truth, would probably be held by a family of judicial officials.

The men who held the priesthood as a secondary profession were part-time personnel at the temple and were divided into four groups. Each group worked at the temple for one month, thus completing three months of duty in a year. In serving at the temple, the priests also helped their fellow men, for in addition to their religious duties they were expected to undertake educational, administrative and medical tasks, thus creating in the temples centers of learning for scribes, artists and doctors. The temple also provided a place of retreat for those who were troubled in mind, or were in search of miraculous cures; these were accommodated in sanatoria attached to the temples and were attended to by the priests. It appears that at least some of the patients were successful in their quest and were healed.

Obviously the temples required permanent personnel as well, for the administrative duties were extensive. The high priest, the king's delegate who performed the ritual, was also an administrator who organized the business of the great temple estates. Minor clergy, singers, dancers and musicians (often female), gardeners, cooks and butchers who prepared the meat offerings made to the god, all helped to run the huge complex and lived near their place of work. Certain priests were specialists in branches of learning which were necessary in the temple – the liturgy, the interpretation of dreams for those who attended the temple in search of cures, animal cults, astronomy and so forth.

Since the Egyptian temple was obviously a force to be reckoned with, its origin and role in society take on importance. At the beginning of Egyptian civilization every tribe possessed its own deity whose image was enclosed and protected by a reed shelter – the first primitive "temple." This was probably placed close to the hut of the tribal chieftain since it was his duty to attend to the god's needs. The reed shrine was a simple hut lying in a small courtyard, enclosed by a wall with a single entrance. On either side of the entrance a flag-pole was placed. This basic design was to continue virtually unchanged throughout the thousands of years of Egyptian history, although it was of course greatly elaborated. The simple layout of the shrine and its enclosure is still apparent in the form of the later Pharaonic and Ptolemaic temples which consisted of a sanctuary, hypostyle halls, open forecourts and an enclosing wall into which was set a great main gateway, flanked by two stone towers or pylons to which were attached the flag masts.

By the 3rd Dynasty the Egyptians had already started to build "for eternity" by translating the earlier reed and mud-brick structures into stone tombs and temples. However, the original designs dictated by these earlier materials were never changed. Since the design and decoration of the basic temple fulfilled its purpose for the Egyptians, they would have considered any major alteration undesirable and impossible.

Let us now imagine how one of the great stone temples of the Pharaonic or Ptolemaic period would have looked to the spectator. Every temple was built more or less to the same plan. It was rectangular in shape, consisted of four main sections and stood in the center of a large enclosure which often contained subsidiary outbuildings,

The temple of Abu Simbel on the Nile near Aswan. The sketch on the left illustrates how the temple's entrance was so oriented that twice a year the rays of the sun penetrated the interior and illuminated a statue of Ramesses II (*right*).

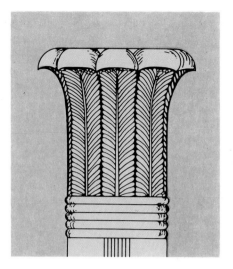

Egyptian temple columns. *Left:* the colonnade at Luxor with lotus-bud capitals. *Middle and right:* two different capitals with palm motifs. The floral decorations represented the flowers on the original "Island of Creation."

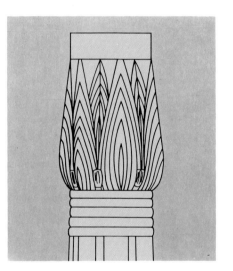

Above: the lotus motif (closed on the *far right*). *Below, left:* the mortuary temple of Ramesses III at Medinet Habu, with Ptolemaic capitals. *Middle:* elaborate lotus capital. *Right:* Hathor-headed column, a particular feature at Denderah.

The mortuary temple of Ramesses III at Medinet Habu. The reliefs show pharaoh killing a captive.

and the whole complex was encircled by a thick mud-brick wall. On approaching the temple complex, one would have been faced by the main gateway, set between two massive stone towers which supported the flag masts, and on which were usually carved enormous incised reliefs showing the king striking with a mace-head cringing figures of captive prisoners. These great towers in fact imitated in stone the towers of woven reeds which had protected the entrance to the primitive reed shrine. On passing through the tall bronze doors, the first of the court-yards would have been reached, with its stone-flagged floor, colonnade and incised wall reliefs which often showed the king undertaking campaigns on behalf of the gods. Beyond this first courtyard there was sometimes another, both open to the sky and often strewn with statues. Possibly certain important laymen may have been permitted to enter these outer courts on festival days when the statue of the god would have been carried out into the open by the priests. The ordinary people who flocked to the festivals would doubtless have been kept outside the temple wall where they would have offered their prayers and deposited their humble presents to the god. Some-where outside the temple building, but within the en-closure, there would have been a Sacred Lake where the priests performed their ablutions and cleaned the temple equipment.

Beyond the open courts lay the sacred roofed area of the temple proper, which only the priests could enter. As one passed through the great bronze doors of the temple, set on the main axis, it would have become apparent that "the mansion of the god" was no empty phrase. The Egyptian temple was indeed the "home" of its resident deity in the same way that the tomb was the "home" of the deceased where he would pass eternity. Both were establishments, with their quota of servants – the funerary priests were "servants of the ka" and the temple priests were "servants of the god." While the houses and palaces of the living were constructed of wood and mud-brick, the tombs and temples were built of stone, for they were intended to last for eternity; but in other respects the architecture of the three "dwellings" was similar, and provision was made in all three for "living rooms" and storage space for the owner-occupant's possessions, since the gods and the dead were believed to have the same physical needs as the living – food, drink, clothing, rest and recreation.

The first area of the temple into which one would have entered was the outer hypostyle hall; beyond this often lay an inner hypostyle hall. In these halls the stone columns were massed together and carved to represent plant forms – palm-fronds, lotus and papyrus flowers. These originally would have adorned the delicate reed columns in those early shrines. The halls were illuminated by clerestory lighting; windows (with no glass) would have been inserted on either side of the central row of columns, which were taller than the others. While the rituals were in progress, the priests would have carried torches to give additional light. The reception area in a house was reflected by the hypostyle halls in a temple.

Beyond lay the sanctuary. Here stood the statue of the god, probably within a wooden shrine corresponding to the master's bedroom in a house. Since the temple sanc-tuary formed the culminating point of the priestly pro-cessions, however, the "bedroom" was placed on the main axis of the building, whereas in a house it was usually placed to one side of the main entrance.

The god's sanctuary, an imitation of the earliest reed shrine, was small and dark. Additional shrines were included in the sanctuary area for any other gods who might also reside in the temple with the chief god, whose shrine was always on the main axis. The statue of the god rested in his cult shrine throughout the year; in some temples, where there was sufficient space, a barque shrine was included as well, where the sacred boat rested, complete with a lighter, portable statue of the deity on board, in readiness for the processions which occurred on festival days.

Passing out of the sanctuary, one would have arrived at a series of small rooms grouped around the sanctuary, where various administrative and other duties were carried out and where the god's clothing and possessions were kept.

This briefly describes the general plan of a typical "cultus" temple of the New Kingdom. Variations on the basic design occurred even during the New Kingdom. The remains of temple architecture in the Middle Kingdom are sparse, and in the later Ptolemaic temples (which, because of their excellent state of preservation, afford us a good opportunity of studying their wall reliefs and ascertaining the purpose of the various halls and rooms) there were minor structural differences from the New Kingdom temples.

The cultus temple was an isolated building where the resident god was worshiped by means of rituals and festivals. The "mortuary" temple, the second major type of temple, was often attached to a royal tomb or in the time of the Old Kingdom, to a pyramid. Its main function was to provide a place where the dead king could receive worship and the funerary cult. By the New Kingdom the king's tomb and his mortuary temple were no longer close; he would be buried in the Valley of the Kings but his temple would be elsewhere. Indeed, it is not unusual to find that mortuary and cultus functions were combined in the same building. One area would be reserved for the ritual and festivals of the deity while the cult of the dead king would be celebrated elsewhere in the same temple.

During the reign of the "heretic" pharaoh Akhenaten the temples built for the worship of Aten were still basically places where the king could approach the god. Architecturally, however, they differed from the traditional temples since they were open to the sky and did not contain a resting place for any divine statue.

The role of the Egyptian temple in society can best be explained by examining the Egyptian's beliefs about the origin of his temples, and attempting to reconstruct the rituals which occurred behind the closed doors of the temple, and their purpose.

The meaning of ritual. The temple was at the center of Egyptian religion. Its very existence, to the minds of the Egyptians, ensured the survival of their land and way of life. We have seen how the Egyptians explained the creation of the universe. Along with the other institutions of

society, it was believed that "the Temple" had been established on that "First Occasion." A group of "Building Texts" in the Greco-Roman temples of Edfu and Denderah summarize the beliefs which the Egyptians held regarding the mythological and historical origin of their temples.

Each new temple was regarded not only as a reflection of the first mythical temple, built on the "First Occasion," but also as an actual representation of the Sacred Island which had emerged from the muddy waters of the great primeval ocean. Here the god in the form of a falcon had alighted, perched on a reed and established his resting place. In time, a reed temple was constructed around the god and the island became the center of all creation.

From this, mythological explanations were derived for the architectural features of the temple. The temple and its contents were intended to represent reality – a desired situation – in the same way as did the art in the tombs. The temple wall-reliefs, the columns, ceilings, floors – all had magical powers and could be "brought to life" by special rituals. They were not primarily intended for structural support or artistic decoration.

The walls of every Egyptian temple are covered with registers of scenes in which the reigning pharaoh performs a series of religious rites on behalf of various deities. In the mortuary temples the gods sometimes perform certain rites for the king. The reliefs are carved with great skill and are one of the best examples of Egyptian art, yet they often occur even at the top of the walls where they can scarcely be seen; they are also found on the columns. Never intended to beautify the building, or to inspire the worshiper, their purpose was functional in the same way that the tomb reliefs were functional.

In the outer courts, the king is often shown in battle;

Relief sculpture showing an offering scene, Late period. The style is crude compared with earlier and finer work.

Head of Ramesses II, wearing the double crown, at the Ramasseum in Thebes. It is typical of the grandiose art of the period.

these scenes provide useful historical data – the geographical order of campaigns, names of conquered peoples and so forth – but their original purpose was not to narrate history but to glorify the deeds of pharaoh, always shown as a conquering hero. In the inner chambers of the temple each room is decorated with registers of scenes showing religious rites. In some instances these merely commemorate great religious events, such as the foundation and consecration of the temple, or the coronation of the king and his acceptance by the gods. However, in the majority of cases the scenes illustrate religious rites which were customarily performed in each particular room or hall. If an order can be established for reading the scenes correctly, together with their accompanying inscriptions, then it is possible to reconstruct the rituals which once took place in the various parts of the temple.

Usually there was only sufficient wall space to accommodate a selection of rites from the original longer and more elaborate ritual. It was believed that these scenes could be "brought to life" by the performance of the ceremony of "Opening of the Mouth," when all the figures on the walls and all the statues in the temple, as well as the temple itself, were animated. Once "alive," the temple possessed potent magical force, and it was believed that, should the actual performance of the rituals cease, the animated wall reliefs would ensure their magical continuance. This ceremony was performed when the temple was consecrated and was repeated annually.

The continuance of the rituals for the gods ensured that the king, and the land of Egypt and its inhabitants, received in return the bounties of life. In all temple scenes throughout Egypt, it is the king himself who is shown performing the rituals for the gods; in theory, he alone could attend to their needs, for he held the unique position of divine son. Part-human, part-divine, the king in theory built every temple and performed all the necessary rituals to ensure the safety and fertility of Egypt and its people, and maintain his own power, prosperity and victory. As the divine heir, he had been created by the gods to serve their needs and to act as mediator between them and mankind. As their son, the king alone could meet the gods. When he approached the gods through the medium of rituals he represented the Egyptians and Egypt.

The fruits of Egypt and of its people – food, drink and other offerings, the building of monuments, booty from campaigns – these were all presented to the gods through the agency of the king. In return, the gods provided the required benefits. If ever the rituals and worship ceased, the Egyptians fully expected disaster, famine and obliteration to follow. The temple rituals ensured their very survival.

The reliefs and inscriptions in the temples where the king, without the assistance of the priests, performs every rite for his fathers, illustrates this idealized situation. In early times, the tribal chieftain doubtless had complete control of the ritual, which changed little in later times. But when the tribal leader became king of a great state and his responsibilities increased, and when the number of temples multiplied, it would have been impossible for him to have performed every ritual in every temple in Egypt. The duties were therefore delegated to the high priest of every temple, although the king may have personally performed the daily ritual in the main temple of the chief god, and perhaps attended foundation ceremonies and certain of the festivals throughout the country.

From the original notion that the temple was the Island of Creation, chosen by the falcon god as his home, there grew up another, secondary belief – that every temple was the home of the resident deity and a resting place for his statue. Here, through attending to the needs of the deity, mankind could approach his god by means of a ritual. Basically, there were two kinds of ritual – the great festivals held at intervals throughout the year and varying to some degree from temple to temple, and the daily worship of the god, which never varied. Since the Egyptian deity, like his followers, required rest, recreation, food, drink, clothing, perfuming and washing, the daily ritual was a means of attending to these needs and of regular worship. All the elements which had been present in the earliest ritual in the reed shrine were probably retained in the later, more elaborate rites. These also incorporated elements from the solar and Osirian cults.

Every morning the king (or high priest) entered the sanctuary, and opening the doors of the innermost shrine lifted out the statue of the god. Removing the ointment and clothing of the previous day and censing the statue, he adorned it with fresh clothing and ointment and presented to it the insignia of kingship. Finally, it was provided with a selection of food and the priest left the sanctuary, closing the door behind him with a final purification. The ceremony was accompanied by many prayers and purificatory censings. This daily ceremony symbolized the daily rebirth of the sun, and also the resurrection of Osiris – the king had restored his father to life. As such, the ritual was a vital factor in the lives of those countless Egyptians, toiling away in the fields or on the building sites, who would never see the rites which, it was believed, would ensure their very existence.

The ritual was performed three times daily – in the morning, at midday and in the evening, when the statue was again "fed" and returned to the wooden shrine for his rest, to await the renewal of his life on the morrow. The food offered to the god's statue remained untouched. It was carried out of his sanctuary and offered, with another series of rites, to the Royal Ancestors in another area of the temple. The king was expected to fulfil certain obligations on behalf of all the Ancestors – former kings of Egypt since the times of Menes, with certain exceptions such as Akhenaten. By this ritual the king ensured that the

Ancestors would support his claim to rule Egypt. The offerings were placed before a list of kings' names, engraved on a wall of the temple.

This ritual was performed in many temples from the New Kingdom onward and again the high priest deputized for the king. The food – in theory offered twice, to the deity and to the Ancestors – still remained uneaten. The Egyptians, always a practical people, would have considered such a daily waste quite inexcusable and the problem was neatly solved by carrying the food outside the temple proper and dividing it among the priests as a daily stipend. Thus the god was appeased and continued to bestow his blessings, the Ancestors were well-satisfied with their son and heir and the priests ate hearty meals three times a day!

Great festivals, held at intervals throughout the year, provided special occasions for the gods and for the people who flocked, if possible, to different parts of Egypt to take part in these festivities with religious fervor. The daily rituals imitated the events of day-to-day living, but the festivals were times of great rejoicing when the gods visited each other's temples with the priests carrying the god's statue in its sacred barque, or were celebrations of seasonal events, such as the coming of spring or the New Year. Again, in these festivals, the "human" element of the deities may be seen. Perhaps only the Festival of Osiris could be said to have symbolized an event which did not merely imitate the highlights of mortal existence. Held yearly at Abydos, this was an occasion of great sanctity when the resurrection of the god from death was celebrated. Intense mourning preceded the eventual rejoicing, and religious plays were performed by the pilgrims to Abydos who reenacted the events of the life, death and resurrection of Osiris.

Perhaps on the surface these religious rituals and festivals appear to be rather trivial, if colorful, ceremonies. We may scoff at the robing, anointing and feeding of the god, and the outings which punctuated his year, but the system appeared to work well for the Egyptians for thousands of years, until the Christians finally overthrew the temples and their pagan rites. The rituals certainly produced the hoped-for results – a powerful god-king, a great empire and a magnificent civilization. When the gods were neglected, as during the Amarna period, and their temples fell into disuse the Egyptians felt that they had experienced the withdrawal of the gods' favor.

The priests, highly educated, intelligent men, must have felt that the temples had, apart from material comforts, something more to offer. We can only assume that behind the facade of religious formulas and repetitive actions – the only evidence we have on which to base our judgments – they had discovered at least some of the answers to the problems of their lives.

Painted wooden figure of the goddess Nephthis, sister of Isis and protectress of the dead. Late Ptolemaic period.

The Amarna heresy. One great religious revolution, as we have seen, shattered the traditions of ancient Egypt. Towards the end of the 18th Dynasty, Pharaoh Amenophis IV moved his capital from Thebes to a virgin site some 250 miles to the north. The new city was called Akhetaten (now Tell el-Amarna) and the pharaoh changed his own name from Amenophis ("Amun-is-satisfied") to Akhenaten ("Servant-of-the-Aten") and established as the official religion a form of solar monotheism. This revolution has been regarded by scholars either as a vision of a Messiah who was before his time, or as a reasoned calculation on the part of a weak ruler who, threatened by the great power of the priesthood of Amun, used this new faith as a tool to enhance the divinity of pharaoh, as well as to obliterate the traditional priesthood. Moreover, Akhenaten is blamed, to some degree, for the gradual disintegration of the Egyptian Empire.

The new faith was based on the worship of the sun as the source of all life and creation, whose power was made manifest through the life-giving rays of the sun-disk, or Aten. The sole agent of the deity on earth was pharaoh, who acted as an intermediary. Prayers to the god could only be addressed through the king, and he and the royal family are pictured on the walls of the tombs, replacing the former gods of the dead. As the only high priest of the god, Akhenaten was able to disperse local priesthoods and close down the temples of rival deities.

The Aten was not, however, a newcomer to the Egyptian scene. His existence can be traced even back to the Middle Kingdom and has been noted during the reigns of several of the 18th-Dynasty rulers. It was Amenophis III, father of Akhenaten, who first brought his worship to prominence, but Akhenaten himself did what no other pharaoh was prepared to do – he ordered the complete exclusion of all other deities. Abolishing the traditional temples, rituals, festivals and statues, he even obliterated the names of the other gods and at Akhetaten, his new capital, together with his family and courtiers who had followed him there, he worshiped the one god. It is unlikely that the new beliefs, which emphasized the power of an intangible deity, were understood or accepted by the majority of ordinary people who continued to pray to their household deities. After the end of his reign, most of the courtiers doubtless also returned to traditional beliefs.

Nefertiti, the beautiful wife of Akhenaten and mother of his six daughters, is perhaps one of the most mysterious of these "heretics." There is some reason to believe that she played a major part in this revolution; research and analysis of the scenes which occur on the stone blocks which once comprised the Aten Temple at Thebes suggest that Nefertiti had considerable influence on the new faith.

The deity nevertheless withheld from his prophet the ultimate blessing of a monarch – a son to carry on his father's work – and Akhenaten was obliged to nominate as his successor Smenkhkare, the husband of his eldest daughter. The boy died in early manhood, without issue, and another of Akhenaten's sons-in-law, Tutankhaten, succeeded to the throne and changed his name to Tutankhamun, signifying the change of allegiance back to Amun. The preservation, virtually intact, of his mummy and burial treasures would doubtless have been construed by the ancient Egyptians as his just reward!

Horemheb, the last pharaoh of the 18th Dynasty, attempted to obliterate all memory of the Amarna heresy. Akhetaten was deserted – the magnificent temples, palaces and villas, the many examples of the revolutionary art forms which had flourished in this city – all were abandoned to the encroaching sand and the jackals. The city had been an economic drain on the country. Egypt had lost much of her foreign power and wealth and the established order had been overthrown in favor of the pharaoh's desire for "truth" in art and religion. Akhenaten's memory was hated and his beliefs were soon forgotten.

Whether he was a scheming politician or a monotheist and idealist who advocated an early form of "internationalism" – or something between the two – his dreams were not realized. Yet in the famous hymn addressed to the Aten, which is attributed to Akhenaten, his ideas live on – that the power of the sun created all life, and that the sun was the father of all the races of men; that this sole divinity placed mankind in various regions and gave them different languages and physical attributes and that the creator determined every important aspect of a man's life.

Funerary beliefs and customs. The ancient Egyptians were devoted to life, not death. Perhaps more than any other people they wished to live forever, and they were the first people known to have formulated definite ideas regarding the immortality of the individual human soul.

The afterlife of the king, who was part divine, was always considered to be different from that of his subjects. Here we shall consider only the afterlife of the non-royals.

The Egyptian concept of the human "personality" was complex. The body (and eventually the corpse), the shadow, the individual's name and his "ba" and "ka" – all together were thought to comprise the essence of every human being. The "ba" was depicted with a human head and the body of a bird. Loosely translated as "soul," the ba was believed to be the immortal part of a person which remained tied to the body after death, but which could act independently as the representative of the dead man, leaving the tomb and visiting his favorite lifetime haunts. Free from the limitations of space, it could from time to time continue to experience the joys of earth on behalf of the deceased.

An accurate description of the word "ka" presents an even greater difficulty; to some extent the individual "ka" was the "double" of a man, ever-present to guide and help

Painted relief of Sethos I lifting up a tray of food offerings to Isis. From the temple of the Pharaoh Sethos I at Abydos.

him during his lifetime. After death the ka continued to exist in the tomb – indeed, the name for a tomb was "Mansion of the Ka," the priests who attended to the needs of the deceased were known as "Ka-priests," and all offerings of food and drink were made to a man's ka. Perhaps the ka is best described as a creative force, the vital energy, the very essence of life, which continued after death to sustain an individual's existence, whereas in life it had acted as a man's constant adviser and conscience. The ka was always shown as two arms upraised in an attitude of prayer, often placed on top of the head of a human figure.

The tomb – whether it was a pit-burial, mastaba or rock-cut tomb (true pyramids being reserved for royalty) – provided the place where a man could be reunited after death with his ba and ka, and could continue his existence for eternity. It has been pointed out, with some truth, that either the gods with their temples, or the dead with their tombs claimed most of Egypt's resources. Not only the royal family, but also the nobles and the well-to-do made every provision to build and equip tombs for their own eternity and to ensure that their bodies were preserved by means of mummification.

There were three basic schools of thought concerning the hereafter. The most ancient and simple belief, that a man carried on his existence in his tomb, continued throughout the years to be the most popular. In the tomb he had the same faculties and needs as in life – for food and possessions. In the earliest pit-burials simple cooking equipment and jewelry were placed with the body. In later times the tomb walls were decorated with scenes of daily life and a banquet of food and drink for the tomb owner to enjoy. He also took with him a complete set of funerary equipment – clothes, jewelry, wigs, domestic requisites, his favorite possessions in life and sets of servant models. These, and later the ushabti figures, replaced the earlier custom of burying servants with their master to care for his needs after death.

The body was mummified by an elaborate process. This developed over the years and became a highly professional and lucrative concern, but it is probable that the idea had originated from the remains of their ancestors which the early Egyptians found desiccated and preserved in the sand. The mummified body was swathed in bandages, between which were placed amulets to protect the body against all evils and disasters, for the continued existence of the body was considered essential for the afterlife. A model boat was also often included in the tomb to enable the deceased to make a pilgrimage to the sacred city of Abydos.

At death, the ba was believed to leave the body. It returned after the mummification process was complete, when the ceremony of the Opening of the Mouth was performed on the mummy at the funeral, restoring life to the deceased for eternity. The dead needed the living – to perform the funerary rites and, later, to continue to present offerings of food and drink at the deceased's tomb, to satisfy his ka. The heir to a man's estate was not necessarily

his eldest son, but the one who had carried out his funerary rites (although, in most cases, the eldest son performed this duty). An Egyptian's greatest fear was that he might die outside Egypt, where the correct burial procedure would be ignored, or that his corpse might be destroyed by fire or drowning.

It soon became apparent that a man's heirs could not continue indefinitely to bring food and drink to his tomb – after a few generations, and the accumulation of numbers of dead relatives, tomb-visiting would have become a full-time occupation! It thus became the custom to set aside in life a property which would continue to provide sufficient revenue to provision the tomb and to employ a "ka-priest" to make the necessary offerings in perpetuity. Ka-priesthoods tended to become family professions, generation after generation. This system had very obvious disadvantages – it became an economic drain, as time went by, on a family's income, and also the ka-priests could not be relied upon to carry out their duties. Eventually, these practical provisions for the dead man's ka were replaced by magic – the inclusion of paintings of food on the tomb walls, to be brought to life at the tomb owner's will. Even today a custom prevails in modern Egypt of distributing food among the poor on certain feast days, in order to bless the souls of the dead. It is unlikely that the participants realize that this custom has its roots in their pharaonic past.

In time, Osirian and solar elements were added to the basic funerary beliefs and customs. Originally the king was believed either to enter heaven where he became a star in the sky or traveled the heavens with his father, the sun god Re', in his day and night barques; or he became assimilated upon death with Osiris, the king of the dead and god of the underworld. After the First Intermediate Period funerary beliefs became more democratic. Every man and woman might accompany Re' on his everlasting journey around the heavens or, alternatively, he might become an "Osiris" in his own right, however humble his station. He would then have to make the treacherous journey, overcome many dangers and be judged for his deeds upon earth before finally passing on to the Kingdom of Osiris where all men were equal. There he would till a small plot of land and continue his former earthly existence. For the toiling peasant, the afterlife of Osirian belief must have offered great hope. Not surprisingly, the beliefs were very popular.

Thus there seemed to be a satisfactory belief for every level of society. One could hardly expect the poor man, his body wrapped in a straw mat and placed in a hole in the ground, buried communally or thrown into the Nile, to dream of an afterlife in a well-equipped tomb; his one hope lay in Osiris. The wealthier, however, could plan an affluent eternity in paradise – a second Egypt, one free from plagues and wars. As the funerary beliefs of the Egyptians were so complex, they compromised and, at least officially, an amalgamation of beliefs was considered quite acceptable and not at all illogical. But belief in life

Anubis, the jackal-headed god of embalming, prepares a body for burial. The mummy has been placed on a lion-bier and the ritual of Osiris is being performed. The deceased is Sennedjem, tomb official of the New Kingdom, 18th Dynasty.

after death was universal throughout Egyptian society.

Did anyone doubt the efficacy of these elaborate funerary preparations? It seems that they did, for passages have survived, such as the following (quoted in Montet, *Eternal Egypt*), which show a different attitude to death:

"The gods who once lived and who rest in their pyramids, the nobles, and the glorious departed likewise are buried in their tombs. They built houses the sites of which no longer exist. What has become of them? . . . Their walls have crumbled, their places no longer exist; it is as if they had never been.

No one returns from those distant regions to tell us how they fare, or what their needs are. Therefore follow the happy day and be not weary therein. See, no one takes his goods with him. Behold, no one returns who has once departed."

One of the most interesting aspects of the Egyptians' beliefs is their preoccupation with the final judgment of the individual soul. Upon death, a man was thought to face judgment by an incorruptible court of gods who assessed his life and deeds on earth and sentenced him accordingly to eternal bliss or destruction.

"Thou knowest that the court which judges transgressors is not lenient at the hour when it passes sentence on the wretched and carries out its function . . . Do not trust in the length of years, for they look upon a life's span as but an hour. When a man remains after death, his deeds are heaped beside him. What is there, is there for all eternity. He who practises what is condemned is a madman, but he who reaches the other world without wrongdoing shall exist there like a god." (Montet)

Osiris, the Great Judge, presided over the court of 42 divine assessors and the proceedings were supervised by Thoth, god of writing, who recorded the results of the enquiry on his tablet. The deceased was required to recite the "Negative Confession" – 36 negative statements denying his participation in various aspects of wrongdoing – and then formally to declare his innocence. Finally, he recounted the good deeds which he had performed. His heart was weighed in the divine balance against the feather of Ma'at – symbol of truth – and if the two sides balanced exactly, the deceased passed on to his eternal happiness. If he had led an evil life, he was condemned to a horrible fate.

Perhaps the most outstanding characteristic of the Egyptians was their firm conviction that human existence continued after death. The modern world should be grateful that the Egyptians took such care with their preparations for eternity, for they provide an incomparable insight into the skills and beliefs of a great people.

THE EGYPTIAN TEMPLE

VISUAL STORY

The basic plan and architecture of the Egyptian temple varied little from the New Kingdom to the Ptolemaic period. Each represented the dwelling of the god. Its massive pylon or gateway, like that of the Ptolemaic temple of Horus at Edfu (*left*), led into a series of open courts and pillared hypostyle halls to the sanctuary of the god. There were two main types of temple – the so-called cultus temple for the worship of the deity who lived within it, and the mortuary temple dedicated to the worship of a dead and deified pharaoh. The temple of Horus at Edfu is an example of the cultus temple; the Ramasseum at Thebes, whose huge pillars are shown below, is a mortuary temple dedicated to the warrior king,

Ramesses II. The temple's great pylons led into a forecourt, open to the sky and often surrounded by a colonnade. Festival processions would enter the temple through the pylons into the open court on their way towards the shrine, where the most sacred rituals were performed. Laymen were probably not allowed to go beyond the court, but here they could pray, make offerings and watch the processions. The processional way rose gradually in height as one approached the sanctuary, increasing the sense of awe as the "Holy of Holies" was reached. Every temple represented the original "Island of Creation," and its columns – shaped after palms, papyrus and the lotus – the island vegetation.

Portico of the courtyard of the temple of Horus at Edfu, as drawn by a traveler in 1838. Many of the great temples, when first discovered by the western world in the 19th century, were partially covered in sand. Originally they had been built in thriving, populated areas but today most are in isolated locations.

Another print, of 1847, showing a colossus standing before the hypostyle hall, records the desolation of the ruins at Karnak before they were cleaned up and partially restored in recent times. Karnak and Luxor, both near Thebes, were great centers for the cult of the god Amun. In the typical temple the pillared hypostyle hall provided an impressive final approach to the sanctuary.

A section through the main temple at Karnak (*below*) shows several hypostyle halls leading from the pylon to the sanctuary (*left*) containing the god-statue standing in its bark. The lotus- or papyrus-headed pillars of the typical hypostyle hall were decorated with scenes showing the king with the deities. *Bottom*, clerestory lighting for the halls of the 4th pylon at Karnak.

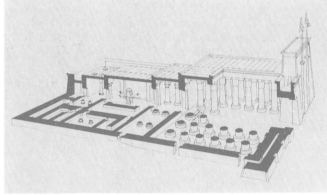

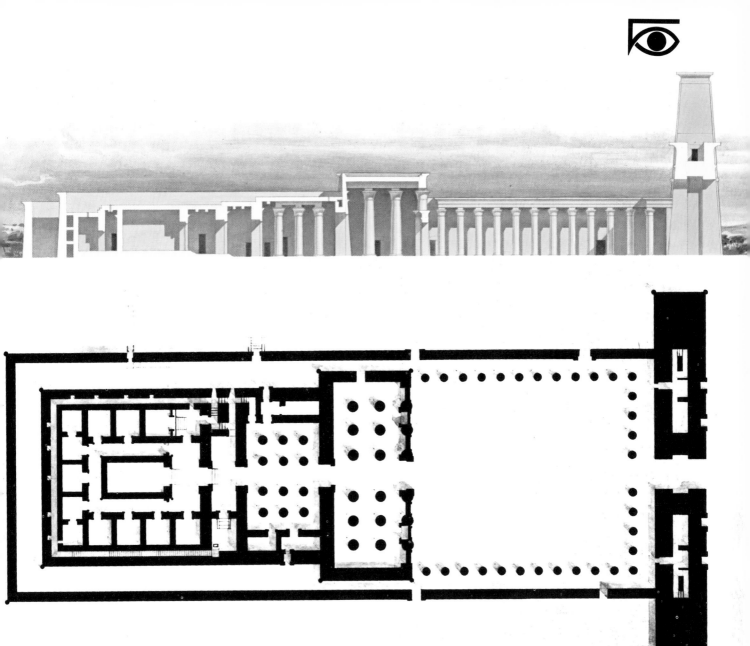

The Ptolemaic temple of Horus at Edfu, shown *above* in plan and section, is a typical example of the Egyptian temple, with its great pylon (to the right), its forecourt, hypostyle halls and sanctuary.

The sanctuary was a simple room, simulating the reed hut which held the statue of the local god in earliest times. The cult-image was small enough to be carried in its bark in processions.

The Ptolemaic double temple of Kom Ombo (*right*). While similar to earlier temples in most ways, the capitals on its pillars betray Greco-Roman influence. So many temples survive in a fair state of preservation in Egypt today because, unlike the palaces and houses, they were built of durable stone.

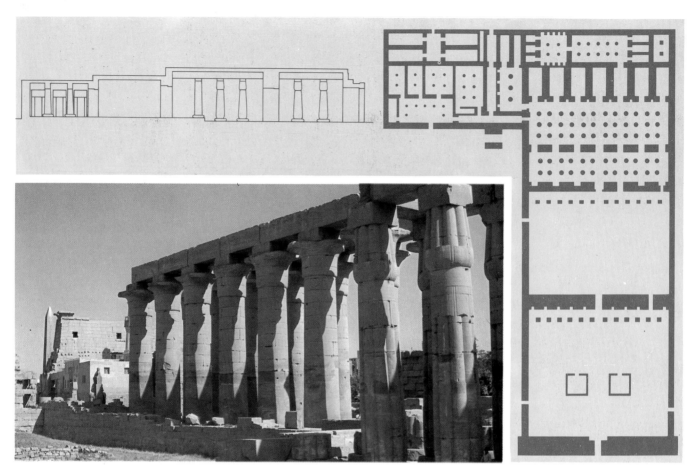

The temple of Sethos I at Abydos (shown at *top*, in plan and section) had a unique L-shaped plan and, instead of one, seven shrines dedicated to six gods and the deified pharaoh. It was also the center of Osiris worship to which pilgrims came to witness the annual drama enacting the death and resurrection of the god, most of which took place outdoors. The plan shows (from the bottom) two courts and two hypostyle halls, the seven chapels, and behind these special rooms for secret rites connected with the Osiris drama. The wing to the left contained storage and ceremonial rooms.

The most famous of columned porticoes and halls are those of the temples of Amun at Luxor (*above*, *left*), and particularly those of Karnak, which represents the overblown, grandiose ideas of the New Kingdom pharaohs who ruled Egypt at the time of the empire. A transverse section through the great hypostyle hall of Sethos I and Ramesses II at Karnak, the largest columned hall in the world, is shown *below*. The hall alone covers 54,000 square feet, and the central pillars are 69 feet high. The complex at Karnak as a whole includes 20 temples, shrines and ceremonial halls, dedicated to various gods.

Thebes had two main temples to Amun, that at Karnak, which was the central shrine, and another, smaller one a mile and a half to the south near the modern town of Luxor (*left*). The Luxor temple was built by Amenophis III of the 18th Dynasty on the site of an earlier sanctuary. Before his death he added a double colonnade of 14 columns, each 52 feet high, in front of his temple. The space between the two was later filled in by that insatiable builder, Ramesses II, with a second forecourt and a new great pylon (*left*), adorned with two obelisks and six colossal statues of himself, four standing, two seated. Amenophis' original temple, however, is much more graceful and well planned than this heavy later work, reflecting the height of New Kingdom artistic achievment under its builder. A 19th-century print (*below, left*) shows Luxor before partial restoration, with a huge Ramesses colossus fallen.

The two Theban shrines of Amun were closely linked, especially by the yearly festival during the inundation when Amun's god-image was carried from Karnak to Luxor by sacred barge up the Nile, where it resided for several weeks each year. At first merely the local god of Thebes, Amun rose with the fortunes of that city, first during the Middle Kingdom, then as the god of the New Kingdom pharaohs (joined with Re). During the empire Amun became immensely wealthy and at the time of Ramesses III, his Theban estate, including the temples of Karnak and Luxor, comprised some 86,000 workers, almost 700,000 acres of land, 65 cities and towns and untold other assets.

The Egyptian temple as a whole – its pylon, courts and halls – was built around and focused on one small room, the sanctuary where the god lived, using his cult-image as a resting place. It was here that the most sacred rituals took place. These were of two types – the daily ritual, carried out by the priests, and the periodic festivals celebrating events in the lives of the gods, the change of seasons, the coronation or jubilee of a pharaoh. The festivals were perhaps the only religious ceremonies in which the people of Egypt could take an active part. The most important part of the daily ritual was carried out by the pharaoh – or by the high priest in place of the king. Every temple was decorated throughout with reliefs and inscriptions, many of which commemorated some great event – a royal coronation, or the founding of the temple itself. Others often illustrated in detail the religious rites carried out in each room or hall, thus providing a matchless record of what these rituals were like. At Abydos in particular the ritual scenes are well preserved. A selection on these pages gives aspects of the daily ritual as carried out for the gods Amen-Re' and Osiris by Pharaoh Sethos I.

The ritual begins when King Sethos enters the sanctuary and takes the statue of Amen-Re' (*above, right*) out of its small shrine (naos). Meantime he has offered prayers, purified the sanctuary and presented incense and a libation (*below*) to the image. The god's clothes and ointments are then changed (*opposite page, left*), he is offered a great collar (Osiris, with Isis behind him); then, back in his naos, Osiris is presented with scepters, a flail, anklets and bracelets (*below*). More presentations and finally an offering of food complete the ritual. In other rooms the food is then offered to a "King List" of all the pharaohs (the ancestors) from the beginning, and is finally divided among the priests.

A festival procession of the fertility god Min, as redrawn
from the walls of Ramesses III's mortuary temple at Medinet
Habu, is shown below. A statue of the god (*center*) has been
drawn out from the sanctuary into the outer courts amidst
throngs of rejoicing people. The pharaoh rides in his sedan
chair (*left*), censes the god-image (*center*) and walks before
another portable god-image (*right*).

V
KING AND COMMONER

Two different art styles. *Left:* head of Chephren (Old Kingdom). *Right:* head of Ramesses II in a later, more decadent style. He is wearing the blue (war) crown.

No brief survey can do more than give a superficial picture of the social conditions prevalent in ancient Egypt. Moreover the material remains, abundant as they are, still give us only the sketchiest idea of Egyptian houses, furniture, clothing, burial customs, jewelry and so forth. When the evidence is from time to time more detailed and abundant, as with the royal workmen of Deir el-Medineh, there is every reason to ponder over the material, including the refuse, which they have left us; for in so doing we can gain an insight into the personality of the average Egyptian that no tomb, temple or statue can provide.

In attempting to pinpoint some of the main features of the Egyptian way of life the subject has been approached from two angles, first, the structure of society – the royal family, nobility, craftsmen, officials, slaves and so forth – which remained a basic factor of Egyptian civilization over the years, and secondly, those aspects of society, such as marriage, education, illness, the army which crossed all barriers of status and wealth and affected all Egyptians. In these latter aspects we find the Egyptians comfortingly similar to ourselves.

The Pharaoh. The name "Pharaoh," from the Egyptian word "pr-'3," meaning "great house," was originally the name for the royal palace. In time, it became the name applied to the ruler himself. The pharaoh, as agent of the gods but executing his duties in a mortal world, was a busy man. He was commander-in-chief of the army, head of the administration and treasury, high priest of every temple and chief judge. In earliest times he had probably fulfilled these duties in person, but as the organization of the country became increasingly complicated he delegated some of the duties to officials. By Old Kingdom times this system had become highly organized, although the king did retain certain duties. He remained the final appeal in criminal cases, with the power to pardon or confirm death sentences. He was the upholder of Ma'at, the concept of truth and justice and the established order of the universe. He fought battles and visited temples to make offerings; indeed, all the temple and battle records preserve the fictitious idea that he alone performed the rituals and killed the enemy.

Thus to a large extent the power of Egypt was dependent upon the ability of the king, whom the gods had

created, to carry out the necessary duties, for he alone could mediate between gods and men. In earliest times there had been pastoral chiefs to look after the different localities, but eventually, under the rule of one king, the Egyptians achieved a national unity unlike any other early civilization, which brought them all the benefits of a centralized state and enabled them to carry out land reclamation, irrigation, and pyramid-building.

At first they regarded their kings as gods incarnate; the pyramids ensured the continuance of the god-king's existence after death, and upon this his subjects were dependent for their eternity. By the 5th Dynasty the king came to be regarded as the physical son of the god Re', and this belief persisted, throughout Egyptian history. The king was also theoretically the incarnation of the god Horus, the son of Osiris; and upon death he became Osiris. During the Middle Kingdom the kings were less remote from the people – the collapse of royal power at the end of the Old Kingdom had greatly affected the former attitudes, and the kings, though still divine, were seen rather as the protectors and saviors of the people. By the New Kingdom, the kings were acclaimed as warriors who built and maintained a great empire, based upon the overthrow and expulsion of the Hyksos.

Akhenaten, with his generally unacceptable monotheism, broke this pattern when, as the gods' sole agent on earth, he tried to assert the special position of the pharaoh. His concept was reminiscent of the king's exclusively divine status in earlier times. In the Late Period, successive foreign conquerors adopted the role of pharaoh with all its traditional trappings; for in order to rule Egypt they required the traditionally absolute power of the monarchy. The Ptolemies in particular, as we have seen, used the position of pharaoh to exploit Egypt, and the Romans similarly exploited the concept of power as it had belonged to the pharaohs.

The pharaohs lived in palaces built of brick and wood, few of which have survived. We can imagine the pharaoh carrying out his typical duties – giving audience, surrounded by his advisers, to officials, architects, engineers;

Temple relief. The king wears the Atef crown and stands before a god and goddess. Christians later defaced the figures.

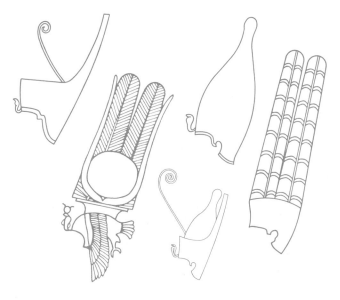

Egyptian crowns. *Left to right:* red crown; queen's crown (with two feathers, sun disk and Hathor horns); white crown *(top)*; double crown; and *(far right)* the crown worn by Amun.

listening to reports; considering pardons for criminals; welcoming ambassadors from other lands, and awarding favors to worthy subjects. His religious duties would include the daily performance of the ritual for the chief god of the state. Early in his reign he would commence the preparations for the building of his tomb and would pay regular visits of inspection to the site. His pleasures were energetic – hunting for gazelle, antelope or deer at home or, as in the case of the 18th-Dynasty kings, pursuing lions and elephants beyond the River Euphrates. He also enjoyed chariot practise and archery and was entertained with banqueting, music and song.

Eventually he died, and was placed in his elaborate tomb. His heir, usually the eldest son by his chief wife, succeeded him. After a short period of time the coronation took place, greeted with rejoicing and festivities throughout the land. The Double Crown – the Red Crown of Lower Egypt and the White Crown of Upper Egypt – was

placed on his brow, signifying the unification of Egypt. The new king was given a royal name, consisting of five titles, which stressed his position as the divine son and his power to rule the two lands. Each king ruled by the assent of the gods.

All the royal princes were probably given the same training, for the eldest son not infrequently died before his father. They were taught to read and write, and were trained in warfare, sport, hunting and religion. Co-regency – when a king was joined on the throne by his eldest son for a length of time – may have always been a feature of the kingship, but it is in the 12th Dynasty that its use is most frequently recorded. It ensured a smooth continuation from one reign to the next, and was perhaps employed at times when the succession could be disputed.

After a number of years – often 30 – the pharaoh celebrated a jubilee festival, the meaning of which has been much debated by scholars, although it probably included elements of thanksgiving and the ritual renewal of the king's ability to rule.

To the Egyptians "kingship" was an immortal, unassailable institution. Reverence for the ruler was one of the basic characteristics of Egyptian society. Good, bad, indifferent – kings came and went. Nominally, their power was absolute, but from an early age the prospective rulers were taught to uphold certain principles and to try to conform to the Egyptian idea of a "good" ruler, who was expected to care for the helpless, to stamp out bribery and oppression, to treat all men equally, to uphold the concept of justice, and to utter no evil.

We can assume that for most of the time the pharaonic system worked well for the Egyptians. From the moment the king ascended the throne he was their link with the gods, assuring them of peace, prosperity and eternal life. His duties would continue unabated until his death; the god's son could never abdicate or retire. A king's accession was always greeted with joy, and there is no reason to suppose that they were expressing empty formalities when the people cried out, "What a happy day! Heaven and earth rejoice (for) thou art the great lord of Egypt!"

Sculpted versions of some of the Egyptian crowns. The cartouche bears the name of Ramesses II.

An area of the western cliffs at Thebes showing many rock-cut tombs of the nobles (New Kingdom).

The nobles. The Egyptian nobility comprised the administrative officials, scribes, lawyers, doctors, priests and army officers. Of these, one of the most important groups was that of the high administrative officials. In Egypt, the state economy depended to a large extent on taxes collected from individuals and institutions owning vast estates, in addition to the tribute levied from conquered countries. Taxes were paid in kind – meat and agricultural produce – and this was used as a means of payment to employees who were not engaged in growing their own food – craftsmen, officials, priests and soldiers. To deal with this complex system the Egyptians required a network of administrative officials.

Originally, when the king delegated his duties, these tasks were undertaken by younger royal sons and close relatives. But in time officials were drawn from a wider social area and, provided a man showed ability, he could rise to high office from humble origins. The offices, however, tended to become hereditary, although the appointment of a new official was always subject to pharaoh's approval. The highest administrative position in the land was that of Vizier whose duties, as listed in the tomb of Vizier Rekhmire in the 18th Dynasty, appear to have been onerous. In the Old Kingdom high administrative officials had to be prepared to undertake a variety of duties for which they were not specially trained, such as mounting military expeditions. Organizing ability, rather than specialized technical skill, was thus required.

The nobles dwelt in fine houses, and lived in an elegant manner. In the towns the best houses were usually several stories high, since building space was valuable. Country houses or villas, such as those built at Tell el-Amarna, were usually one-storied buildings, with public reception rooms. The villas were set in beautiful gardens, planted with flowers and often containing a pool and a shrine for the family devotions. The Egyptians delighted in their gardens which they often had depicted on the walls of their tombs. The kitchens, servants' quarters and animal pens were all situated outside the main building, so that the associated odors would not trouble the master and his family.

At Amarna the villas, unlike those of other periods, had no special quarters reserved for the women, who seem to have shared the same part of the house as the master. The houses were equipped with fine furniture – chairs, beds with headrests, stools and chests for clothes. The women possessed elaborate toilet sets, and fine jewelry. They wore gauzy, flowing garments of linen, and possessed a selection of wigs. Their children played with manufactured toys – some of which are quite sophisticated – and joined their parents on hunting and fowling expeditions to the marshes.

Entertainments were lavish. The guests were waited on by young female servants, and dancers and musicians were employed for the evening to provide amusement. The female guests, in addition to their fine clothes, wore cones of scented wax perched on top of the thick wigs, which in the course of the evening would melt and give forth a pleasant odor. Each female guest was also presented with a lotus flower which she attached to the front of her headband.

The workmen. The laborers and artisans who constructed and decorated the temples, pyramids and tombs played a major part in Egyptian society. This labor force was divided into two types, the ordinary workmen and the craftsmen. The heavy work was done by huge gangs of unskilled labor consisting mostly of conscripted peasants –

although prisoners-of-war, soldiers on duty in Egypt and prisoners sentenced by the law courts were also included. In theory every male Egyptian was expected to spend part of his time on the public works programs, but in actual fact this burden fell almost exclusively on the peasantry, who in any case were forced to find alternative employment for a period of time each year because it was impossible to work on their own lands during the annual inundation of the Nile. Since the government paid for the subsistence of the laborer during his period of conscription, the public works programs in fact provided a means of regular, paid employment for the poorer classes, many of whom, together with their families, might otherwise have starved.

Thus it is simply not true that these massive building projects, as has so often been stated, were an economic drain on the country's resources and a crushing burden on Egypt's manpower. Nor were they in any sense achieved by slave labor, although during the New Kingdom foreign captives were present in Egypt in larger numbers than before, and some were certainly committed

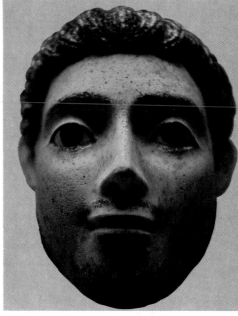

Above: painting on plaster of the Lady Thepeu, in the tomb of the chief sculptor Nebamun at Thebes. The painting shows his mother, dressed in the costume of the court of King Amenophis III.

Left: statue of Methyethy, an official of King Unas. He is shown in the usual style of the Old Kingdom period as a vigorous young man in striding pose wearing a broad bead collar.

Below right: originally a sphinx of the 12th Dynasty, representing the daughter of Anenemath, this head was subjected to drastic remodeling by Roman artists around 130 AD to grace the palace of the Emperor Hadrian at Tivoli near Rome.

to heavy labor. The work was undoubtedly arduous and unpleasant, but the common belief that only the despotism of pharaoh and the harshness of the system could have forced through these almost superhuman building feats is quite unacceptable. It was the nature of the land that created the situation, and the government provided a system which at least ensured paid employment, and against which there seems to have been little sign of revolt.

The second class of workmen was, at least in their own minds, quite superior to the laboring peasants. These were the craftsmen who executed the carving, painting and highly skilled processes involved in finishing off the buildings. These men seem to have been organized into groups or workshops, belonging either to the state or to the temples. Many must have used some of their time (either in working or leisure hours) to carry out private commissions for which there would have been a great demand. The most successful of them were able to emulate middle-class standards and provide themselves with comfortable houses and quite elaborate tombs. The sculptors and goldsmiths appear to have become more prosperous than the painters, probably because of the great demand for private funerary statuary and fashionable gold jewelry and trinkets of all kinds.

The trade secrets, passed on from father to son, were doubtless closely guarded, and although many of the craftsmen were able to achieve a fair standard of living, there is reason to believe that the lower officials of the middle class resented the ambitions of these aspiring craftsmen.

The craftsmen lived in specially-built "work-cities" near the site of the building in progress. Various "work-cities," which housed the workmen employed on royal buildings of various kinds, have been discovered, and perhaps the most informative of such towns is that of Deir el-Medineh, known to the Egyptians as the "Place of Truth," which is situated not far from the Theban necropolis. The ruins of the houses, their tombs, religious shrines, papyri and ostraka reflecting their day-to-day concerns – all these have been discovered and provide a fascinating, firsthand account of the lives of these craftsmen. In addition, we have the finished product of their efforts – the decorated New Kingdom tombs in the Valley of the Kings and the Valley of the Queens.

Before considering the organization and work of this unique group of royal workmen, let us look at their town. An expedition of the *Institut français d'archéologie orientale*, headed by B. Bruyère, excavated this isolated site for over 20 years. (A full description of the site from which much of this information is taken is given by J. Černý in *Cambridge Ancient History: Egypt from the Death of Ramesses III to the End of the Twenty-First Dynasty*.) In comparison with the numerous temples and tombs, which were built "for eternity" and are in a better state of preservation, it is one of the few well-preserved town sites discovered in Egypt. The town was founded at the beginning of the 18th

Dynasty. Amenophis I was regarded as the town patron and was later worshiped, together with his mother Ahmose Nefertari, by the workmen. The town was probably actually founded by Tuthmosis I, but Amenophis I was perhaps the king who first established a gang of royal workmen there.

Today the visitor approaches this barren valley site across rugged, desert country. It is possible to see the plan of the town quite clearly, and to wander at will among the rows of terraced houses. The settlement was originally surrounded by a thick mud-brick enclosure wall. Later, other buildings were added outside this area. In the latest stage there were no fewer than 70 houses built inside the enclosure – unimaginative terraced dwellings which faced directly onto the street. The average house was one story high and had four rooms, all set behind each other. The basic structure was of mud-brick. The artisans decorated their walls with charming scenes according to their own taste – sometimes of a religious, sometimes of a more general nature.

About 50 houses of a more spacious design, probably intended for the priests of the community, were built on to the northeast side of the enclosure. There were also police posts, and chapels were erected on the north side parallel to the enclosure. Though the village had no water supply of its own, a storage tank which was available to all the inhabitants was placed outside the main gate as a public water supply. Few towns could have possessed rubbish heaps more interesting than those of Deir el-Medineh; here were found ostraka, inscribed with details of the payment of wages and legal matters as well as the freehand sketches by the workmen which have provided such invaluable insights into their lives and attitudes.

These self-styled "Servants in the Place of Truth" built and decorated their own tombs in their necropolis near the town. The techniques which they employed on the pharaonic tombs were used to advantage on the workmen's own eternal dwellings, and they produced fairly ambitious results. There were two basic types of tomb: one, a pyramid chapel, had a doorway and pylon leading into a small garden or court, at the back of which a small pyramid was constructed on a rock-cut or brick podium (or terrace wall). The building contained a small chapel and various chambers, one to contain the coffins of the family. The other kind, a rock tomb with a pyramid, was of a slightly more elaborate design. The chambers of these tombs were sometimes decorated with paintings, executed by skilled craftsmen. It is perhaps strange that, at a time when the pharaohs themselves had abandoned the pyramid type of burial place, the necropolis workmen were designing their own small pyramid tombs.

The working conditions of these men are known to us. Their main task was to build and decorate the tomb of the pharaoh and those of the major queens; if time permitted, it is probable that they were also instructed to work on the tombs of specially favored nobles. The workmen were

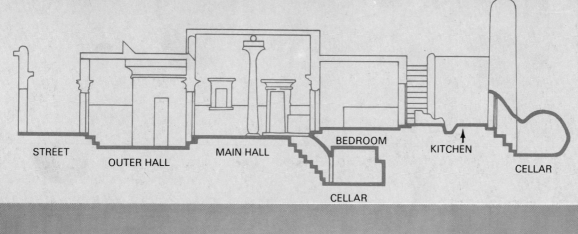

STREET   OUTER HALL   MAIN HALL   BEDROOM   KITCHEN   CELLAR

CELLAR

Deir el-Medineh workmen's village near Thebes, founded in the 18th Dynasty for tomb workers. *Above:* section through a typical house. *Below:* layout of the village and necropolis, showing the rows of terraced houses built of mud-brick.

organized into gangs, each gang divided into a "right" and a "left" side to work on the two sides of the tomb, each side being under a foreman. The gang consisted of the foreman, quarrymen, carpenters, sculptors and painters, and came under the control of the royal scribe. There were usually about 60 men in a gang, occasionally more. Supervised by the scribe and the foremen, the men worked to a plan provided by the royal architect. The scribe kept a detailed report of their progress, including absenteeism and its reasons, and this report was submitted to the vizier who made regular visits to the site. The workmen had official holidays – the 10th, 20th and 30th days of each month, when they returned to their town at Deir el-Medineh – in addition to the festival days of the great deities.

The men worked an eight-hour day, and at night were accommodated in huts near the tomb they were working on, returning to the village only for their rest days. They cut the tomb out of the rock and then prepared it for decoration. The cutting was not too difficult because of the comparative softness of the rock in that area, but the decoration of the king's tomb was often not completed by the time of his death. They received payment in kind – wheat and barley, supplied monthly by the Royal Granary. The taxes paid by the peasants of the Theban district met this demand. There were also regular supplies of fish, vegetables, and wood for fuel; fats, oil and clothing were also distributed to them from time to time. The gang had its own assistants – women to grind the corn, water-suppliers and washermen; and certain "tradesmen" – potters, fishermen and wood-cutters – were nominated to supply the gang with vessels, fish and fuel. Pharaoh also granted special benefits from time to time, including wine, imported Asiatic beer, salt, meat and natron (used as soap).

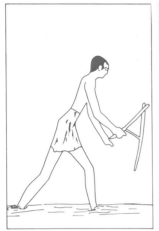

Working people. *Top register:* redrawn from tomb models (*left and right*) and a painting (*middle*) of agricultural workers hoeing and plowing (Middle Kingdom, 12th Dynasty). *Middle register:* brick-making (New Kingdom). *Lower register:* scenes of workers in the process of constructing a pyramid. The architectural achievements of the ancient Egyptians were indeed remarkable but the oppressiveness of their slave system has often been exaggerated by modern writers.

The men were also supplied with copper tools and equipment for their work, including lamps made of baked clay with a wick of old rags. These were used in the darker parts of the tombs.

Back in the village, the life of the community rested very largely on the womenfolk, since most of the men were usually away from home. The village had its own tribunal (knbt), composed of the villagers themselves – a foreman and scribe, and some of the workmen and their wives. The tribunal sat in judgment on local crimes and disputes, and had the power to pass judgment and prescribe the necessary punishment for all except cases resulting in capital punishment. Only the vizier and the pharaoh could sentence a man to death, and they alone also had the power of pardon.

In religious matters as well, the workmen arranged for the priests to be drawn from their own number. The villagers appear to have worshiped such gods as Bes and Tauert at local shrines. There was also a large sanctuary dedicated to the goddess Hathor.

It is obvious that the villagers had a certain independence in both religious and legal affairs. This aspect of their character is also expressed in other ways. The sketches on ostraka, now thousands of years old, which show scenes of noblemen and women in the guise of mice being waited on by servants in the form of cats, underline the somewhat satirical approach which these artists had towards the Egyptian hierarchy. But perhaps their attitude is most clearly shown by their readiness to take strike action when their rights were threatened. On occasion, when the royal granaries were short of grain, and the workmen's food supplies delayed or when the country was under stress – either from external or internal sources – the adminis-

Below: tomb model of a serving girl with a bird in one hand and a basket of offerings on her head. She represents eternal service to the deceased in the hereafter. Middle Kingdom tombs were furnished with models of this type representing an entire staff at the service of the deceased.

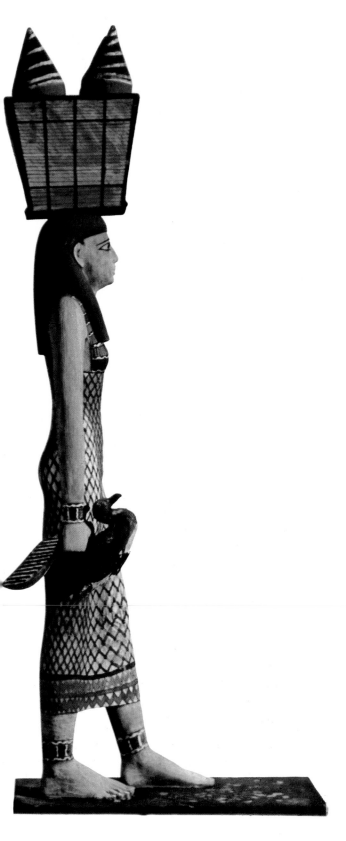

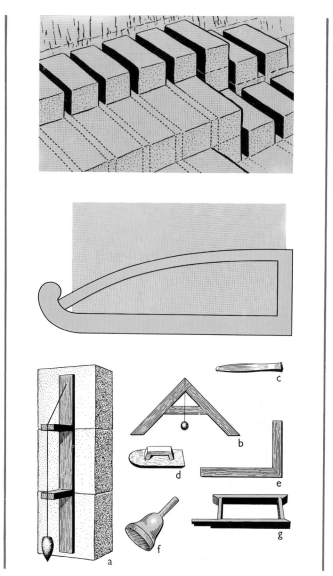

Above: some tools and techniques involved in ancient Egyptian building. *Top:* brick courses. *Middle:* a sledge for hauling heavy stones. *Bottom:* two plumb-lines, chisel, T-square, mold for bricks, mallet, and tool for smoothing mud plaster.

tration was liable to become erratic and not enough food was delivered. In the 20th Dynasty in particular, unrest over the delay of supplies to the royal workmen led to tomb robberies and strikes. In the scribal records of the period there is some mention of "foreigners" in connection with these strikes, and it would appear that some workmen had reason to fear these people, whoever they were.

These strikes, staged over dissatisfaction with conditions of employment, are the first known example of collective protest by employees. They were, moreover, successful, since the workmen had a very powerful weapon – the importance of their work. It was vital that the pharaoh's tomb, the resting place of the divine son, should be completed to receive him, and the workmen's delaying tactics seriously jeopardized this goal. The authorities were therefore anxious to meet the demands of the workmen of Deir el-Medineh, and these grievances are recorded in the scribal records. The workmen, we are told, sat down behind the funerary temple of Tuthmosis III. Officials tried to make them return to work, "but the workmen remained in the same place all day." The food finally arrived and the men went back to their work.

Because of their unique position as royal craftsmen, and also perhaps because of their independent temperament, the workmen at this isolated town were able to twist the pharaonic arm. The records show them as endearing people; lively, independent, proud of their skills and perhaps a little conceited, they were able, in their isolated valley, to preserve a surprising degree of autonomy. The reality of the Egyptian workman is a far cry indeed from the "slave labor" which is too often featured in films and novels dealing with ancient Egypt.

Peasants and slaves. On the lowest rung of the social ladder were the peasants and the slaves – two distinct groups. The peasants worked in the fields, reaping and sowing and tending their animals. When the inundation of the Nile made it impossible to work the land, numbers of the men, as we have seen, were employed as laborers on various royal building projects. Other peasants were employed in the houses of the wealthy. Both men and women worked as servants, indoors and out-of-doors, and the women were usually concerned with making the bread for the noble's family. The houses of these people were simple mud-brick structures; the only burial they could hope for was to be placed in a straw mat and laid in the sand. Yet it is apparent from the tomb-paintings that they possessed an endearing sense of humor. High officials frowned upon snobbery, and the wisdom literature advised them to treat the peasants with consideration. Their main adversary appears to have been the minor official who, full of his own importance, regarded the manual workers with contempt, not realizing that the power of Egypt was maintained, to a large extent, by their patient toiling.

Slavery, if defined as the deprivation of one man's freedom by another, existed in Egypt. The slaves were war captives and refugees. There is no evidence that foreign captives or slave laborers were used in the Old Kingdom to build the pyramids. Egypt's territorial expansion, with its resulting prisoners of war, had not developed at this period. Not until the Middle Kingdom is there evidence for the use of a number of foreigners – Nubians and Asiatics – as domestic servants in Egypt. By the New Kingdom, with the large increase in foreign wars, numerous captives were brought to Egypt and were given to temples and to private estates and owners as domestic servants. Some were used as serving girls and some as children's nannies. Others of the male captives were assigned to the royal building sites as laborers.

The slave's position in Egypt was not too unbearable,

Wooden models of a man and wife, Old Kingdom, 5th Dynasty: typical realistic portraiture of the period.

particularly if he happened to be assigned to the private house of a nobleman. By Ramesside times many foreigners, like the Biblical Joseph, held high positions in the government and at court, and at all periods it was not unusual for a slave to reach a position of trust in Egypt.

Marriage and the family. One of the most firmly established institutions in Egypt was the family. Everything we know about Egyptian society and culture supports the belief that the Egyptians loved, above all else, their close family circle. Throughout the vicissitudes of their history the strength of the family unit provided them with a focus, and was surely a major factor in their continuous and unparalleled ability to rise, phoenix-like, from the disasters, both internal and external, which so often threatened them and their land.

The family unit was compact, consisting usually of husband, wife and children, and perhaps including, in some instances, other close female relatives who had never married or were widowed. A young man became nominally "head of the house" upon marriage, when he moved out of the parental home and set up his own establishment.

Marriage was considered an eminently desirable state. For women, there was really no alternative. Young men were urged to take a wife as soon as they were able to support her financially. Except within the royal family, it is unlikely that arranged marriages were the custom, although doubtless every effort was made to ensure that the daughters of the family were introduced to suitable young men. There is little evidence in the many family genealogies which have been studied that consanguineous marriages – between brother and sister – occurred outside the royal family before the Ptolemaic era. The terms "brother" and "sister," which occur frequently in the love poems of pharaonic Egypt, were probably merely endearments. Some of these surviving poems show that young love has changed little over the centuries, and that Egyptian courtship does appear to have been a matter of inclination rather than parental organization. Here are a few extracts:

"My brother, it is pleasant to go to the [pond] in order to bathe me in thy presence, that I may let thee see my beauty in my tunic of finest linen, when it is wet. . . . I go down with thee into the water, and come forth again to thee with a red fish, which lieth beautiful in my fingers . . . Come and look at me."

"If I kiss her and her lips are opened, I am happy [even] without beer. . . ."

"Mine arms are full of branches of the persea, and my hair is weighed down with unguent. I am like a [princess] . . . when I am in thine arms."

"Mine heart recalleth thy love. The half of my temple [only] is braided, when I come running to seek thee. I trouble myself no [longer] over my hair-dressing, yet, if thou still lovest me, I will put on my curls [i.e. wig], that I may be ready in a moment."

Once a young man's choice was made, he was expected to take presents to the girl's home, and finally the marriage arrangements were made. We know nothing of the actual ceremony, although doubtless there would have been feasting and dancing and general jollification. The god of marriage – the dwarf Bes – was also god of dancing and happiness. It is not certain that the ceremony had any religious significance, but probably prayers would have been offered to Bes to ensure the couple's future success.

The ancient records do throw some light on the legal aspects. It seems that a marriage settlement was drawn up at the time of the wedding, to safeguard the position of the wife and her subsequent children. The husband was required to settle a certain amount of wealth on his bride, and to agree to compensate her if he divorced her later. The bride brought certain possessions to the marital home, which remained hers throughout the marriage and in the event of a divorce, and finally passed directly to her children. The modern parallel can still be seen in Egypt today.

The legal position of a wife in ancient Egypt was safeguarded in several ways. Bigamy was rare; economically and perhaps emotionally the non-royal Egyptian preferred one wife. Kings, sometimes from political necessity, were on the other hand usually polygamous. In non-royal households a man could, and in some instances did, introduce concubines into the household; their status, however, did not jeopardize that of the legal wife, the "mistress of the house." If a couple had no children, a serf concubine was sometimes acquired, with the hope of obtaining an heir; if the girl bore children, they could be allowed to inherit the master's property at his death, and would be expected to carry out the burial rites for him.

Another protection for the wife and her children was a law which prevented a man from transferring a valuable object to a third person without his wife's knowledge and consent, as well as the agreement of the eldest son as representative of his children.

Theoretically, divorce for the man was straightforward – simple repudiation of his wife. In practise divorce was not such an easy proposition, hemmed in as it was by financial commitments, and from the tomb scenes it is apparent that, although legally marriage was not necessarily for life, a man expected and very probably wished that his wife should accompany him not only in this world but also in the next.

The great sin in marriage was adultery. If a woman was found guilty of adultery she could be punished by burning or stoning; it was one of the most obvious reasons for divorce. We are not informed if the same strictness was applied to men as well as to women, but certainly in the wisdom literature the wise old men warned about the lures of the fair sex:

"If thou wouldst prolong friendship in a house to which thou hast admittance, as master, or as brother, or as friend, into whatsoever place thou enterest, beware of approaching the women. The place where they are is not good. On that account a thousand go to perdition. Men are made fools by their gleaming limbs. . . . A trifle, a little, the likeness of a dream, and death cometh as the end. . . ."

It can be seen that the Egyptian family structure included strong legal safeguards. A wife could also expect to be well treated by her husband. The wisdom literature again gives excellent advice:

"Do not let your conduct in the household be too high-and-mighty, and never lord it over your wife, if you know that she is a gentle-hearted woman. Do not say to her: 'Where is so and so? Bring it here,' when she has put it away carefully in some safe place. Keep her beneath your eye and watch her silently in appreciation of her worth. She is contented when your hand rests upon hers."

The Egyptian woman was well-loved, respected and adored by her children. Financially secure, she could expect to share her husband's home and eventually his tomb and afterlife, as the tomb scenes and funerary stelae indicate. At home, she was responsible for the running of the household; the "harem" in an Egyptian house was simply a part of the building reserved for the women's activities – sewing, weaving, playing with the children – and was never a place of restriction.

The customs of the royal family were quite different. Brother and sister marriages between the heir to the throne and the eldest surviving daughter of the reigning king and his major queen, the Great Royal Wife, were not only condoned but expected. This usually, but not always, meant a marriage between a full brother and sister; it could also be a marriage between a half-brother and sister, particularly if the male heir to the throne was the king's child by a minor wife or concubine, and he wished to strengthen his claim to rule. Sometimes a man with an even weaker claim to the throne would attempt to ensure his succession by marrying the king's eldest daughter, the Great Royal Daughter.

It was believed that the Great Royal Wife, or major queen, was visited by the chief state god, and the result of this union was the rightful heir to the throne. Thus the queen had a unique position and it was through the female line that the divine seed was passed on, although in practise queens regnant were extremely rare, Queen Hatshepsut being the most famous and the most successful. The custom of the king's marriage to the Great Royal Daughter was perhaps strongest during the 18th Dynasty, although towards the end of the period the pharaohs began marrying outside the royal family. Amenophis III completely broke with tradition by choosing as his Great Royal Wife the girl Tiye, a child of commoners. In Ptolemaic times the Royal Family, which was then of Hellenistic Greek origin, again intensified this custom of consanguineous marriages to such an extent that the practise began to be imitated by the Egyptian people, particularly those sectors wishing to appear "hellenized."

The pharaohs usually had several secondary wives, some of whom were relatives, Egyptian noblewomen or foreign princesses whose role and presence at the Egyptian court were to some extent diplomatic. It was also customary for the king to reserve quarters at the palace for his favorite concubines. Many of the kings, as will be apparent, were fathers of large families.

The royal women, despite the obvious advantages of almost unlimited wealth and considerable prestige, appear to have been regarded as the king's "property" to a much greater extent than their non-royal counterparts were considered to "belong" to their husbands. There were, of course, exceptions, such as the commoner Tiye, who

Tomb models of a mother and child, carved in wood and painted. New Kingdom, 19th Dynasty.

against a considerable number of rivals, maintained her position as Great Royal Wife, and presumably her husband's affection, until his death. She is known to have wielded power in diplomatic circles even during the reign of her son.

In some ways perhaps the average Egyptian woman had the best of both worlds – she was protected in society, together with her children, and her legal rights were well defined. Moreover her husband was required to clothe and feed her and to respect her. Yet there were no women lawyers or female scribes to ensure that the rights of women were protected. Egypt was ruled almost entirely by men. It is worth noting, however, that the legal status of women and the importance of the family were established and upheld by generations of wise and enlightened men.

Education. The educational system of the ancient Egyptians, like many other aspects of their everyday existence, is not clearly explained in any of the papyri. However, it is obvious from various sources that great attention was given to the training of young people, and that the ability to read and write was considered to be the ultimate academic achievement – an open door leading to power and prestige: "Give thy heart to learning and love her like a mother, for there is nothing so precious" – thus were young Egyptian boys advised.

The children remained in their mothers' care until they were probably about four years of age, living in the "harem" or women's quarters in the large houses and palaces. Doubtless it was here that they received basic training in good manners and behavior – an aspect of upbringing much emphasized by the Egyptians. Regard for the mother is particularly stressed in the ancient texts. A wise man, Any, whose maxims have come down to us, wrote:

"Remember how your mother brought you into the world, and with what embracing care she nurtured you. Never give her cause to accuse you and lift up her hands towards God in condemnation of your conduct, and never give God reason to listen to your mother's complaints."

At four years of age a boy started to learn his lessons. We know, from the career of a priest, Bak-en-Khonsu, that his schooling was fairly lengthy. He was a trainee for twelve years, from four to sixteen, when he started his temple service as a libation priest.

The various groups in society were educated in different ways. The royal children, who were often numerous, were privately tutored at the palace. They were frequently joined by the sons of the great noble families, thus forming an "elite" palace school. This created a bond between the heir to the throne and those who would become his most influential subjects which would last throughout their lives, and would thus ensure loyalty to the king. In some cases, the princesses and even the daughters of the nobility may also have attended these schools.

The most sought-after profession in Egypt was that of scribe. With a scribal training a man could be employed in the temples, the main administrative centers, or the prisons. In addition, certain nobles kept a staff of personal scribes to assist with the running of the great estates. It is therefore not surprising that boys were urged to: "Set to work and become a scribe, and you will become a leader of men." Scribes alone were considered to be independent of any master, and the most prestige attached to the scholarly scribes in the temples, who taught others. Usually a boy took up his father's profession, although in some cases he might be able to persuade his parents to allow him to choose his own career.

The boys who were to enter the professions – whether scribal, medical or legal – seem to have been educated at schools attached to and run by the temples, where they were instructed by the resident specialist priests, or at schools attached to the government departments where their fathers were employed.

What kind of education did these privileged children receive? The most important subjects were reading and writing. Equipped with a scribal palette and a reed brush, the boys learned to write in the hieroglyphic script (the

Traditional writing case, with inscription in Coptic Greek, accompanied by reed pens and dried red and black ink, the usual writing materials of ancient Egypt.

sacred language of ancient Egypt), as well as its cursive derivative, Hieratic, which was used for everyday business. Any student who has attempted to copy the intricate symbols of the hieroglyphic script will sympathize with the small boy who declared, thousands of years ago: "Lesson-time endured forever, like the mountains!" The boys slowly learned how to write the signs, and gradually built up a vocabulary of words. They wrote out texts, dictated by the teacher, not on expensive papyrus but on ostraka – broken potsherds and pieces of limestone which were to be found in the debris of every town and village.

Most instruction, it seems, was oral; the children's copies of ancient stories survive – sometimes providing our only source of a particular text – and the margins of these copy books are decorated with scribbles and sometimes rapid sketches of animals. The boys would eventually progress to composition, enabling them to write letters on a variety of topics. Some would ultimately use this skill as a means of livelihood, acting as petition scribes employed to write such letters. Hieroglyphs, which at a very early date were replaced by Hieratic, and later by Demotic, as a script for everyday use, were probably regarded in these schools as a classical background and a training of the mind in much the same way as Latin has been in our own schools. The pupils were also taught how to read, by chanting stories and recitations. In the course of their reading and writing exercises the Egyptians would also have learned, indirectly, about a variety of other topics – history, literature, geography, ethics. Arithmetic was almost certainly part of the curriculum. In the government service, with its elaborate taxation system, a working knowledge of arithmetic was essential for a scribe.

Particularly in the New Kingdom, Egypt was to have contact with many countries of the ancient Near East. There was an exchange of both people and ideas, and some of the affairs of the court must have been conducted in foreign languages.

In the New Kingdom the *lingua franca* of diplomatic circles was Akkadian. Specialists who could read and write this language were certainly employed at the Egyptian court, and were probably trained for this work while still at school.

The Egyptians firmly believed that knowledge and virtue went hand in hand. Indeed ancient peoples, such as the Greeks, often remarked upon the wisdom and good manners of the Egyptians. Herodotus, the Greek historian, was impressed with the customary politeness of Egyptian youngsters, and noted their regard for their elders. Children were expected to stand up in the presence of older people, and to control their excessive appetites at mealtimes. Dishonesty, bad temper, lack of respect or courtesy, idleness and continuous chatter were all considered to be grave faults; also curiosity – questioning the beliefs of elders and betters – was severely frowned upon. These ideals were probably taught at home, by parental example and chiding.

However, more formal instruction was given at school. Moral "codes" attributed to various sages were produced for study, in the form of instructions to be handed on from father to son. These stressed the virtues of delivering messages faithfully, guarding one's tongue – "a man's ruin lies in his tongue" – entering into the house of another only after an invitation had been given, and then not gazing around at the man's possessions with open curiosity. Altogether, the "instructions" put forward a mode of behavior for almost every situation in which a young person might find himself, and aimed to equip him with the ability to deal with society in general – whether with his superiors, equals or inferiors. When he had acquired all this knowledge, he was then warned against pride, and urged to "learn from the ignorant as well as from the wise man, for there are no limits that have been decreed for art. There is no artist who attains entire excellence."

How were these high standards of behavior inculcated? Children were undoubtedly punished: "A boy's ear is on his back – he listens when he is beaten!" a maxim puts it. The Egyptians loved their children, but they saw nothing amiss in corporal punishment, and indeed regarded it as a necessary part of correction, in one instance likening the young human to a young animal in need of training and chastisement. "Spend no day in idleness, or you will be flogged!" state the ancient texts. Learning "lines" was also a familiar punishment for the Egyptian child. Today, some of these laboriously copied texts still survive. Modern schoolboys could discover in their ancient counterparts the same failings – inability to rise early for lessons, and a readiness to daydream.

In addition to the usual curriculum, boys who were to specialize in medicine, law or religious liturgy would perhaps have devoted some of their time to elementary studies in these fields, although their main training would not take place until they took up more advanced courses of study.

The boys also indulged in various games and sports, such as swimming, boating, ball games, wrestling and accompanying their fathers on hunting and fowling expeditions. It is clear, however, that the Egyptians believed character-training was to be achieved mainly by the discipline of learning to write, and by indoctrination in morals and ethics.

The boys, at least until later times, seem to have been free of the terror of many modern schoolchildren – the examination system. As training centers, the schools appear to have been organized for day pupils only, although later on residence in the temples for periods of time was required. Lessons started early in the morning and finished at noon, because of the heat, and the children eagerly awaited the arrival of their mothers with the mid-day meal of "three rolls of bread and two jugs of barley wine." Education was probably not free, each family paying the temple or government center in kind, from the produce of their land.

Advanced education continued for the professional classes who were to specialize in the subjects which would ultimately lead to their chosen careers. A period of training was required in the temple or government center, where they worked alongside men (usually including their fathers) who could pass on to them their skill and knowledge. It would appear from ancient texts, however, that the students caused their tutors as much concern as in more recent times. The misdemeanors related here by an aged scribe have a curiously modern note:

"I am told that you neglect your studies and devote yourself entirely to pleasure. You trail from street to street, smelling of beer. Beer robs you of all human respect, it affects your mind, and here you are, like a broken rudder, good for nothing . . . You have been found performing acrobatics on a wall! Ah, if only you knew that wine was an abomination, if only you would renounce liquor and think of something other than tankards of beer!"

Formal education for the sons of the lower classes existed only on a very basic level. A boy's career was not selected for him because he wished to become an artist or a goldsmith or a farmer, nor because he showed ability in any particular direction; he entered a trade because it was

Model of a serving girl carrying a pot and wearing the side-lock of youth. From a New Kingdom grave at Thebes (18th Dynasty).

his father's work. The sons of craftsmen and artisans were apprenticed and went to train at one of the temples or state workshops, where they probably learned their skills direct from their own fathers. When his son reached the age of four, the father probably took over from his wife the responsibility for teaching him the skills he would need in his life, before the boy was formally apprenticed to a Master Craftsman at a particular workshop. Likewise, the sons of peasants would have joined their fathers in the fields at an early age.

So far, little mention has been made of the education of girls. It seems that the Egyptian girl did not, for the most part, share in her brother's education. Few "careers" were open to women, although they could "pass on" a professional position, from the woman's own father to her son. It is most likely, as we have seen, that some of the royal princesses and even some of the nobles' daughters joined in the classes held at the palace, and learned how to read and write. Highly intelligent and astute queens are not lacking in Egyptian history, and they could, when the opportunity presented itself, organize many aspects of the court business. However, the role which the majority of girls played was that of wife and mother, and for this they were trained in household management by their own mothers.

Some women pursued other courses. Temple dancers and singers were frequently female and their training at the temples started at quite an early age; similarly, dancers who entertained at banquets would have practised their art from childhood. Women were also employed as professional mourners, and again, from the tomb paintings, it is evident that these girls served an "apprenticeship," learning their trade from more experienced performers. In every community there has always been a need for midwives; the women who performed this task in Egypt probably received no formal training, although again knowledge would have been passed down the generations. Other women were employed on a commercial basis in the weaving and baking centers of the great estates and temples and would have been trained at their place of work.

The Egyptian education system, based as it was on the concept that a son would follow in his father's career, whether profession or trade, placed great emphasis on the idea of teaching by example. However, in certain cases it was possible for a boy of humble origins to rise, by sheer ability, to a position of great influence and power in the land. The system must therefore have been flexible enough to accommodate individuals of outstanding brilliance. Again, although boys were not given a wide choice of careers, it would seem from the achievements of the Egyptians, medical, scribal and artistic, that many persons displayed instinctive ability and sometimes genius in the fields which were chosen for them.

There were faults in the system. There was no equality of opportunity, and few could expect their lot in life to differ radically from that of their forebears. Women were certainly not equiped to work beside men in professions

Hieratic script on the Eber papyrus of medical texts. New Kingdom, 18th Dynasty.

Egyptian learning and wisdom became a byword to later civilizations. Their educational system appears to have produced a man who understood himself and his relative position in society, and who was, moreover, content. Perhaps one reason for the stability of Egyptian civilization for so many centuries lay in this cultivation of the whole personality.

Medicine. That remarkable process known today as mummification was developed by the Egyptians in their attempt to preserve the bodies of their dead for the afterlife. In the process, the internal organs, except for the heart, were removed from the body and treated separately, while the body cavities were filled with preservatives. The body was then packed and surrounded with natron and left until it was dehydrated. It was then washed, treated with special unguents, and wrapped in layers of fine gauze.

From their funerary experiments the Egyptians gained an invaluable first-hand knowledge of the anatomy of the human body. Unfettered by religious taboos forbidding human dissection, they were able to lay the foundations of medical science; and from this the Greeks in particular, the Romans, Persians, Arabs and medieval Europe were to benefit. Mummification has even yielded benefits to modern science in that a study of ancient mummies has allowed us to determine some of the diseases from which an ancient people suffered.

The Egyptians had studied medicine from earliest times. Manetho, the historian of the Egyptians, records that King Djer of the First Dynasty was a noted physician who was credited with having written a treatise on anatomy. In the Third Dynasty, Imhotep, the architect of the first pyramid at Saqqara, was also a famous physician who was later worshiped by the Greeks as a god of medicine.

Our knowledge of Egyptian medicine is mainly derived from written sources, including the Ebers, Hearst, Edwin Smith and Chester-Beatty papyri. These medical "books" vary considerably; some are little more than collections of magical recipes, while others, notably the Edwin Smith surgical papyrus, are methodical and scientific in their approach. From the start, the Egyptians made a clear distinction between those illnesses the cause of which was apparent, such as injuries resulting from accidents, falls and blows, and other diseases the causes of which were unknown. The former were treated with rational, practical medical methods, the latter with a mixture of magic and medicine.

To the Egyptian, the doctor was also a priest and a magician. The illnesses not caused by an obvious accident were believed to be the work of some hostile agent, such as an angry deity or a dead person, and magic was used to free the sufferer from this evil influence. The illness, addressed by the physician as a demon, was exhorted to leave the patient's body, and a magical incantation was often recited over a "medicine," containing particularly

and trades, and only those with the prestige and power of a royal background were able, occasionally, to assert their authority – either directly like Hatshepsut, or perhaps more subtly like Tiye and Nefertiti. However, the educational system is to be commended for its attempt to produce a "rounded" individual – not only one who possessed the requisite scientific knowledge or manual ability, but who had also learned to respect the traditions of his ancestors, to listen to advice, and to express moderation in all things. The Egyptian child, in addition to his formal training, was taught how to live in his society – how to act in the presence of others, how to use self-control and commonsense. He was not, however, taught to question the established order of things. It has been said, with some truth, that the Egyptians always asked the question "How?" whereas the Greeks asked the question "Why?"

unpleasant ingredients, designed to drive the demon away when the sufferer swallowed the draught. The ingredients of such a dose might include the fat and blood of various animals as well as ground-up horns, bones and hoofs, the whole dissolved in water, milk, wine or beer, and sweetened with honey to lessen the disgust. Perhaps the physician, if his treatment had proved successful, came in time to rely increasingly on medicine rather than magic, but magic continued to be used together with medicine, almost as a last resort, throughout Egypt's long history.

These "doctor-magicians" received a thorough education. As medical students they underwent a preliminary training as scribes, to enable them to read the medical papyri. They were then apprenticed to a fully qualified doctor, often a close relative, and were attached to a temple, since they were priests as well as doctors – often priests of the goddess Sekhmet, who had power to bring on as well as to terminate widespread epidemics.

The Egyptians successfully recorded and amassed medical facts, but unfortunately the wrong conclusions were often drawn and useless treatment was prescribed.

These medical practitioners also compiled the first extensive medical and anatomical vocabulary – there are different hieroglyphs which distinguish between the various organs and their functions. They came to understand the relative position of the organs in the body, but as their knowledge of the working of these organs was mostly restricted to conclusions drawn from the dissection of inanimate corpses, they misunderstood the functions of the bodily organs and regarded the nerves, muscles, veins and arteries as parts of a common network, centered on the heart. The importance of the heart as the seat of life was realized; indeed, this organ was credited with an additional role as the seat of thoughts and emotions, whereas no importance was attached to the brain. Again, the circulation of the blood was not understood.

The Egyptians made the first known experiments in surgery, which was employed when other, simpler methods had failed. They knew how to use splints, bandages and compresses. Certain tomb scenes show the application of splints around fractured bones, and the setting of a dislocated shoulder. They also made use of medicines and balms. The papyri list the names and uses of certain medicinal plants. Ointments were made up, using a basis of honey or fats, and applied externally to wounds and sores. For certain ailments special diets were suggested, such as honey, cream and milk for chest and throat complaints. They were also aware of the need for hygiene and cleanliness, both personal and in the home, and to this end recipes are given in the medical papyri to rid the house of fleas, flies, vermin and other pests.

The ailments the Egyptians suffered from seem to have been as varied as our own, although sometimes it is difficult to find exact translations for the names of the illnesses. Their teeth must have caused them considerable discomfort – the attrition caused by the particles of grit present in

their bread, and probably lack of general oral hygiene, resulted in some obviously painful conditions in rich and poor alike. Thus their approach to medicine varied. They gave fairly accurate descriptions of illnesses, but usually suggested inadequate treatments. One of the most interesting aspects of Egyptian medicine was the use of sanatoria attached to temples, where people in search of cures could spend a period of time praying to the resident deity. The psychological benefits of a break from routine tasks and the reassurances of the priests, together with the supplicants' faith, appear to have brought mental and physical relief to many.

An aspect of Egyptian medicine with which we can easily identify was their recourse to cosmetic surgery, and "cures" for the ageing process. These remedies ranged from a surgical cure for pendulous breasts and the manufacture of aphrodisiac medicines, to readily available cures for graying hair, baldness, and the ageing and wrinkling of the skin. Indeed, one papyrus gives a formula entitled, "How to turn an old man into a youth," and also supplies methods for the removal of wrinkles, pimples, spots and

A Late-period mummy case, decorated with spells and incantations. The Egyptian obsession with mummification led to the acquisition of much medical knowledge.

unseemly blemishes. The toilet equipment of the noble-woman included costly anti-wrinkle and cleansing creams, cosmetics and deodorants – much like that of the modern woman.

With all its limitations Egyptian medicine, with its often misguided attempts, paved the way for the future by providing the basis of our present knowledge and, more important, our readiness to examine the human body for causes of illness.

The army. The Egyptians were never a truly military people but they were often forced to take measures of self-defense against would-be invaders, who saw in Egypt a fertile, wealthy prize; thus in time they built up a military establishment. In the Old Kingdom there was no standing army. Troops were levied by local governors when the need arose, and in peacetime were used to assist with quarrying, building projects, and policing the frontiers. Possibly a small group of professional soldiers was formed to guard the king, although there is no evidence of this, and military expeditions were led by administrators with no military background. The local armies contributed to the decentralization and strife of the First Intermediate Period. In the Middle Kingdom they continued to exist until the reign of Sesostris III, who abolished the old system and instituted conscription of native Egyptians, with a quota of Nubian volunteers, to build up a royal army centered on his own personal retainers. The army assisted the king in curtailing the powers of the nobles once and for all, and was also used on building projects and public works. Some soldiers were armed with bows and arrows, others with axes. Although they carried big shields covered with hide, they wore no armor.

One of the greatest achievements of the Middle Kingdom was the string of fortresses built in Nubia near the second cataract. Designed to command the river as well as the hinterland, they were sited either along the riverbank or on islands in the Nile, and controlled Egypt's trading and military interests in the area. From them soldiers were dispatched against raiding parties of Nubians. The fortresses were occupied by the governor, soldiers, administrators and army families. The design of these fortresses was so successful that this experiment provided the basis for Egyptian enterprise in controlling and policing on a large scale the land Egypt was to acquire beyond its borders.

After the Hyksos' invasion and expulsion, Egypt's attitude to warfare underwent a radical change. The need for constant self-defense and the fear of conquest were now recognized, and the Hyksos had themselves introduced the Egyptians to new weapons and military ideas. In the New Kingdom Egypt became a foremost military nation. The army and navy were organized on a national basis, and there was a fully trained, professional standing army which undertook frequent and successful campaigns.

Pharaoh, commander-in-chief, took the field in these campaigns; the "minister-of-war" was the vizier; an army council, formed of senior officers, assisted and advised pharaoh at home and in the field. The field corps, divided into divisions of about 5,000 men each, included the chariotry and the infantry. The divisions were named after the principal state gods, and presumably came under their protection. At the Battle of Kadesh, the divisions were commanded personally by pharaoh and several royal princes. In service at home the army was divided into two corps – stationed in Upper and in Lower Egypt – each under a lieutenant commander responsible to the general, and they escorted royal processions, dealt with riots, garrisoned frontier forts and provided part of the labor force for public works.

The chariotry, probably a Hyksos innovation, was divided into squadrons made up of 25 chariots. Each was under the command of a "Charioteer of the Residence," who was responsible to the "Lieutenant Commander of Cavalry." The chariot, drawn by two horses, had two wheels and carried a driver and a soldier equipped with bows, arrows, javelin, shield and sword. There was no cavalry as such, probably because the breed of horse was not large or strong enough to carry a rider. The horses were trained in chariotry by a royal stable master, who held an influential position.

The Infantry was divided into regiments, each commanded by a "standard-bearer," and was made up of recruits, trained men and specialist fighters – the "Braves of the King." The recruits were quite often from Nubia or were war captives from foreign countries. In the late 18th Dynasty, and increasingly in the later periods, the Egyptian army possessed a substantial number of foreign recruits. These included Libyans, Nubians, "Asiatics" and "Sea Peoples," and in the 26th Dynasty large numbers of Greek mercenaries were employed to fight Egypt's battles. Egypt could not maintain her necessarily large standing army from her own population, but it is possible that the increasing numbers of foreign troops, one-time prisoners-of-war, together with the superior weapons of the Assyrians and Persians, contributed to Egypt's military decline. The foreigners' loyalty to their former conquerors must have been suspect at times. Egyptian natives were conscripted by the "Scribe of Recruits."

When a man entered the army voluntarily, it could also provide a career. It was possible to gain rapid promotion and considerable riches in the service, and veterans were often given lands, gold decorations and war captives as domestic servants. Although the highest army posts were reserved for well-educated men, since these were partly administrative, the army offered the uneducated man a means of acquiring some wealth, and foreigners who entered the service gained their freedom. An additional incentive was provided by the regulation which enabled the sons of a regular soldier to inherit their father's land – the gift of the king – only if they followed in their father's career.

From the "regulars" the officers were recruited. The hierarchy consisted of the "greatest of 50"; standard-bearers in charge of 200 men; the captain of a troop; the commander of a troop who was at the head of a brigade or commanded a fortress; the overseer of garrison troops; the overseer of fortresses (there were two such posts – one for the Nubian frontier and one for the Mediterranean coast); the lieutenant commander, and the general. Often important positions at court, such as Royal Tutor, were granted to ex-army men. The army offered considerable rewards, and several army generals who became pharaohs emphasize the power of the military in Egyptian history.

There were also administrators – mostly scribes who were responsible for assembling and organizing the supplies for the army, which were usually obtained en route to the battleground. The scribes also recorded the daily events and listed the booty acquired. Supplies were transported by mule, packass and ox-drawn wagon.

Perhaps the most important innovation of the 18th Dynasty was the use of the horse and chariot. The earliest chariots display Canaanite influence, and the words used by the Egyptians for horses and chariots and their trappings also suggest a Canaanite connection. The small horse was probably introduced into Egypt by the Hyksos, although the pre-Hyksos horse-burial found at the Middle Kingdom fortress at Buhen in Nubia has caused some scholarly dispute over the exact date of the horse's arrival in Egypt. The number of horses was increased by the carrying off into Egypt of some of the enemy's horses, captured at the Battle of Megiddo. The "First Charioteer of His Majesty" also appears to have undertaken foreign missions, possibly to acquire stud horses.

The pharaohs set off on frequent campaigns, sometimes yearly, and marched their troops to Syria/Palestine and beyond where, led by the chariotry, they made many assaults on fortified towns. These Syrian and Palestinian fortifications in turn influenced the military architecture of the New Kingdom. Compared with other conquerors of the ancient world, the Egyptians usually showed clemency to the enemy towns, which were not brutally sacked. Nor were the soldiers allowed to loot them, since the booty, which belonged to pharaoh and ultimately to

Tomb models of Nubian soldiers marching to war. From a Middle Kingdom grave. Recruits to the infantry were quite often from Nubia. Some were prisoners of war from other countries. The models are skillfully made from wood.

the gods of Egypt and their temples, was meticulously recorded by the scribes and transported home. Many captives were also brought back to Egypt. A chosen few would be killed ceremonially by pharaoh, wielding his mace; the remainder would enter servitude. Some of the princes of the conquered kingdoms would also be brought back to Egypt as hostages. They were educated with Egyptian royalty, thus laying the foundation of future comradeship when these vassal princes returned home to rule their lands subject to pharaoh's wishes.

The establishment of a professional army in Egypt brought obvious benefits – wealth, empire and captives – but it also imposed a considerable burden of recruitment on the country, which could not eventually be met by native Egyptians. It also enabled certain professional soldiers to threaten the power of pharaoh. Horemheb, Ramesses I, and Herihor were all army officers who achieved rule in Egypt, and in the Late Period weak pharaohs were constantly aware of the threat which the army offered to their rule. The army, like the priesthood, was created on a grand scale and made rich and glorious by the all-powerful pharaohs of the 18th Dynasty. These great warriors, secure in their own strength, can have had little notion of the dangers which their military policies unleashed for later, less secure rulers.

The navy. The navy, as an extension of the army, was used more as a means of transporting troops and merchandise than for active warfare. Vessels were sometimes used as mobile headquarters for operations, as in the expulsion of the Hyksos; occasionally they were used in fighting, as a relief of Ramesses III at the Temple of Medinet Habu shows. Ships were also successfully used in trading expeditions, such as the voyages to Punt. The navy was employed by Tuthmosis III to reach Phoenicia. Once there,

he sailed into the harbors of the various coastal cities and forced them into submission, then made arrangements with them for the supplies necessary for his forthcoming military campaigns in the interior. The naval base near Memphis was the port from which the 18th-Dynasty fleet set forth for Syria/Palestine. The Egyptians built their own ships. From earliest times they had designed their own craft and these were able to reach Nubia and Punt.

The organization of the navy is not fully explained in the records; it appears that recruits were assigned to training crews under a "standard-bearer of rowers," then were sent to join the crew of a ship. The number of a crew varied according to the ship, and a recruit could be promoted either to a higher rank, such as "commander of rowers," or to a larger ship. Soldiers and sailors were interchangeable and could be transferred or promoted from one service to the other. From a "standard bearer" on a ship a man could rise to a higher land position, such as "commander of troops," more suitable for an older man. At the top of the naval hierarchy came the "ship's captain" and the "chief of ships' captains," belonging either to the royal fleet or the fleet of a temple, and finally the admirals, who controlled the royal fleet under the commander-in-chief – the crown prince. The ultimate authority was the king. The chief administrator was "chief-of-all-the-king's-ships"; the vizier had no direct responsibility for the fleet, although he could arbitrate in naval disputes.

The navy in wartime was a necessary but secondary service; in peacetime it really came into its own as an efficient merchant service, useful in expanding Egypt's trading interests. Unlike earlier naval facilities, which had been provided as the occasion demanded, the navy under the 18th Dynasty was a fully organized facility, and was one creation of these warlike pharaohs which served the nation well.

Model of a private boat showing rowers and the owner, from the grave of Mectine at Deir el-Bahri. Middle Kingdom.

TELL EL-AMARNA

An Egyptian City

VISUAL STORY

Tell el-Amarna was once the great capital city of Akhetaten, founded by the heretic pharaoh Akhenaten (*left*) and inhabited for only about 15 years. It was then deserted, after Tutankhamun and the royal court had returned to orthodoxy and to the traditional New Kingdom capital of Thebes. The site lies about 300 miles north of Luxor (the ancient Thebes), on the east bank of the Nile. Built on the narrow strip of cultivated land along the banks of the river the ancient city, bordered by the desert mountains, was long (9 kilometres) and narrow, curving towards the river bank at the north and south ends. The site first came into prominence in 1887 when a peasant woman unearthed some baked clay tablets there, inscribed in cuneiform, which proved to be part of the diplomatic correspondence sent to the ancient Egyptian court from the north Syrian region and subsequently buried in the ruins of the royal archives. These were the famous "Amarna letters." After they had finally been acknowledged as genuine, excavation of the site began. Flinders Petrie excavated many of the official buildings in 1891–92, the Germans continued, and in 1921 the Egypt Exploration Society took over the work. The city has never been fully excavated.

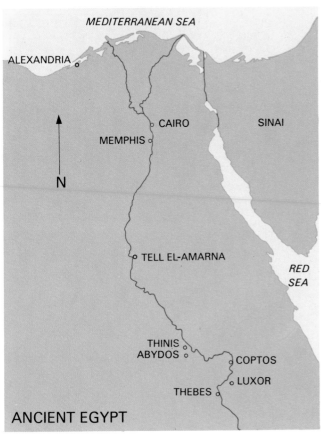

ANCIENT EGYPT

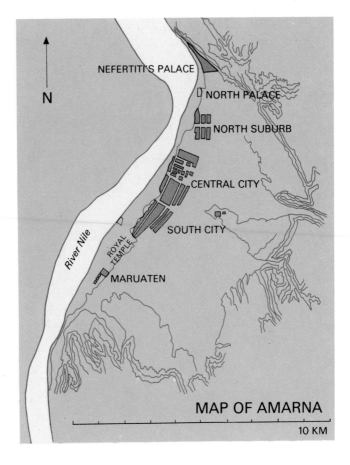

MAP OF AMARNA

10 KM

BLOCK PLAN OF THE CENTRAL CITY IN AMARNA

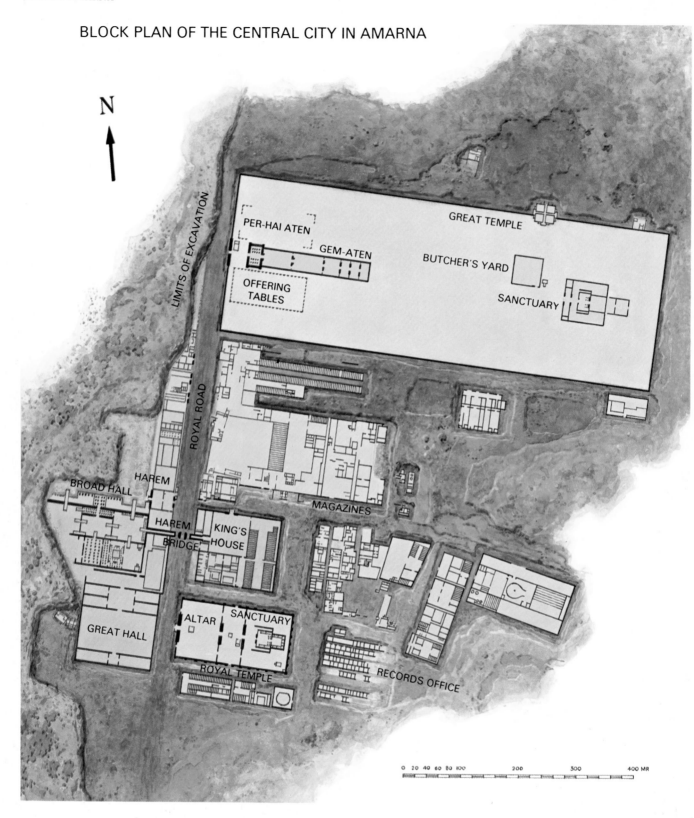

N

GREAT TEMPLE

PER-HAI ATEN

GEM-ATEN

BUTCHER'S YARD

OFFERING TABLES

SANCTUARY

LIMITS OF EXCAVATION

ROYAL ROAD

HAREM

BROAD HALL

MAGAZINES

HAREM BRIDGE

KING'S HOUSE

GREAT HALL

ALTAR

SANCTUARY

ROYAL TEMPLE

RECORDS OFFICE

0 20 40 60 80 100   200   300   400 MR

Tell el-Amarna, the ancient Akhetaten, consisted of a central city containing the palaces, temples, government offices and magazines; the south city, a residential area; a northern suburb, the business area, and several outlying palaces. *Above* is a plan of the central city, and on the *opposite page* an artist's reconstruction of part of the central city, both looking south.

In Akhetaten, unlike crowded Thebes, there was building space t spare, and it was therefore possible to lay out one-story houses se in spacious gardens. Since it was so briefly occupied, the site of Akhetaten is unique in that the excavators had to deal with only one level of occupation, and the original plan was never radically altered.

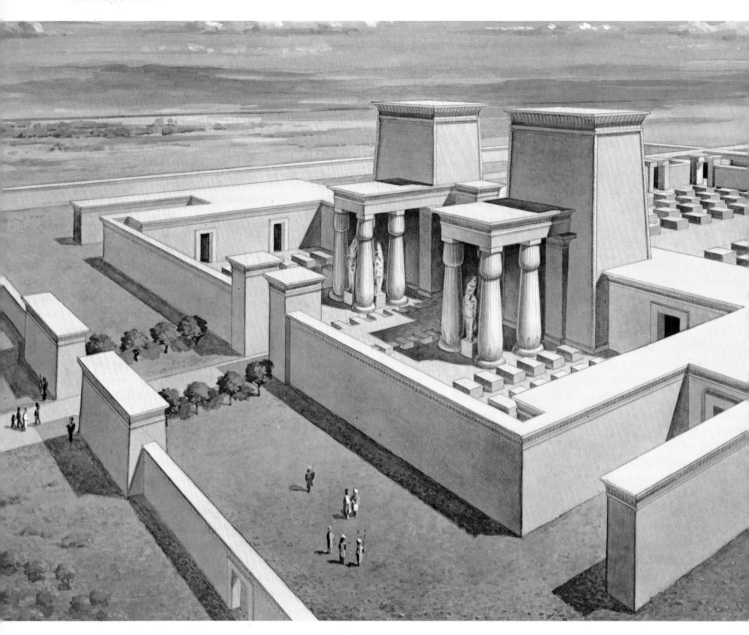

The sanctuary, or central shrine, of the city's
Great Temple of the Aten is shown *above*
in reconstruction. Because Akhenaten had
instituted the cult of sun worship in his
capital city, the temples of Akhenaten
differed markedly from the traditional
temples of Egypt. There was no enclosed
shrine holding its cult statue, nor priests to
wash, anoint, clothe, feed and worship the
statue daily. Instead the Amarna temples
were open to the sun, the god Aten, whose
beneficent rays appear so often in Amarna
art reaching down from the sun disk. A
series of courts led up to the high altar in
the sanctuary where, to the accompaniment
of music and singing, offerings of food,
drink and flowers were placed on altars or
offering tables for the god.

Akhenaten's beautiful queen, Nefertiti, at worship. Nefertiti seems to have played as important a part in the temple ceremonies as the king himself. In fact, the two together seem to have dominated the sophisticated life of the city, presiding as one over the bold innovations in religion and the arts that characterized the Amarna period.

Excavations have shown that the Great Temple underwent three phases of construction. A fragment of a raised relief from Amarna (*below*) shows laborers, one perhaps a Negro or Nubian, at work building some part of the Great Temple complex. There were other temples at Amarna, notably the smaller Royal Temple close to the palace.

The chief center of sun worship at Tell el-Amarna was the Great Temple of the Aten, whose sanctuary is shown *above*. The temple as a whole consisted of a huge enclosure with the sanctuary at the far end. A causeway ascended gradually from the entrance through a series of narrow courts to the high altar in the sanctuary. Hundreds of stone or mud-brick offering tables flanked the causeway or were set up in the enclosure, most of them probably intended for ceremonial use by those who were not permitted to enter the sanctuary itself. Other offering tables were placed in the courts and in the sanctuary itself, which also contained a number of colossal statues of the king. The entrance courts, named Per-Hai ("House of Rejoicing") and Gem-Aten ("Finding the Aten"), were entered through a pylon and bordered by columned porticoes. A limestone relief from Amarna (*opposite page, left*) shows a scene in the Great Temple, probably just such a colonnaded court with offering tables piled high with fruit and flowers and flanked by incense burners.

Akhetaten was a notably civilized city, spacious, orderly and elegant, a city of temples, palaces and comfortable houses with open courts and columned porticoes. There were gardens everywhere, green with palms, willows and sycamore trees, bright with beds of flowers, flowering shrubs and lotus ponds. Several luxurious palaces housed the royal family. For a young Amarna princess like the one pictured here (*left*) life was easy and pleasant. Everybody in Akhetaten lived well. Both men and women wore pleated linen robes, loosely fitting with wide, fringed sleeves. Elaborate wigs were in vogue. The arts flourished, and the frequent ceremonies in palace or temple were both dignified and colorful.

Of the Amarna palaces, the Great Palace in the central city, with its state halls, was the most important. The plan (*opposite page*) shows the main building, with the broad hall on the left. To the right was a large columned coronation hall, and on the other side servants' quarters and the harem. The palace was set on a hill, with three terraced gardens leading down to the Nile landing stage, and was connected with the king's house and royal nursery by an arched bridge across the royal road.

A limestone relief from Amarna (*left*) depicts the "window of appearances" where the king and the royal family would show themselves to the multitude, sometimes throwing down gifts to their favorites as they leaned on the cushioned sill. The window, reached through the small doors, most likely faced an open court from the broad hall. Servants are shown sweeping this courtyard and laying the dust with water, while an overseer stands by the grounded shields and weapons of the guard. Other palaces included the North Palace, a rest house with gardens, a zoo and aviaries, and Maruaten, a pleasure palace where the royal family picnicked.

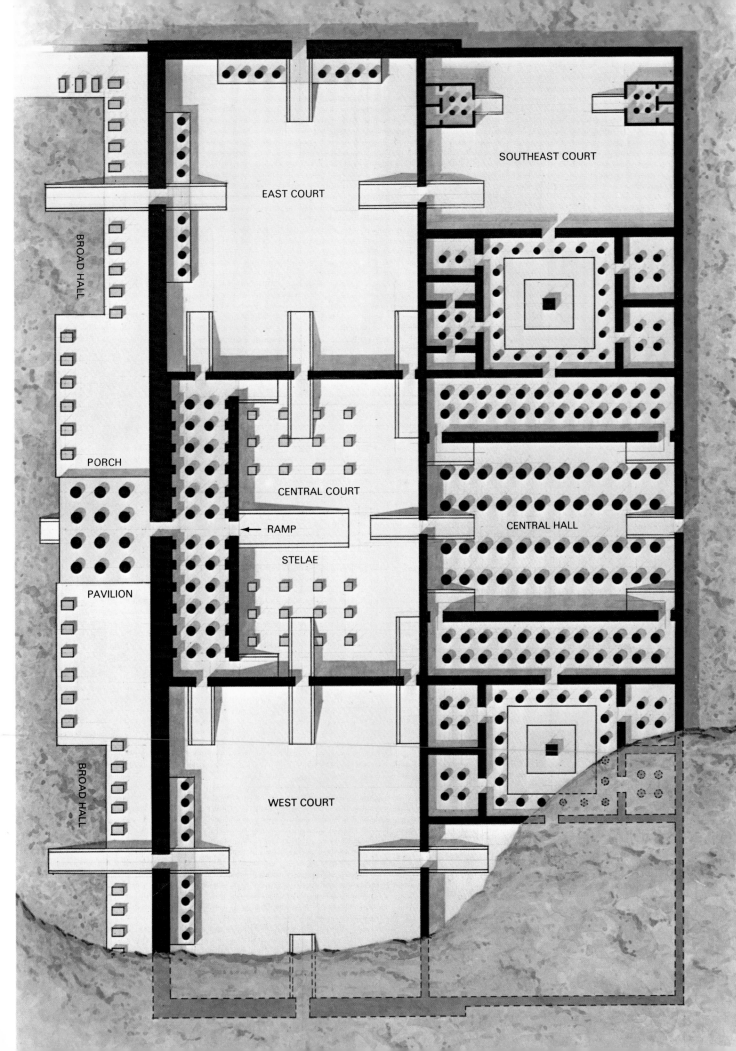

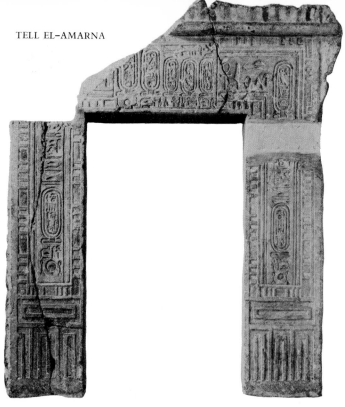

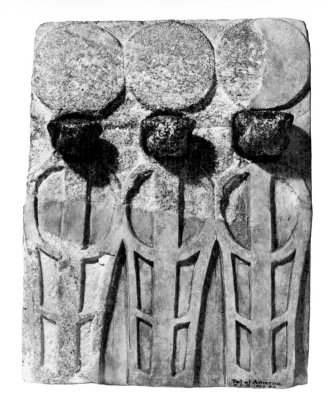

Amarna's palaces and temples were lavishly decorated. A fragment of a brightly colored fresco (*left*) came from the king's house. It shows two of the six royal princesses sitting on cushions while the legs of three others appear above. The doorway (*above, left*), once in the Great Palace, is embellished with the cartouches (names) of Akhenaten, Nefertiti and the Aten. Cobras crowned with solar disks, as on this slab from a temple (*above*), represented the uraeus, a protective deity. Friezes of these cobras were a common architectural motif in Amarna. The relief (*below, left*), found in the Great Temple, shows a charioteer awaiting his master at a religious ceremony in the temple. While royalty and nobles rode around the city in such chariots, the ordinary inhabitants no doubt walked. Their houses, too, were modest. A section and plan of a typical small villa in the North Suburb are shown *below* and *opposite*.

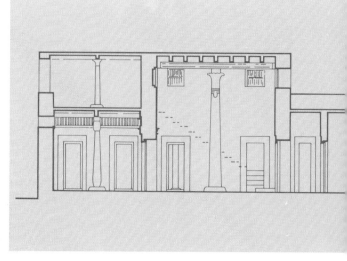

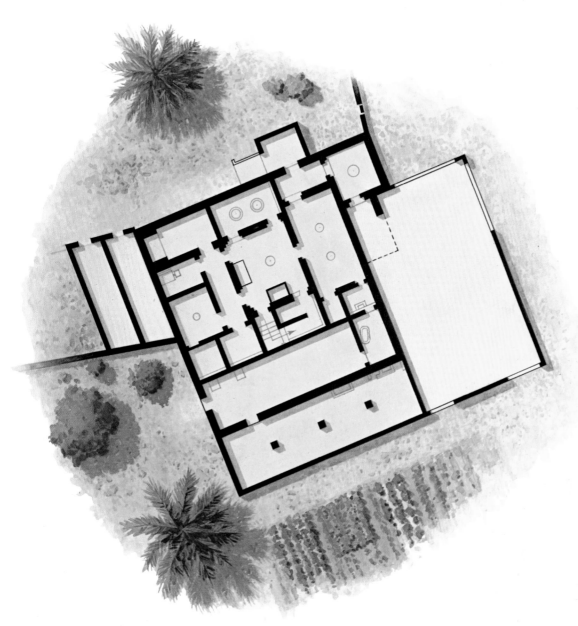

This modest villa in the North Suburb (the section on the *opposite page* cuts the house plan left to right) had its kitchen and servants' quarters in the main building. There was an entrance lobby (bottom of the plan) and loggias to the left and at the bottom, each with two columns, and a central two-storied hall with staircase leading to the upper floor. The private section to the right included hall, bedroom, smaller rooms and bathroom and latrine. Domestic buildings were constructed of plastered mud-brick, with stone and wood used for certain parts.

A gardener waters his garden from the Nile. Akhetaten depended greatly on the river for its crops, garden and transportation.

Akhenaten's brave experiment in
setting up a new life and a new
religion in a city of his founding
began between the fourth and sixth
years of his reign, when he had 14
boundary stelae erected to demarcate
the exact limits of his dream city. It
ended, after his death in the 17th year
of his reign, with the savage
destruction of his city and repudiation
of his beliefs. But the heart had already
gone out of the enterprise about three
years earlier when Queen Nefertiti
(*above, right*) seems to have died. To
fill the void Akhenaten took on
Smenkhkare, possibly a younger
brother, as co-regent and married
him to his eldest daughter Merytaten
The charming painted relief (*below,
right*) is generally accepted as
representing the young couple.

But Smenkhkare himself died in a few
years. The nine-year-old child,
Tutankhamun, then became king and
had no choice but to return to Thebes
and to the old ways again. For in
following his dream Akhenaten had
thrown over the powerful state
church of Amun in favor of his sun-
god, the Aten, and had antagonized
the ruling classes of Egypt with his
unorthodox ideas. Moreover, in his
preoccupation with religious affairs
he had allowed Egypt's empire to
disintegrate and had left Egypt itself
in an economic mess.

The reaction against Akhenaten's ideas
was even more brutal than his own
repudiation of Egypt's traditional
ways. His monuments were
mutilated and his very name cursed
and removed from the records. His
city of Akhetaten was first deserted
and its buildings desecrated, then
finally pulled down stone by stone to
be used in building projects elsewhere. The recovery of many of
these stones, including many reliefs,
and the excavation of the site itself
have enabled archaeologists to regain
some of the life and shape of
Akhetaten as illustrated here.

VI
BUILDING AND PLANTING

The Egyptians were an immensely practical people who devoted great thought and energy to the problems involved in coming to terms with their very special environment. Since ancient Egypt was predominantly an agricultural country, most of its inhabitants were involved in one way or another with the cultivation of the land and the processing and marketing of its products. A peculiarity of the growing cycle, as we have seen, was that during the period of inundation, about three months annually, agricultural work became impossible because the Nile waters rose and spread over the land. In late November and early December the waters subsided and plowing and sowing then commenced. We have an invaluable and detailed record of the agricultural cycle and the kind of tools that were used in the paintings in the tombs of the nobles.

The plow was developed at an early date, and at first it seems to have been pulled by two oxen with the yoke attached to their horns. Later the shoulder yoke was introduced. This could be fitted over the animals' shoulders and made pulling the plow a much easier task. There is evidence that the earliest plows consisted of simple forked branches which the animals pulled through the soil. The handles of the fork were used as handles to guide the plow. These primitive plows produced very narrow furrows so that the larger clods of earth had to be hacked apart with a hoe. The work was doubtless relentless and tiring, but even this simple plow eased the life of the farmer and was one of the most important of early innovations.

The seed could then be scattered in the soil; barley and emmer wheat were the main grain crops. Where the ground was soft and muddy, sheep or pigs were used to trample the seed into the ground. On harder soil a pick was used to cover the seed with soil. The harvest was gathered, often to the accompaniment of singing and flute-playing, in March or April, and the crops were cut with sickles consisting of a line of short flint blades set into bone or wooden handles. Donkeys – the traditional beasts of burden in Egypt – then carried the sheaves away to the villages, where they were emptied from the panniers on to the threshing floor. Sheep, oxen or donkeys again played their part in treading out the grain, and after the separated

Stone model of a man kneading dough, from Saqqara. Old Kingdom, 5th Dynasty.

material had been winnowed it was again packed on donkeys and taken away to the grain silos.

Agricultural processes in Egypt were dependent to a considerable degree on the amount of water available. In a land where rainfall is scarce, the Egyptians came to rely very largely on the Nile waters. The inundation which supplied this water annually originated in central Africa, and there was nothing which the Egyptians could do to regulate the quantity of water or the force with which it entered Upper Egypt. Thus the inundation could bring tragedy as well as blessings. If excessive, the waters could drown villages and people, and yet a scanty Nile often resulted in drought and even famine. The Egyptians of course were aware of their dependence upon the "Nile-god," and took practical measures to ensure a more even, widespread and longer-lasting flow of water. Irrigation was vital. Indeed, Egyptian engineering projects connected with water-direction were among their most important developments.

Channels were dug to allow the water to reach the fields, and the fields themselves were divided into small squares by ditches. From these ditches the water was spread over the fields by means of a shaduf, a water-lifting device that can still be seen in use in Egypt today. The shaduf consists of a long pole pivoted on top of a vertical post. On one end of the pole is a rope and a bucket and on the other end is a counterweight. It is worked manually. The bucket is lowered into the water; when full, the counterweight swings it up to the level of the ground. The saqqieh (water wheel) was a later innovation and can still be seen in Egypt. It provided a more effective and less onerous alternative to the shaduf. Where the river and irrigation channels met, dams were constructed and were used as roads. When the river rose these were broken down to allow the water into the fields. By this process a much larger area of land could be watered, and during the period of germination sufficient water would be stored in the ground to feed the growing crops. During the summer months the ground again became hard, until the inundation once again brought life.

This system of irrigation required constant attention and supervision, and this could only be achieved when the government was stable and men were able to go about their tasks in peace. The constant demands of the land – which had to be met if life was to survive – must have greatly influenced the Egyptian character, with its stability, immutability and love of peace. Tussling with nature, the Egyptians had little time to ponder theoretical questions or alternative systems of government. The maintenance of agriculture and the irrigation system was so important that, from earliest times, it was considered one of the principal duties of the king to perform ceremonial tasks connected with the agricultural cycle. Indeed, it was believed that an early legendary king had been responsible for the introduction of irrigation into Egypt.

Other engineering projects included the experiment in the Fayoum Basin in the 12th Dynasty where a reservoir for storing water was successfully created, with the attendant reclamation of land. There was also the periodic and necessary clearing of the Nile cataracts to enable easier access to Nubia, and the construction of a canal or waterway between the Nile and the Red Sea, part of which was artificial. Despite Egyptian dependence on the river, little attention appears to have been given to bridge building, and small craft were used to transport men and goods from one bank to another.

The ingenious Egyptians thus improved upon nature, enlarging and enriching a very fertile strip of land which was covered annually with rich black Nile mud. Crops other than grain were grown – grapes, olives, dates and figs. Their animals included cattle, sheep, antelopes, goats, pigs, geese, ducks, pigeons and cranes, and dogs, cats and donkeys. The Egyptian diet – at least that of the nobles – was quite varied, and included various kinds of meat from

Painting from a tomb at Thebes showing building workers making mud-bricks and carrying stones for tomb building.

New Kingdom, 18th Dynasty. A detail of the original from which the drawing on page 106 was made.

dates back to the predynastic period, and as early as the Old Kingdom workshops employed women on a large scale to carry out spinning and weaving. The linen produced was of a fine weave, and was usually plain white, although red, yellow and blue linens, achieved by using basic dyes, were not uncommon. Patterned material was probably rare, and wool, even in wintertime, was only used for light cloaks.

A thriving industry existed then, as it does today, for beauty preparations – cosmetics compounded of animal fats or plant oils, and scented with aromatic substances pressed out of plants; and wigs, produced either from real hair or from vegetable fibers.

Glass and pottery, glazed and unglazed, were manufactured primarily for the domestic market, and although serviceable and often attractive, never became an art form. The earliest clay vessels of predynastic times were handmade by tedious and slow methods, either by forcing slabs of clay into preformed molds or by building up the pot with rings of clay. Kilns came into use sometime before the 5th Dynasty. These were tall structures resembling chimneys, with openings at the top partly blocked with mud or stones. The introduction of the potter's wheel revolutionized the process; production became far more rapid and efficient. The clay was softened by treading, and the wares were then prepared for the kiln on a low turntable, probably made of wood or clay. This was quite unlike the modern potter's wheel in that it could not rotate continuously.

Glass was manufactured in Egypt from the 18th Dynasty, although blown glass was unknown before

Figures making pottery. Various stages in the process are shown, from molding the clay to baking the pots in a kiln.

Roman times. The glass objects included small vessels and beads. Some glass was colored, using manganese, copper, cobalt and iron, and was often used for inlay to imitate semi-precious stones.

Glazing dates from predynastic times. "Egyptian faience," a distinctive blue, green or turquoise glaze, was used for beads, amulets, inlaid work, ushabtis, vases and jewelry to simulate rare, imported lapis lazuli. Other colors, such as red, cream or black, were also produced.

Upper register: Old Kingdom frieze of carpenters constructing beds and headrests. *Lower register:* men and women making bread. They are shown pounding wheat to make flour and kneading the dough.

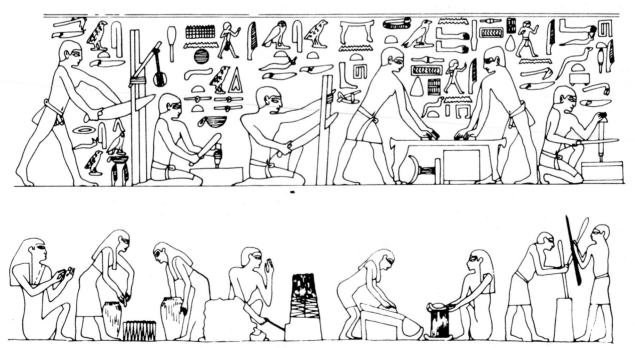

"Egyptian faience" consisted of a core of quartz, covered with a thin glaze and colored blue by heating the material with copper ores. It differed from modern faience, and today can only be found in remote parts of Persia.

An outstanding feature of Egyptian technology is the way in which stone tools – such as the carefully shaped flint and obsidian knives – were never entirely replaced even by copper or bronze tools – and certainly never by iron. The older forms continued to be used alongside the new. Nevertheless the natural resources of Egypt were great, and abundant supplies of stone and gold ensured great advances in these crafts. In fact Egypt's glut of gold enabled her to purchase from other countries the commodities which she lacked – notably timber. Her craftsmen – whether architects, sculptors, painters, stonemasons or carpenters – were extremely versatile. They could produce both massive buildings and colossal statuary which defied the passage of time, or exclusive jewelry which, in its perfection and attention to minute detail, has seldom been matched.

Moreover the Egyptians developed for practical purposes, in connection with their engineering and architectural feats, an impressive command of mathematics and astronomy. Systems of measurement for length, area and weight were established, a decimal system of calculation was in use and a calendar, based on the agricultural seasons, existed. In Ptolemaic times, a research institute of engineering studies was set up at the newly-built Museum of Alexandria; here three outstanding inventors – Hero, Ctesibius and Philo of Byzantium – produced various hydraulic devices, including a water clock, a water organ, a fire engine and a device to open temple doors. These are known to us only from literary sources. Another inventor, Archimedes, made, among other things, a screw-pump for raising water from mines. Military equipment, such as the catapult and crossbow, was also studied here and possibly it was at this Museum that the water-wheel, known in Egypt and elsewhere by the 1st century AD, was developed.

However, scientific research, even at this institution, was limited in its objectives, and no new sources of power were discovered to increase the prosperity of the country, nor were any efficient methods developed to ease the lot of the peasant and to improve industry. Egyptian technology, like so much else in Egypt, changed little over the centuries. Techniques established long ago were acceptable to succeeding generations, and advances in most fields came early, often during the years of the Old Kingdom, when the foundations of the civilization were being laid.

The wisdom of the ancient Egyptians is legendary, and they made significant contributions to many branches of learning. In their continuing quest for eternity and in their attempt to conquer both death and their earthly environment, they stand out among ancient peoples. Perhaps their greatest legacy to succeeding generations lies in their indestructible belief in the ability and supremacy of man.

Further Reading

GENERAL

Aldred, C., *The Egyptians* (Ancient Peoples and Places) (London, 1961).

Baines, J. and **Málek, J.,** *Atlas of Ancient Egypt* (Oxford, 1980).

David, A. R. and **A. E.,** *Ancient Egypt* (History as Evidence series, London, 1984).

Desroches-Noblecourt, C., *Tutankhamen* (London, 1971).

Drower, M. S., *Flinders Petrie — A Life in Archaeology* (London, 1985).

Edwards, I. E. S., *The Pyramids of Egypt* (London, 1961).

Emery, W. B., *Archaic Egypt* (London, 1961).

Gardiner, A. H., *Egypt of the Pharaohs* (Oxford, 1961).

Hayes, W. C., *The Scepter of Egypt*—A background for the study of the Egyptian antiquities in the Metropolitan Museum of Art, New York, Parts 1 and 2 (New York, 1959 and 1960).

Lewis, N., *Life in Egypt under Roman Rule* (Oxford, 1985).

Posener, G., *A Dictionary of Egyptian Civilization* (English edition, London, 1962).

Trigger, B. G., Kemp, B. J., O'Connor, D., and **Lloyd, A. B.,** *Ancient Egypt: A Social History* (Cambridge, 1983).

Wilson, J. A., *The Burden of Egypt* (Chicago, 1954).

ART

Aldred, C., *Old Kingdom Art in Ancient Egypt* (London, 1949); *Middle Kingdom Art in Ancient Egypt* (London, 1950); *New Kingdom Art in Ancient Egypt during the 18th Dynasty* (London, 1961).

Davies, N. M., *Ancient Egyptian Paintings*, 3 vols. (Chicago, 1936).

Iversen, E., *Canon and Proportions in Egyptian Art* (Warminster, 1975).

Peck, W. H., *Drawings from Ancient Egypt* (London, 1978).

Rochewiltz, B. de, *An Introduction to Egyptian Art* (English translation, London, 1967).

Schäfer, H., *Principles of Egyptian Art* (English translation, Oxford, 1974).

Stevenson Smith, W., *The Art and Architecture of Ancient Egypt* (Pelican History of Art, London, 1958).

RELIGION

Černý, J., *Ancient Egyptian Religion* (London, 1952).

David, A. R., *A Guide to Religious Ritual at Abydos* (Warminster, 1981).

—— *The Ancient Egyptians: Religious Beliefs and Practices* (London, 1982).

David, A. R. and **Tapp, E.,** *Evidence Embalmed: Modern Medicine and the Mummies of Ancient Egypt* (Manchester, 1984).

Dawson, W. R. and **Gray, P. H. K.,** *Mummies and Human Remains* (London, 1968).

Fairman, H. W., "Worship and Festivals in an Egyptian Temple" in the *Bulletin of the John Rylands Library, Manchester*, Vol. 37, No. 1, Sept. 1954.

TRAVELERS

Wortham, J. D., *British Egyptology 1549–1906* (Newton Abbot, England, 1971).

HIEROGLYPHS

Gardiner, A. H., *Egyptian Grammar* (3rd ed., Oxford, 1957).

TECHNOLOGY

David, A. R., *The Pyramid Builders of Ancient Egypt: A Modern Investigation of Pharaoh's Workforce* (London, 1986).

Hodges, H., *Technology in the Ancient World* (London, 1970).

Lucas, A., *Ancient Egyptian Materials and Industries* (4th ed., London, 1962).

Acknowledgments

Unless otherwise stated all the illustrations on a given page are credited to the same source.

Ashmolean Museum, Oxford 57 (bottom right) 58 (exc. center) 60 (exc. bottom left) 61 (left top and bottom) 62 (exc. bottom right) 64 (top left) 76 (left) 79 (top) 123 (top right) 126 (top and center) 128 (top)

A. M. Badawy (after *A History of Egyptian Architecture*) 105 (top) 119 (bottom left) 125 126 (bottom right) 127 (top)

Boston Museum of Fine Arts 124 (bottom)

British Museum 50 (right)

Brooklyn Museum, New York, 122 (bottom left) 123 (bottom right) 127 (bottom)

E. Brunner-Traut (from *Die altägyptischen Scherbenbilder*) 69

J. L. Burckhardt (from *Denkmäler Nubian*) 54

Cairo Museum 107 (left)

A. M. Calverley (after *The Temple of King Sethos I at Abydos*) 96 (top and bottom) 98 99 (exc. bottom)

A. R. David 19 (bottom left exc. insets)

Description de l'Égypte 2 47 (bottom) 49 (inset) 81 (top right) 94 (bottom left)

C. Desroches-Noblecourt (after *Tutankhamen*) 57 (bottom left)

EDITO Service, Photo Rencontre, Geneva 108

Egypt Exploration Society 89

Elsevier Amsterdam 13 19 (bottom left insets) 30 33 (bottom) 35 (bottom) 36 37 38 39 42 50 52 76 (top right) 79 (bottom)

82 83 96 (center) 100 106 107 (right) 111 119 (top left) 120 121 122 (top) 125 126 (bottom left) 127 (top)

W. B. Emery (after *Archaic Egypt*) 35 (top)

Fairman (after *Worship and Festival*) 95 (center)

A. Held, Ecublems 31 80 105 (center) 130 131

A. A. M. van der Heyden, Amsterdam 9 10 (bottom) 15 16 17 20 21 (exc. inset) 22 24 25 26 27 28 34 40 41 44 (bottom) 46 (inset) 48 49 (exc. inset) 50 (left) 52 53 (left) 55 56 65 66 68 70 72 73 74 77 78 84 85 86 87 91 94 (bottom right) 97 (top) 101 102 103 107 (left) 115

Holle Verlag GmbH, Baden-Baden 10 (right) 11 12 19 (top and right) 21 (inset) 30 (far left top and bottom) 51 53 (right) 59 60 (bottom left) 63 67 71 73 76 (bottom right) 92 93 110 113 114 118 128 (bottom) 129 133 135

F. L. Kennett, London 61 (right)

Manchester Museum 4, 5, 6, 7

Metropolitan Museum, New York 29 (right)

H. W. Müller, München 32 (left)

E. Otto (after *Egyptian Art and the Cults of Osiris and Amon*) 99 (bottom)

J. D. S. Pendlebury (after *The City of Akhenaten*) 120 121

Photographie Giraudon, Paris 124 (top)

Photographie Viollet, Paris 64 (bottom right) 95 (bottom)

Photo Scala, Florence 117

D. Roberts, G. Croly and W. Brockendon (from *The Holy Land*) 33 (top) 44 (left) 45 46 (left) 47 (top) 81 (bottom left) 94 (top 97 (bottom)

The Publishers have attempted to observe the legal requirements with respect to the rights of the suppliers of photographic material. Nevertheless, persons who have claims are invited to apply to the Publishers.

Glossary

Adze A metal instrument which was used in ancient Egypt in the "Ceremony of Opening of the Mouth," when the statues and mummies were believed to be reanimated by a vital force and to "come to life" with the performance of a ritual which included the priest touching the face of the statue of the mummy with the adze.

Alabaster Egyptian "alabaster" is a calcite, white or yellow in color and used widely in Egypt, for building, vases and the inlay of eyes in statues etc. It occurs in various localities in the desert to the east of the Nile, the most famous perhaps being the ancient Hatnub.

Alexandria, Museum and Library Alexandria was founded by Alexander the Great and grew from a small native village into one of the greatest of ancient cities and sea-ports. With the development of Hellenistic civilization, Alexandria became a great cultural center and the Museum and Library were places of learning renowned throughout the world.

Amethyst One of the most popular semi-precious stones used in jewelry and inlay work by Egyptian craftsmen. Amethyst was acquired from Nubia.

Ammianus Marcellinus In his *Roman History* this writer (born c. 330 AD) gives details of monuments, hieroglyphs and the flora and fauna of the Nile Valley.

Amulet A charm, made of stone, glass, gold, bronze or often of faience, which was used by the Egyptians as a means of magical protection, both in life and in death. They were worn as jewelry in life and inserted in the mummy-wrappings in death. Amulets have many forms – little figurines of gods, royal emblems, hieroglyphs and special forms such as the wedjat-eye, scarab, djed-pillar etc. The idea behind some amuletic forms was imitation – parts of the body in amulet form gave protection to the various limbs and organs of the body.

Amun Originally the local tribal god of the Theban district. When the Theban princes seized the throne of Egypt, Amun rose with them to great power, becoming the supreme deity of the state pantheon in the 18th Dynasty. His greatest temple was Karnak at Thebes, where he was associated

with Re' and became Amen-Re'. His priesthood eventually rivaled the power of the king.

Ankh, the symbol of life

Ankh Sign This was the hieroglyphic sign meaning "life," and was depicted in tomb and temple scenes, often held in the hands of deities. It had a magical, protective force for the bearer. The sign symbolizes a sandal as seen from above – the ancient Egyptian word for a "sandal" was pronounced in a similar way to the word for "life" and therefore the sandal was also used in hieroglyphic writing to represent the word "life."

Annealing In this process the copper, hammered to make it increasingly hard, is annealed before it becomes too brittle and cracks; the metal is gently re-heated and allowed to cool, which makes it soft and malleable again. The annealing process is often repeated several times.

Anubis The jackal-headed god who had embalmed Osiris and was in control of mummification, as well as being the patron of embalmers and "Lord of the Necropolis." His center was at Cynopolis, but he was also worshiped widely elsewhere. One of the most famous statues of Anubis is that which was discovered in Tutankhamun's tomb, crouching in protection of his royal master.

Atef Crown The most elaborate of Egyptian crowns, this combines various elements and is shown on the heads of gods or kings; the White Crown, sun's disk, uraei, two feathers and ram's horns are common components of it. It was worn by the king at his coronation.

Aten The "Aten" was the disk of the sun. It became the central symbol of Pharaoh Akhenaten's solar monotheism in the 18th Dynasty when the sun's disk was regarded as

the agent of the universal power, dispensing light, warmth and life to mankind. Although the word occurs much earlier in Egyptian texts, Akhenaten gave the word a special significance, changing his own name from Amenophis to Akhen*aten* and giving his city and his children names which incorporated the word.

Aten

Azurite A deep blue basic carbonate of copper, occurring in copper deposits. It was used as a source of metallic copper and as a pigment, and probably in the production of blue glaze. It was found in Sinai and the eastern desert.

Basalt See under **Dolerite**.

Bas-relief (Low Relief) The Egyptians decorated the surfaces of tomb and temple walls, stelae and parts of statues with carved reliefs, which have the appearance of tomb-paintings but are modeled in relief to give added interest. In antiquity the reliefs were painted with bright colors, although today much of the color has been worn away.

Bas-relief from the pyramid of Unas

Two basic types of relief were used: bas-relief, which produced finer results, was achieved by cutting away the background, leaving the figures to stand out from the wall with gentle rounded forms; this type of relief was usually employed on inside walls, away from weathering processes. See also **Relief en-Creux**.

Bastet The cat-headed goddess, worshiped at Bubastis. She was the goddess of joy and of the warmth of the sun.

Bedouin The "sand-dwellers," constant insurgents against Egyptian authority from earliest times. They lived on the desert fringes of Egypt and constantly infiltrated into Egypt. They are mentioned on several Egyptian stones, and probably joined in with some of the large-scale invasions of Egypt such as that of the Hyksos.

Belzoni, Giovanni An Italian who was Henry Salt's first agent in Egypt. He had received some training as an engineer and performed various tasks in Egypt such as transporting antiquities up the Nile and cleaning the sand from the temple of Abu Simbel. He also revealed the tomb of King Sethos I in the Valley of the Kings. His crude methods have earned him a notorious reputation in the history of Egyptology.

Lapis lazuli figurine of Bes

Bes The ugly dwarf-like god who was worshiped throughout Egypt as a household deity and fertility god. He was the god of music, jollity, marriage and dancing and was probably worshiped in local shrines, never possessing a temple. Bes was introduced into Egypt probably from Asia Minor.

Black Land "Kemet" or "Black Land" was the name given by the ancient Egyptians to their country – the stretch of country consisting of the Delta and the area bordering on either side of the Nile. It was called "black" on account of the color of the rich mud deposits which the Nile floods annually spread over the land. The Greeks later called the country Aigyptios and its modern name is Misr.

Bruce, James An 18th-century explorer. Hoping to reach the source of the Nile, Bruce went first to Alexandria and then, seeking the source of the Blue Nile, visited many Egyptian sites, paying great attention to the hieroglyphs, especially at Luxor and Karnak.

Bubastis This was the site of a town situated in the Delta, where the inhabitants worshiped the cat-goddess, Bast. The temple of Bast was at Bubastis, and here hundreds of cats were mummified and buried in a necropolis. Bubastis became the capital of Egypt in the 22nd Dynasty.

Burckhardt, Johann Ludwig He explored Nubia between 1813 and 1817, financed by the London-based African Association. His

interest lay in the Islamic rather than the pharaonic culture in Egypt, but he is famous for his discovery of the sand-covered temple complex at Abu Simbel.

Calcite The geological term for "Egyptian alabaster." See under **Alabaster**.

Capital The upper part of a column. In Egyptian architecture there were various styles of capital – representing palm leaves, or a closed or open lotus-bud, or the top of a payrus plant, or the form of a sistrum, Hathor's musical instrument. There were other less common or late composite forms.

Carnarvon (Lord George Edward Stanhope Molyneux, 5th Earl of Carnarvon) (1866–1923) Due to a serious motoring accident, Lord Carnarvon spent his winters in Egypt from 1903; here he met Howard Carter and they began their excavations at Thebes. Apart from the discovery of Tutankhamun's tomb in 1922, other discoveries were also made. Carnarvon died in Egypt of pneumonia and blood poisoning resulting from a mosquito bite. He was present at the opening of Tutankhamun's tomb, but did not live to see the completion of the excavation and clearance.

Carnelian From Nubia, a reddish-brown semi-precious stone widely used in jewelry by the Egyptians.

Carter, Howard (1874–1939) The British Egyptologist who discovered the tomb of Tutankhamun in the Valley of the Kings in 1922. Carter was born in London and commenced his career as an Egyptologist by joining the Archaeological Survey, under Newberry, in 1891; he went out to Egypt in 1892 to join Petrie's excavation at Amarna. In 1899 he was appointed Inspector General of Monuments of Upper Egypt and later became Inspector of Lower Egypt. Finally, in 1907, he joined Lord Carnarvon and from 1919 he searched the Valley of the Kings for the tomb of Tutankhamun. Carter and his staff worked for ten years on the packing and removal of the treasures from this tomb. He was the author of various works, including a popular book on Tutankhamun's tomb. He died in London in 1939, 17 years after the tomb of Tutankhamun had been discovered.

Cartonnage Gesso (whiting and glue) was applied to linen in layers to form cartonnage mummy masks and coffins, which were painted and gilded.

Cartouche A loop of rope with a knot at one end, the so-called cartouche probably represented the universe; the custom of writing the pharaoh's name inside was meant to convey his dominion over the universe. Of the five royal names in the title of the king,

two are written inside cartouches. In translation from hieroglyphs, it is an immediate assistance in identifying a royal name.

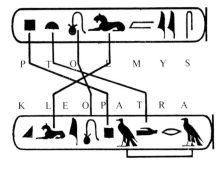

Cartouches of Ptolemys and Kleopatra

Caviglia, Giovanni Battista A former Italian sea-captain, Caviglia made various discoveries in his excavation of the Great Pyramid at Gizeh in the early 19th century. He also removed the sand from the Sphinx and carried out the first exploration of the nobles' tombs at Gizeh.

Champollion, Jean Francois One of the most famous of Egyptologists. His decipherment of hieroglyphs enabled the study of Egyptology to develop rapidly over the last hundred years. Born in 1790 in France, Champollion lived to be 42, finally becoming a professor at the Collège de France in 1831. In 1822, having studied the Coptic language and all other attempts at the decipherment of hieroglyphs, he explained his discovery of the correct interpretation of the language and writing of the ancient Egyptians.

Chasing The process of hammering or punching a design on metal.

Cheops A 4th-Dynasty king who was responsible for the building of the Great Pyramid at Gizeh as his tomb. His mother Hetepheres was buried at Gizeh and the furniture from her tomb has been reconstituted and includes bed, chair, canopy etc. She was one of Sneferu's several wives. The length of Cheops' reign is uncertain – Manetho gives him 63 years, but another source states 23 years.

Chephren (Khafre) The successor of his father Cheops, Chephren ruled for 66 years, according to Manetho. His pyramid is the second largest at Gizeh, where the Funerary Temple can also be seen; the Sphinx was probably carved out of a natural outcrop of rock during this reign, and given the pharaoh's facial features.

Chrysocolla A bluish-green or blue ore of copper, used in ancient Egypt as a source of metallic copper, and occasionally as an eye-paint, worked either in Sinai or the eastern desert.

Cire-perdue (Lost Wax) A method of casting which involved the making of a wax mold of the object to be cast, covered with clay to form the mold; this was embedded in sand and heated until the wax melted and disappeared, leaving the mold ready to receive the molten metal which was poured into the mold. Once the metal had cooled, the mold was broken away to reveal the statue or object.

City State A self-governing city, ruled by a king or leader, and sometimes a group of councilors, which was entirely responsible for its own internal and external policies. Sometimes a group of such city states would share a common culture, as with the Sumerian and Greek city states, but they were nevertheless politically and economically independent of each other. Often such states were theocracies, under the direct control of a particular deity whose supposed wishes were implicitly obeyed. Warfare between neighboring city states was a common feature.

Claudius Ptolemaeus Author of a *Geography* (c. 510 AD), which includes a brief account of the districts and towns of Egypt.

Clement of Alexandria This writer (c. 150–215 AD) gives one of the earliest descriptions of Egyptian hieroglyphs, which, although less extraordinary than some accounts, was still incorrect.

Clerestory The method of lighting employed in the hypostyle halls of the pharaonic temples; stone grids were inserted between the top of the walls and the roof slabs, to allow the penetration of shafts of daylight.

Cloisonné Enamels and glass were set with their surfaces flush to the surrounding metal; the enamel was set into a sunken area, or, in the case of cloisonné work, the enamel, glass or stones were set into wire, often gold, soldered on to the metal background. The ancient Egyptians were particularly skillful at this type of work.

Cobalt Compounds were used by artists as a deep blue pigment and also to color glass. Colbalt compounds were probably imported from Persia or the Caucasus region.

Coffin Texts In the Middle Kingdom, when the ordinary man gained the right to expect an afterlife, the magical formulas, used originally to protect the king in the hereafter, were converted to the use of the ordinary citizen. The texts were painted on the inside of wooden coffins and thus are known today as "Coffin Texts." This type of usage is limited to the Middle Kingdom and a brief resurgence in the 26th Dynasty.

Colossi of Memnon These two enormous statues, now to be seen dominating the Theban plain on the west bank of the Nile at Luxor, were statues of Amenophis III of the New Kingdom which once stood before the pylon of a great temple. The temple has now completely disappeared.

Colossus A statue, usually of a god or king, which is many times larger than life-size.

Coptic The final form of the ancient Egyptian language, which was written in the Greek script with the addition of several new signs. This form was in general use until the Middle Ages in Egypt and continues today in the liturgy of the Coptic Church. "Coptic" is also a general term referring to the aspects of art, architecture and literature which relate to the Christian community in Egypt.

Crucible A container with a lip on one side used for casting bronze.

Ctesibius The son of a local barber, he entered the Alexandrian Museum and was responsible for a number of inventions, including pieces of artillery, a weapon that worked by means of compressed air, a fire-engine and a water-organ which utilized air and water. The piece of artillery which was designed to work on compressed air, however, was never in use because of the inadequacy of materials employed in its manufacture.

Cultus Temple An Egyptian temple where the daily ritual was performed in honor of the god or group of deities. Cultus temples also included areas where the festivals of the temple deity were held.

Cuneiform The term applied to the symbols used in Mesopotamia in ancient times, and in which the various languages of the area – Sumerian, Babylonian, Assyrian etc. – were written. The method employed was to impose the symbols using a wedge-shaped tool on wet mud, which, when sun-dried, has preserved cuneiform texts until today.

Cursive The rounded scripts, such as Hieratic and Demotic, developed from hieroglyphs, often referred to as "cursive." They were written with a reed pen and ink on papyrus or ostraca; hieroglyphs, on the other hand, although sometimes written in this way, were more often used in stone carving.

Cylinder Seal A cylindrical piece of stone with an inscription carved on the outside which, when rolled out on clay, produced an impression of either a name or a title. Such seals were used throughout the ancient Near East to indicate ownership. The cylinder seal was perhaps introduced into Egypt just before the Archaic Period.

Middle Kingdom cylinder seal

Dahibeyeh A type of boat in use in Egypt for transporting people and goods on the Nile; many of the early travelers to Egypt in the last two and a half centuries rented this type of boat and made the slow voyage up the Nile from Cairo to Aswan and beyond.

Death Mask A mask of gold, silver, wood or cartonnage, molded and painted in the likeness of an idealized man or woman, which was placed over the face of the mummified body. Some masks were likenesses of the deceased, such as the famous gold mask of Tutankhamun.

Demotic This cursive script appeared towards the end of the 7th century BC and was a development of the hieroglyphic script. New vocabulary and grammatical structure were also introduced. As its name suggests, it was the script generally used for day-to-day legal and administrative business, continuing alongside hieroglyphs and Hieratic which were retained for religious texts.

Diorite One of the types of stone used by the ancient Egyptians for vases and statuary; their source of diorite has been discovered 40 miles north-west of Abu Simbel.

Dolerite The name given to the coarser varieties of basalt, a black rock used in the Old Kingdom for architecture, especially for paving-stones. It probably came from the Fayoum and in general is widely distributed throughout Egypt. It was also used for vases, axeheads etc.

Dynasty Manetho, the historian, divided Egypt's history into dynasties. The exact meaning of this term is uncertain; often a dynasty consists of the members of one family of rulers, but sometimes consecutive dynasties are related. Because Manetho's scheme provides modern Egyptologists with a concise system, the division into dynasties has been retained.

Ebers Papyrus The famous medical papyrus which Georg Ebers acquired from Edwin Smith at Luxor and which he published with an introduction and glossary by Edwin Stern. Ebers was a German Egyptologist who lived 1837–1898 AD.

Edwin Smith Papyrus An important medical papyrus, acquired by Edwin Smith, an American adventurer and dealer who lived at Luxor until 1876 AD. The papyrus deals mainly with Egyptian surgical treatments.

Egypt Exploration Society With the assistance of Reginald Stuart Poole and Sir Erasmus Wilson, Miss Amelia Edwards founded the Egypt Exploration Fund in 1882 to carry out the scientific exploration and accurate publication of Egyptian monuments and antiquities. Miss Edwards acted as secretary and excavations were carried out by Petrie and Naville. Today the Egypt Exploration Society continues the tradition of British excavation in Egypt; it produces various academic publications, including the annual *Journal of Egyptian Archaeology*, and organizes a yearly series of specialized lectures.

Electrum Originally a natural alloy of gold and silver, producing a pale gold-colored metal. It came to Egypt from Kush (Nubia), Punt (on the Red Sea coast) and various other sites south of Egypt. It was used for jewelry and overlaying obelisks.

Embalming The process of preserving a body after death by artificial means. The ancient Egyptians used the method known as "mummification," by which they dehydrated the skin tissue and applied ointments to the desiccated corpse, attemping to preserve the features of the person as he had appeared in life.

Eusebius (earth 4th cent. AD) and **Sextus Julius Africanus** (early 3rd cent. AD) Christian writers in whose works was preserved a shortened version of Manetho's writings.

Faience Egyptian faience, not to be confused with true "faience," is made from glazed quartz frit (powdered quartz) and was usually a greenish-blue color. There were several varieties of faience, but the typical ware consisted of a cone coated with a vitreous alkaline glaze. Small objects – scarabs, amulets, beads, pieces for inlay – as well as ushabti figures, statues and vases were made of it.

Felspar Also known as Amazon stone, felspar is an opaque green stone, found in various of the Egyptian wadis and used for beads in ancient Egypt, especially in Middle Kingdom jewelry and for amulets and inlay in Tutankhamun's tomb.

"First Occasion" The term applied in the texts to the time of the creation of the universe, a time when perfection was the norm and when all the laws, ethics and religious ideas were established for all time. The Egyptians forever attempted to return to this "First Occasion."

Flake A by-product of the process whereby implements and weapons were chiseled out of stone.

Flax Some of the tomb scenes in Egypt show the cultivation of flax, which grew in abundance in Egypt and was used from predynastic times onwards, particularly for fine linen, but also for matting, cordage and basketry.

Frit An artificial compound used as early as the 4th Dynasty in ancient Egypt, which consisted of a crystalline compound of silica, copper and calcium; it was made by heating together silica, a copper compound, calcium carbonate and natron. It was used as a blue pigment, and also in the manufacture of beads, amulets and blue or green pottery vases.

Glaze It has been suggested that glaze was first probably produced by accident, and the basic necessary ingredients for the blue glaze of ancient Egypt were "an alkali, copper or a copper compound, a stone to form a base for the glaze and a fire" (Lucas, *Ancient Egyptian Materials and Industries*, 1962).

Grave Goods The equipment – domestic articles, jewelry, cosmetics, clothes, food, drink, magical protective devices – which was placed in the tombs or graves of the ancient Egyptians, to provide all the requirements for survival after death.

Great Papyrus Harris Papyrus Harris No. 1 is in the possession of the British Museum, and it dates to the 20th Dynasty, perhaps forming part of the archives of the library of the temple at Medinet Habu. It is a state document and gives a wealth of information including the benefactions made by Ramesses III to the various divinities in Egypt and a detailed account of the donations received by the temples from various sources.

Greaves, John He visited Egypt in the mid-17th century and published his *Pyramidographia*, being the first scientific study of the pyramids, with exact measurements which he had made himself. He also entered the Great Pyramid and noted that the walls were not covered with hieroglyphs as earlier writers had claimed.

Gypsum A natural material, varying in color from white to light brown. Gypsum occurred in Egypt to the west of Alexandria, near Suez, in the Fayoum and near the Red Sea coast, in rock formations or scattered just under the desert surface near Cairo, and Alexandria. It was used for mortar and plaster in the Gizeh necropolis and obtained from the Fayoum; also it was employed to plaster walls, statues, to cover bodies, model masks and make molds. It was also used as an adhesive, in eye-paint and as a pigment.

Hand-axe Early man in the Nile Valley used stone implements, chiseled from larger blocks, for all his hunting and domestic needs. Stone implements continued to be used in Egypt alongside copper and bronze tools for many generations. One end of the axe was pointed for cutting, the other rounded for holding in the hand.

Harem The ancient Egyptian harem, unlike the concept of an Oriental harem, was a quarter of the master's house where the women went about their duties – weaving, rearing small children etc. They were never confined to the harem. On a larger scale, the royal harems were organized on an industrial scale, supervised by a male bureaucracy, where textiles were woven by the royal women and their female servants.

Harpocrates "Horus the Child," son of Osiris and Isis, is usually shown wearing the double crown of the pharaohs, the "sidelock of youth" – a lock of hair worn at the side of the head by children – and with his finger in his mouth.

Hathor The goddess of music, love and dancing. Hathor often appeared in the form of a cow; she was also a sky-goddess, nurse of the Egyptian king, and often associated with Isis as mother of Horus. One of her greatest temples was at Denderah and she also had a chapel in Hatshepshut's temple at Deir el-Bahri. Outside Egypt, she was worshiped at Byblos, Punt and by the communities of miners in Sinai.

Hay, Robert A Scottish landowner who explored the ancient monuments of Egypt in the mid-19th century. His party of explorers included artists, an architect and an Arabic scholar.

Hecateus of Miletus A Classical author who visited Egypt c. 500 BC and wrote a *Periegesis* or "Survey of the Earth," which is now lost, but which apparently described some of the geographical aspects of Egypt.

Hellenistic The term applied to the various aspects of the civilization which flourished under the rule of Alexander the Great's generals, after his death. This is also known as the Ptolemaic period in Egypt when a line of Ptolemies, the most famous of whom was Cleopatra, imposed certain Greek values on the Egyptian native population and culture.

Hero The Museum at Alexandria, founded by Ptolemy Soter, became a research institute where scholars came from all over the world. Hero was one of these scholars; he had been a pupil of Strato, a contemporary of Aristotle at the Lyceum in Athens. Hero wrote a textbook of engineering, although many of the ideas may be attributed to Strato. He invented a water-clock, a device for cutting screws and a steam turbine, which was regarded as merely an interesting invention although the principles involved could have been developed to provide a wider source of power. Hero also invented a mechanism for opening temple doors.

Herodotus The most famous of the writers of antiquity to have described the geology, geography, social conditions, religious beliefs and customs of ancient Egypt. This Greek from Halicarnassus, sometimes described as the "Father of History," visited Egypt in 450 BC and includes in his work descriptions of some of the sites he reached. His history of the country is based on the accounts given to him by the priests, and, if not always accurate, his anecdotes are amusing and entertaining. This book, the second in his *Histories*, provides a wealth of first-hand knowledge.

Hieratic A cursive script derived from hieroglyphic writing, which simplified the pictorial hieroglyphs. Hieratic was known to the earliest dynasties and was used until the end of the New Kingdom. It was used in legal and business documents, being written on papyrus or pieces of stone with a reed. It was finally replaced as a popular script by Demotic.

Hieroglyphs The script of ancient Egypt which first appeared, fully developed, c. 3100 BC and which continued until the Roman period. This pictorial script, which consisted of phonograms (sound values) and ideograms (picture signs with no sound value), was used mainly for religious and literary texts, with the Hieratic and Demotic scripts being used for daily business and correspondence.

Horapollo Author of an early work on the decipherment of Egyptian hieroglyphs.

Horus The name Horus was applied, in various forms, to different deities; there was the early sky-god, in the form of a falcon, who protected the ruler; also Horus or Haroeris (Horus the Elder) was the husband of Hathor; Horus the younger, "Horus son of Isis" (Harsiesis), was the child of Osiris and

Isis, who avenged his father's death by fighting Seth; Harmakhis, or "Horus of the Horizon," was the personification of the rising sun and represented eternal life.

Amulet of the Horus falcon

Hypostyle Each Egyptian cultus or mortuary temple possessed one or more hypostyle halls, where the columns supported the slabs of the roof. Placed close together, the columns represented verdant plant life, and the hypostyle hall of a temple may be compared to the reception area in a palace or house.

Sign of Isis

Isis As the wife of Osiris, Isis became the symbol of an ideal help-mate and mother. She played a great part in the Osirian myth and was very popular in Egypt, becoming the typical mother-goddess figure. Although Isis never had her own cult or temple in Egypt until the Roman period, her cult continued and spread outside Egypt after the decline of Egyptian civilization. In Egyptian mythology she was sister of Nephthys and of her own husband Osiris. Her son was Horus the younger, who is usually shown seated on his mother's knee.

Island of Creation The mythological place of origin of Egypt and its inhabitants, described in the Edfu Building Texts. This island was believed to have arisen from the waters of chaos at the time of creation of the world and to have become the first home of both gods and men. Each temple, it was believed, was a re-creation of this island – a protective place for the resident deity – and many of the architectural features of the temples were an attempt to re-create the features of this island.

Josephus This Jewish historian (born c. 38

AD) preserves extracts of the *History of Egypt* written by Manetho.

Juvenal This author (47–127 AD) included in his *Satires* criticisms of the animal worship of the Egyptians.

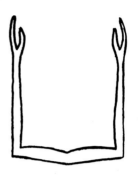

Sign for Ka

Ka The vital energy or spirit of a man, which the Egyptians believed continued after death. The Ka was also envisaged as a person's "double" to whom the food and drink offerings could be offered at the tomb after death. The Ka when depicted is shown as a human figure with both arms upraised above the head, with the palms of the hands to the front. The priests who attended to the provisioning and ritual upkeep of a deceased man's tomb were known as "Ka-priests," and the tomb itself, believed to be the home of the dead man after death, was called the "House of the Ka."

Khnum The ram-headed god of Elephantine who, in one of the creation legends, is said to have created mankind on his potter's wheel. He is shown in scenes of the coronation, making images of the king.

King Lists These lists were placed in the temples of Egypt, where they played a part in the ritual of the Royal Ancestors, when the food which had reverted from the god's altar was then offered to all the king's royal ancestors. The lists are therefore incomplete, giving only the names of the rulers up to the date of the reign of the owner of the temple; also rulers who were not "acceptable" or were considered heretical were not included in these lists. They thus have a limited value to the historian and must not be regarded as accurate historical monuments. However they do provide valuable information regarding the sequence of rulers. The lists include the Abydos List, the Palermo Stone, the Turin Canon, the Table of Saqqara and the Table of Karnak.

Kircher, Athanasius A German scholar who studied the Coptic language in his work *Lingua Aegyptiaca restituta* (1643); this step forward in the understanding of Coptic eventually assisted the decipherment of hieroglyphs, although Kircher's interpretations of hieroglyphs were not sound.

Labyrinth Greek and Roman writers wrote of a "Labyrinth" in Egypt built by the legendary Moeris – a place which inspired their admiration. It was the pyramid and funerary complex of King Amenemmes III, built in the Fayoum, and in antiquity was regarded more highly than the pyramids at Gizeh.

Lapis Lazuli Much prized by the Egyptians for inlay in jewelry, this semi-precious stone was introduced into Egypt from Afghanistan. Blue faience was an attempt to imitate it.

Lepsius, Richard An influential Egyptologist of the 19th century who led a Prussian expedition to Egypt in 1842 and later published his findings in an important report which is of considerable value today. The expedition reached Meroë in the far south.

Limestone Consisting of calcium carbonate and small quantities of other ingredients, limestone occurs throughout Egypt in the hills along the Nile Valley. It was used in tombs and temples until the mid-18th Dynasty and occasionally later, but was largely replaced by sandstone. The most important quarries were at Tura, Gebelein, El Bersheh and El Amarna.

Lotus The flower of the lotus – in bud or full-blown – often occurs in architecture, tomb-paintings or as a decorative motif on mirrors, vases and small objects. In particular, in the banqueting scenes shown in the noblemen's tombs, it appears that a lotus blossom was presented to each guest and worn attached to the front of the head circlet. The lotus had a strong sweet smell which endeared it to the Egyptians.

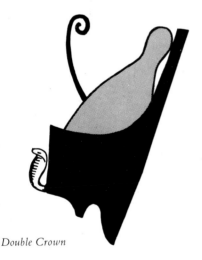

Double Crown

Lower Egypt The northern area of Egypt, centering around the Delta and forming a separate country before 3100 BC; Lower Egypt had its capital at Buto and the goddess was the cobra, Edjo.

This distinction between north and south

was retained throughout Egyptian history. Upper Egypt was called the "White Land" and Lower Egypt the "Red Land." Both originally had distinctive crowns, which were worn by the kings of Egypt after the unification, either on different occasions or amalgamated into the "Double Crown."

Ma'at holding the Ankh sign

Ma'at The goddess of truth and justice in Egypt. Ma'at was represented by a woman wearing an ostrich feather on her head. She symbolized the balance of order in the universe and set down the code of right behavior for human beings. The king was under the guidance of Ma'at, as were his subjects, and he is sometimes shown in temple reliefs presenting a small statue of Ma'at to the gods. She was the daughter of Re', and established order where there had previously been darkness and chaos. On the Day of Judgment the feather of Ma'at was placed in one of the pans of the weighing scales to balance against the heart of the deceased and to establish whether he was "true of voice."

Mace-head Pear-shaped or disk-shaped stone mace-heads were shown from the Archaic Period onwards as symbols of power. Similar implements were found in Mesopotamia. Egyptian kings were shown on wall-reliefs in temples brandishing a mace over a kneeling prisoner-of-war in the ceremonial act of destroying an enemy.

Malachite A green basic carbonate of copper, found in Sinai and the eastern desert of Egypt. This was the earliest ore of copper used in Egypt from the Badarian period onwards, as an eye-paint, a pigment for wall painting and in the coloring of glaze and glass.

Manetho A priest at the temple at Sebennytos, Manetho lived at the beginning of the 3rd century BC. He knew both Greek

and Egyptian hieroglyphs, and is accredited as the author of eight books; his most famous book, unfortunately only preserved in fragments through later writers, was his *History of Egypt*. Although his account is treated with caution, his division of Egyptian history into dynasties is still used by modern Egyptologists.

Manganese Compounds were used in ancient Egypt to give a purple color to glaze and glass, and also rarely as an eye-paint and a pigment for tomb paintings. It is unlikely that it was imported, as only small amounts were used; it was probably acquired from the eastern desert.

Mariette, Auguste One of the most famous French Egyptologists who originally went to Egypt to purchase copies of Coptic manuscripts for the Louvre, and instead discovered the Serapeum at Saqqara. He continued his career in Egypt until his death in 1881 and established the Egyptian Service of Antiquities.

Maspero, Gaston Succeeded Mariette as another French director-general of the Egyptian Service of Antiquities.

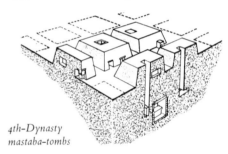

4th-Dynasty mastaba-tombs

Mastaba The modern name given to the private tombs of the nobles of the Old Kingdom at Gizeh and Saqqara. The shape of this type of tomb – rectangular with slightly inclined walls – is reminiscent of a bench, and hence the tomb is referred to by the Arabic word *mastaba*, meaning "bench." These tombs consisted of two parts – buried chamber and chapel, the walls of the latter being decorated with vivid scenes from daily life.

Memphite Theology Memphis, capital city of the newly united Egypt, in 3100 BC established its own religious cosmogony, declaring that Ptah, the local deity, was the creator of the world. The Memphite priests also sought to associate Ptah with Osiris, the god and judge of the dead. This theology was rivaled by the theories of creation prevalent at nearby Heliopolis.

Min The ithyphallic god of fertility. Min's centers were at Koptos and Chemmis. He was also often associated with Amun. He was regarded as a bestower of sexual powers, but also as a rain-god, generating the power to produce growth in the grain. He was associated with various fertility and harvest festivals. His other role was as lord of the foreign lands, and the eastern desert, and as patron of nomadic travelers. His sacred animal was the white bull.

Minoan Civilization The sophisticated civilization which flourished on the island of Crete, centered around the palace of Knossos, and which was destroyed by a catastrophe c. 1400 BC. Trading contacts existed between Egypt and the Aegean islands, and examples of Aegean influence on artifacts may be seen in Egypt.

Monolithic Stone A block of stone, usually used for architectural purposes, and often of considerable size, which has been cut in one piece from the parent rock.

Mortuary Temple Unlike the independent cultus temple, the mortuary temple had strong connections with a deceased pharaoh. In early times, it was usually part of the burial complex but by the New Kingdom the tomb and king's temple were usually separate. In the mortuary temple a ritual was performed to ensure the continued existence of the deceased ruler and his acceptance by previous kings and identification with Osiris. Mortuary temples also accommodated the cult of a deity, whose daily ritual was performed as in the cultus temples. Mortuary temples were frequently completed and presumably used even during a ruler's lifetime.

Mummy The Egyptians mummified the bodies of their dead in order to preserve the body for use by the soul in the life after death. When first buried in the dry sand, the bodies became dehydrated by natural means, but once they began to place the bodies in tombs, it became necessary to develop an artificial process of preservation. Herodotus relates how the internal organs were removed from the body and treated separately, while the body was dehydrated by means of natron and finally annointed and wrapped in layers of bandages.

Naos A small, enclosed shrine to contain the god's statue. Some naoi were similar to small shelters and were included in temple complexes; others were small wooden structures placed in the innermost sanctuary of the god and containing the cult statue of the deity.

Natron A natural compound of sodium carbonate and sodium bicarbonate, today found in Egypt in the Wadi Natrun, the Beheira province and El Kab. In ancient Egypt it was used mainly in mummification, purifying the mouth, making incense, but

also in cooking, making glass and in medicine.

Necropolis The "City of the Dead," an area near to every city, town or village in Egypt which was set aside for the burial of the dead. Usually the necropolis was situated outside the fertile irrigated area of land and was placed on the edge of the desert.

Negada Culture The term applied to the artifacts and way of life of one of the predynastic groups centered around the Theban region. This culture spread to the north and the south and was characterized by its pottery and sculpture.

Nomarch The local governor of a "nome" or province, the nomarch wielded great power at certain periods of Egypt's history when centralized government was weakened; they built local tombs and sometimes ruled as minor kinglets with their own troops. Eventually, in the Middle Kingdom, the king finally crushed their power and threat to the throne.

Norden, Frederick Lewis A Dane, exploring Egypt at the same time as Pocock. He made a particular study of obelisks and he was the first European to visit Nubia and publish an account of the temples there, although he was obliged to turn back at the Second Cataract.

Obelisk These upright stone pencil-like structures, topped by a pointed pyramidion, were directly connected with the solar cult in Egypt. In early times Heliopolis was the center of this cult, but obelisks also occur in cultus temples of the New Kingdom such as Luxor and Karnak; the granite was hewn at Aswan and transported in one piece to Thebes. Obelisks like the so-called "Cleopatra's Needle" were shipped from Egypt to London, Paris, Istanbul and America in later times.

Oblation Table A table made of stone (often alabaster) or pottery, usually flat, large and circular and mounted on a small base, on which offerings of food – fowl, meat, fruit, vegetables – were offered to the gods by the king or the high priest in the temples.

Obsidian A black or green natural glass of volcanic origin, obsidian was probably imported to Egypt from Asia Minor, Abyssinia, Armenia and the Red Sea coast. It was used for implements, statues, amulets, beads, scarabs and as inlay eyes for statues.

Orpiment A natural sulfide of arsenic, used by the Egyptians as a yellow pigment, in addition to yellow ocher. Orpiment was used in the latter half of the 18th Dynasty, at Amarna and in the tomb paintings at Thebes.

It was probably imported into Egypt from Persia or Asia Minor.

Osiris Perhaps the most famous of Egyptian gods, Osiris was believed to have originated as a human king, the bringer of civilization to Egypt, and the devoted husband of Isis. He was killed by his jealous brother Seth and his body dismembered and scattered throughout Egypt. After his death, Isis conceived a son by Osiris – Horus the Younger; she gathered together the limbs of her husband and Horus, when grown, avenged his father's death by fighting and defeating Seth. The Council of Gods was finally called upon to decide the winner of the contest; they favored Horus and Osiris was resurrected and became king of the dead and judge of the underworld. This myth is preserved in Plutarch's writings. Through faith in Osiris ordinary people hoped for continuing life after death.

Apis

Osiris-Apis Apis was the sacred bull in which it was believed that Osiris was incarnate. The Apis bull was a fertility god, whose cult was believed to have originated at Heliopolis, perhaps established by King Menes. Apis was associated with Ptah and Osiris. Widely worshiped in the New Kingdom and in the Late Period, the Apis bull was black with special markings on parts of the body. When a bull with this marking was found, the old bull was ceremonially killed, mummified and buried with royal funerary rites in the Serapeum. The new bull was left at Memphis where it was honored as a god. Apis worship continued throughout the Ptolemaic period and spread eventually to Athens and Rome.

Ostracon A limestone flake, used as a cheap alternative to paper. Letters, accounts and literature were written upon ostraca and more recently these have been excavated from the rubbish heaps of ancient town-sites.

Some ostraca are covered with pen-and-ink sketches – the work of the artisans working on the royal tombs.

Palm-fronds The leaves of the palm tree. They were imitated in stone, to form the capitals of columns in the temples.

Pantheon The term referring to the whole group of deities worshiped by a particular civilization. This usually applies specifically to the great state gods.

Papyrus reeds

Papyrus The papyrus plant was the symbol of vigorous growth and renewal in Egypt; it was believed to have been known in primeval times and was often copied in temple architecture in the capitals of columns. The plant flourished particularly in the Delta, although now it has disappeared completely. It was used to make ropes, sandals, skiffs, baskets and so forth, but particularly as a writing material. By beating together lengths of the pith the Egyptians obtained a fine white kind of paper which was ultimately exported to Greece, Palestine and all parts of the Near East. Our word "paper" comes from the Greek *papyros* which is probably derived from an older Egyptian word.

Pectoral A piece of jewelry worn in life and death; usually rectangular in shape, the pectoral was suspended by a chain or string of beads around the neck and lay on the chest. It was often made of gold, and inlaid with semi-precious stones or glass; the design varied, but, like so much jewelry, it was magically protective in origin.

Perring, John Shae A civil engineer who carried out a scientific study of the pyramids in Upper Egypt in 1837–39. His theories on the pyramids were opposed to the earlier ideas of Wild and Lepsius.

Perry, Charles A doctor who was in Egypt between 1739 and 1742. He was particularly noted for his account of the scenes of the Battle of Kadesh, dating to the reign of Ramesses II, at the Temple of Karnak. His interest in these and the tomb paintings led others to inquire into the activities shown in such scenes.

Persea A type of tree frequently found in Egyptian temple scenes; it occurs in connection with the coronation ceremony, where at his accession the king's name is inscribed by the gods on the persea tree.

Petrie, Sir William Matthew Flinders (1853–1942) One of the greatest Egyptologists, Petrie was the son of William Petrie; he had a considerable knowledge of British archaeology and surveying, and in 1880–82 he went out to Egypt to make a survey of the Gizeh pyramids. His lifelong interest in Egyptology dated from 1866, when he read Piazzi Smyth's controversial book dealing with the Great Pyramid. Amongst the achievements of Petrie's remarkable and successful career were his independent excavations in Egypt, supported financially by wealthy English businessmen; the founding of the Egyptian Research Account in 1894; his excavations carried out for the Egypt Exploration Fund; his appointment to the Edwards Professorship at University College London in 1892, the first chair in Egyptology in England.

He excavated many sites in Egypt, including Kahun and Tell el-Amarna, Abydos and Gizeh, Naqada and Naukratis; he also excavated in Palestine and introduced systematic excavation methods into archaeology in general, insisting upon the examination and recording of all objects found at a site whether large or small.

He published many books and articles and his excavation material is housed in museums throughout the world, including the Petrie Museum at University College London.

He died, aged 89, at Jerusalem.

Pharaoh The word "pharaoh" comes from the ancient Egyptian "great house" (*per-o*); by the New Kingdom the phrase used for the royal palace came to be applied to the king himself, although it was never used as the royal title.

Philo of Byzantium A member of the Museum at Alexandria, Philo wrote widely on the defense and siege of towns, ballistics, the principles of the lever and pneumatics and various other topics. In general, the inventions achieved at the museum were never properly utilized to increase the economic sources of power in Egypt.

Pigment The colors used by the ancient Egyptians in their tomb and temple paintings were achieved by the use of pigments – usually from natural minerals, or manufactured from mineral substances. The colors included black, blue, brown, green, gray, orange, pink, red, white and yellow.

Pit-burial The earliest type of burial in Egypt, for rulers, nobles and commoners. It consisted of a shallow pit about 12 feet below ground level in which was placed the body of the deceased and various possessions for the afterlife. The body was usually placed in a crouching position with the knees drawn up under the chin.

Plato References are made in Plato's writings to the characteristics of various Egyptian divinities.

Pliny the Elder (23–79 AD) He included descriptions of monuments in Egypt and the Egyptian antiquities which had been brought to Rome in his *Natural History*.

Plutarch In earlier times Plutarch's work *De Iside et Osiride* was the most detailed account of Egyptian religion available to the student. He deals with the story of Osiris and it seems that his account is based on original Egyptian texts. Plutarch lived c. 50–120 AD and is one of the most famous of Egypt's Classical historians.

Pocock, Richard An Anglican clergyman who visited Gizeh, Saqqara and Dahshur in 1737 and then continued to the ancient sites in the Fayoum and in Middle and Upper Egypt. His drawings made the architectural wonders of Egypt come to life for Europeans and he made the first sketches of several temples, including Karnak and Luxor.

Porphyry Porphyritic rocks, varying in size and color, occur near Aswan, in Sinai and in the eastern desert of Egypt. Black and white porphyry was used to make stone vessels in the Predynastic and Early Dynastic periods. "Imperial porphyry" was exported from Egypt in later times by the Romans.

Ptah The creator of gods of Memphite theology, always shown mummiform, with a human head. Ptah was husband of Sekhmet and father of Nefertum, and was patron of craftsmen. One of the earliest of Egyptian deities, Ptah was later often associated with Osiris.

Pylons The two great towers which surmounted the main entrance into an Egyptian temple. Built of stone and often supporting two flag-poles, some of the pylons have survived in part until today.

Pyramid The Egyptian pyramid was the

tomb of the king in the Old and Middle Kingdoms. The first pyramid was built by Imhotep for King Djoser at Saqqara, and was probably a development of the earlier mastaba-tomb. After the Middle Kingdom the pyramid was no longer built in Egypt because it provided an immediate target for tomb robbers and was a drain on the country's economy.

Pyramidion The small stone pyramid-shaped structure which topped the obelisk. In ancient times the pyramidion was often gilded and reflected the rays of the rising and setting sun.

Pyramid Texts These texts consisted of a series of magic formulas, placed inside the pyramids of the 6th Dynasty at Saqqara, to protect the kings in their journey after death. As the earliest religious texts in Egypt, they are thought to reflect the conditions, beliefs and language of a period of history before the Old Kingdom.

Quartzite A hard type of sandstone, white, yellowish or red in color, from a number of places in Egypt, especially Gebel Ahmar near Cairo and Wadi Natrum. It was used for building – lining burial chambers, door thresholds and so forth – although not extensively.

The solar barque

Re' The god who symbolized the sun; his cult-center was at Heliopolis and the cult reached its zenith in the 5th Dynasty when the king became known as the "Son of Re'." Re' was king and father of the gods and the creator of mankind. Many myths grew up around Re' and it was believed that after death the pharaoh in his solar barque joined Re' in the heavens.

Red Land In contrast to the irrigated land, the surrounding deserts were called "Deshret" or the "Red Land" by the ancient Egyptians, on account of the color of the barren soil and cliffs. Thus Egypt was a land divided into two main geographical regions, and this had a profound effect on her history.

Reisner, George Andrew (1867–1942) An American Egyptologist who became Professor of Egyptology at Harvard. Reisner's greatest discovery was the tomb of Queen Hetepheres at Gizeh; he was the author of many articles and he continued and improved Petrie's methods of systematic excavation.

Relief en-Creux This "incised" or "sunk" relief was achieved by cutting the outline of the figures and details of the scene deeply into the stone background. It was a more rapid method than bas-relief, but the results do not achieve the same level of delicacy and beauty. Its main use was as a decoration on the outside walls of temples.

Repoussé This was the process of working bronze, so that a design or decoration was caused to stand out in relief; this could be done from the back or the face of the metal.

Roberts, David A Scottish painter who traveled in Egypt and the Holy Land in the 1840s and produced a six-volume work entitled *The Holy Land*. He traveled as far as Wadi Halfa and painted romantic scenes of various sites; these were included in his publication and achieved great popularity.

Rock-cut Tomb In the Middle Kingdom the practice developed of hewing tombs from the rocky cliffs in the provincial areas of Egypt, particularly in Middle Egypt. The interiors of these tombs were decorated with scenes of everyday life. In the Old Kingdom the nobles had been buried in brick-built tombs around the base of the king's pyramid, but with the decline of centralized power they began to be buried in their own provinces, in the cliffs. By the New Kingdom the royal family as well as the nobles had adopted the rock-cut tomb, and were buried at Thebes. It was hoped, vainly, that the rock-cut tomb would provide more of an obstacle than the pyramid to the tomb robber.

Rosellini, Professor I. An Italian who accompanied Champollion on his visit to Egypt to collect hieroglyphic material. Rosellini published a series of drawings in four volumes.

Rosetta Stone This stela, bearing a copy of a decree of Ptolemy V and dating to 196 BC, was discovered by one of Napoleon's officers at Rosetta, near Alexandria, in 1799. The inscription on the stone was written in hieroglyphs, Demotic and Greek and Champollion used it to assist him in his decipherment of Egyptian hieroglyphs. Now in the British Museum, the Rosetta Stone came into the possession of the British in 1801.

Sacred Boat The barque in which the king was believed to journey around the heavens after death. Also the boat which was used to transport the god's statue from its temple to a neighboring temple during the deity's festival.

Sandstone Used generally after the mid-18th Dynasty, this stone, consisting of quartz sand, was one of the main building stones used in Egypt for temples and monumental buildings. The main source was Silsila, 40 miles north of Aswan.

Sandys, George He went to Egypt in 1610 as one of the first gentleman-travelers. He visited the Great Pyramid, Alexandria and Cairo, where he saw numbers of mummified remains. He published a popular account of his *Travels*, which included on-the-spot accounts of what he had seen and accurate sketches of the Pyramids of Gizeh, Dahshur, Saqqara and the Sphinx.

Saqqieh The water-wheel, introduced into Egypt in Greco-Roman times, and still in use until recently.

Sarcophagus The protective container in which a mummified body was placed within the tomb. Various materials were used for sarcophagi – wood, stone, cartonnage, gold and silver; they were carved or painted with inscriptions – magical formulas to protect the dead person – and sometimes inlaid with colored glass or stones. Some were anthropoid, others were rectangular with straight sides. On the outside of a sarcophagus a pair of eyes is frequently shown to enable the deceased to look out at the world.

Satrap The Persian Empire was divided into regions or satrapies, each under the control of a governor or satrap. When the Persians conquered Egypt, she too was placed under such a governor.

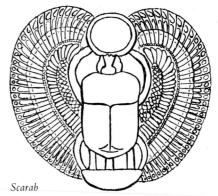

Scarab

Scarab A seal used to stamp clay-sealings on letters, bolts, wine-jars etc. with the mark of the owner. Often made of faience, limestone or steatite, the scarab is carved in the shape of a dung-beetle, and has a design on the base – sometimes a name, title, epithet or decorative motif. The dung-beetle of Egypt (called Kheper in the Egyptian language) was associated in the ancient Egyptian mind with the verb *kheper*, meaning to "come into existence." Because of the similarity of the sound values of the two words and because the beetles were observed coming forth from the sand as if from nowhere (although in fact from eggs laid in the sand some time previously), the scarab came to represent the manifestation of spontaneous creation, and the "Heart scarab" – a larger stone scarab bearing an inscription from the Book of the Dead – was placed between the mummy bandaging to ensure the renewed life of the deceased.

Schist (Graywacke) A hard, fine-grained rock, widely used for bracelets, vessels, statues and sarcophagi. It was quarried in the Wadi Hammamat.

Sculpture in the Round Unlike relief en-creux and bas-relief, used by the Egyptians to decorate tomb and temple walls, sculpture in the round applies to any sculpture – statues, amulets, ushabti figures etc. – which is carved from the stone three-dimensionally, and which may be viewed from front, back and both sides.

Sea Peoples The collective name given to the sea-faring northerners who attempted to force an entry into Egypt in the reigns of Merenptah and Ramesses III, and who were repulsed.

Sekhmet The lion-headed goddess, wife of Ptah, mother of Nefertum, whose center was at Memphis. She was the patron of doctors in her capacity of goddess of healing. But she was also a destroyer, mistress of the deserts and a powerful enemy of all who threatened the king.

Semitic Language A general term applied to languages spoken by the Semitic peoples, including Egyptian hieroglyphs which also contain elements that are non-Semitic in origin.

Sem-priest One of the specialized grades of priest, concerned particularly with the funerary rituals and often shown in a mortuary connection. The Sem-priest was characterized by his clothing which included a leopard-skin slung across his linen undergarment.

Serapeum This subterranean complex of galleries at Saqqara, the necropolis of Memphis, was the burial site of 64 mummified Apis bulls and was discovered by Mariette in 1850–51. When the cult of Serapis was introduced, the Serapeum, in use many years before, became a great religious center.

Serapis The amalgamation into one deity of Apis and Osiris, adopted by the Greeks living at Memphis in the Ptolemaic period. Serapis was chosen by Ptolemy I to be the official god of Egypt in an attempt to unite the Greek and Egyptian elements in Egypt. The cult of Serapis was perhaps more successful outside Egypt, where he remained something of an artificial, royal creation.

Seth The brother of Osiris, Seth was regarded as the embodiment of evil in ancient Egypt, and was represented by the boar-like, but unidentified Seth-animal. Seth was worshiped at certain periods, notably when the Hyksos conquered Egypt. In mythology Seth was finally defeated by Horus, who avenged the death of his father Osiris.

Shaduf Introduced into Egypt in the New Kingdom, the shaduf is still used to irrigate the fields. It consisted of a bucket on a rope, attached to a pole; the bucket could be lowered into the river and easily drawn up again.

Shaw, Thomas An 18th-century explorer who visited Alexandria and Gizeh but who contributed little to the knowledge of Egypt. He believed that the pyramids were temples, which was a more reasonable theory than many advanced on the purpose of the pyramid.

Sherd A piece of pottery, broken off from the main body of a pot; sherds were often used as an inferior writing material.

Sicard A Jesuit priest (1677–1726), Sicard was one of the early explorers of Egypt. In his travels he reached Aswan, the first modern explorer to do so, and visited many tombs and temples. It was also Sicard who rediscovered the lost ancient capital of Thebes.

Slate Palettes These were produced during the Archaic Period and often exhibit a high standard of craftsmanship; they are sometimes decorated with designs of a non-Egyptian type. The larger palettes are ceremonial, the most famous being that attributed to King Narmer. Smaller slate palettes were used to mix eye-paints and cosmetics and were placed in tombs for use in the hereafter.

Slaves Prisoners-of-war from the Middle Kingdom onwards were usually owned by the Crown, the temples or native Egyptians. However they were *not* used in the building of the Old Kingdom pyramids. Even slaves had their own possessions; they could marry whom they wished; their owners could legally free them; they could own and inherit land; and they could even possess native Egyptian servants. Some achieved positions of responsibility in Egypt.

Smyth, Charles Piazzi (1819–1900) British astronomer, the Astronomer Royal of Scotland and Professor of Astronomy at Edinburgh University, Smyth was the author of a controversial book about the Great Pyramid; his work is based on deductions made from the measurements of the Great Pyramid – a study which was very popular

at this period, and which has become known as "pyramidology." Smyth's work influenced Petrie's early interest in the Great Pyramid and in Egyptology.

Sobek The crocodile-headed god, worshiped particularly at Crocodilopolis and at Kôm Ombo, where he shared a temple with Haroeris. A water-god and associated with fertility, Sobek rose to become a state god in the 12th Dynasty.

Sphinx (from the Egyptian "living image" – *shesep ankh*) A royal power, protecting good and repelling evil. Each sphinx possessed a human face, representing the king, and the body of a lion, in a crouching position. The most famous is the Gizeh Sphinx which was carved out of a natural outcrop of rock in the reign of Chephren, builder of the second Gizeh pyramid, whose features it was given.

Stela A rectangular stone slab, with the upper part curved in a semi-circle. They are usually of limestone and are decorated with a picture and inscriptions. The "Royal Stelae," originally set up in temples, quarries etc., give official statements on victories, trading agreements and so forth. Private funerary stelae were placed in tomb-chapels; they give titles, names and epithets of the deceased and were an additional attempt to secure continuing life after death.

Strabo This famous geographer, born at Pontus, lived at Alexandria for some time and journeyed to the First Cataract of the Nile in 25–24 BC. His description of Egypt is given mainly in the seventeenth book of his *Geography*. In addition to geographical facts, he also recounts historical and religious details. His information is still of use to modern scholars.

Sun-disk See under **Aten**. The sun's disk, a source of life to the Egyptians, was called "Aten," as opposed to the sun as a whole, which was "Re'."

Syncellus Also known as George the Monk, Syncellus (c. 800 AD) was a historian and, with Josephus, Africanus and Eusebius, was responsible for preserving the writings of Manetho.

Tauert The goddess who protected women in childbirth, from queens to peasant women. Tauert was shown as a pregnant hippopotamus, standing upright and supporting herself on two emblems representing the hieroglyph for "protection." Like Bes, Tauert was a household deity, worshiped in the home. Many amulets and statuettes were made in the form of Tauert.

Tell el-Amarna Letters The collection of

cuneiform tablets which were discovered at Akhenaten's capital city, Tell el-Amarna. These were sent to the Egyptian capital from Ugarit in Phoenicia and Boghazkoy, the capital city of the Hittites, and from them it has been possible to deduce some of the political-diplomatic background of the time. They throw light on the commerce of the ancient world and the political status which Egypt held.

Thoth The Ibis-headed god of Egypt, who had charge of writing, reading, mathematics and all learned and scribal pursuits. Hermopolis was his main cult center, and he was the patron god of scribes. Through his knowledge of hieroglyphs he also had control over magic and magicians. He is usually shown as the scribe of the gods and played an important part as clerk of the court at the ceremony of weighing the heart on the Day of Judgment.

Trireme A ship with three banks of oars, being built as early as 600 BC by the Syrians and Egyptians. The Greeks feared that the Persians would use these ships against them and therefore began to build their own. Little actual information is available on the trireme – some literary sources, marble reliefs including one from the Acropolis in Athens, a clay model and some uncertain sketches. However it seems that there were three banks of rowers, totaling from 120 to 200, and that triremes were used for warfare and trading purposes.

Upper Egypt The southern area of Egypt which originally formed a separate kingdom before Narmer's unification of Egypt in c. 3100 BC. The ancient capital was at Nekheb and the great goddess was Nekhbet, the vulture.

Ushabti Literally meaning "the answerer." Each of these little figures was believed to play a part in the hereafter. Usually made of wood or faience, sets of these mummiform figures were placed in the tombs of the well-to-do from the Middle Kingdom onwards. They were supposed to act as slaves and to work on behalf of the deceased in the "Fields of Osiris"; the inscription on the figure detailed the willingness of the ushabti to "answer" the call to work.

Valley of the Kings Called Biban el-Moluk, this was the barren area chosen by the kings of the New Kingdom as their burial site. It lies under the protection of the "Peak," the highest point in the cliffs on the west bank of the Nile at Thebes, which is reminiscent of the pyramid shape. The tombs, excavated into the rocky cliff, were all extensively robbed, except for the tomb of Tutankhamun. Originally they had protected the king's mummy, encased in its coffin and sarcophagus and surrounded by treasures for use in the next life. The walls of each tomb were decorated with scenes of the underworld, through which the king had to journey, and funerary texts to protect him on this journey; these scenes were in contrast to the scenes of everyday life in the nobles' tombs. Sixty-one tombs have now been discovered in this valley.

Valley of the Nobles The region on the west bank of the Nile at Thebes, near to the Valleys of the Kings and Queens, where the nobles of the New Kingdom were buried in tombs which are decorated with colorful scenes of many aspects of daily life.

Valley of the Queens This valley is situated on the west bank of the Nile opposite modern Luxor, near the Theban burial sites; it is referred to as Biban el-Harim. Here were buried the wives, daughters and some of the sons of the pharaohs of the Ramesside period. The most famous tomb is perhaps that of Nefertari, wife of Ramesses II.

Vizier The Vizier, or Chancellor, was the chief minister of Egypt, subordinate only to the king. He was often a member of the royal family and was responsible for the administration of the country. He played an important role in legal and economic matters.

Vulture and Cobra Nekhbet and Edjo were the two goddesses of Upper and Lower Egypt in the predynastic period. Nekhbet was a vulture goddess who presided over El-Kab, capital of Upper Egypt, and protected the king; Edjo was the cobra goddess of Buto, capital of Lower Egypt. The goddesses were later incorporated into the royal pantheon as the "Two Ladies" and continued to protect the sovereign throughout Egyptian history.

Vyse, Colonel Richard William Howard He hired Caviglia to direct work on the pyramids of Chephren and Mycerinus, but they quarreled and Vyse continued the exploration of these pyramids by himself, using destructive methods including gunpowder when he deemed necessary.

Warburton, Bishop William He published *The Divine Legation of Moses* in 1741 in which he set forth the first reasonable theories on Egyptian hieroglyphs, attacking the earlier ideas of Kircher. He was the first to realize that hieroglyphs were a system of writing and not just a set of mysterious, religious symbols.

Water-clock The Clepsydra or water-clock is sometimes shown in Egyptian temple reliefs. The water-clock introduced by Hero used water as a means of movement; the even flow of water directed the accuracy of time-keeping.

Water-organ Ctesibius designed a water-organ at Alexandria, which worked on the principle of displacing a volume of air by water. Most of the inventions of this period are known only from literary sources.

Wilkinson, Sir John Gardner Author of *Manners and Customs of the Ancient Egyptians*, based upon his travels in Egypt in 1821. His interest also extended to the tomb paintings at Thebes. His popular book was the best account of Egyptian civilization in the 19th century and made people aware of Egyptian art and religion.

Young, Thomas An English physicist and linguist. He discovered that the cartouches in hieroglyphic inscriptions contained the names of rulers. His results were published in 1819 but, although he made great advances in hieroglyphs and Demotic, he did not achieve the results of Champollion.

Ushabti

Index